PRAISE FOR
Working **Stiff**

"[Stoddard is] the thinking pervert's go-to guy for behind-the-scenes reporting. . . . Consistently hilarious. . . . His self-deprecating style and wonderful appreciation for the absurd serve him well. . . . Smart and appealing."   —*Publishers Weekly*

"Cringingly hilarious. . . . Stoddard's descriptions of his increasingly edgy sex misadventures . . . are enjoyable for their geek-out-of-geekdom charm. . . . This odyssey of luck is often charmingly relayed."
                                                                            —*Kirkus Reviews*

"Grant Stoddard's debut is a sex-memoir with heart: an inspirational true story of how to 'make it' in New York, in every sense of the word. *Working Stiff* is an American (wet) dream come true."
                                                —Jessica Cutler, author of *The Washingtonienne*

"Peek under the dirty sheets of Stoddard's hilarious debut, and you'll find a brave, moving, and, yes, seductive story of a young man's struggle to find his way in a strange city, a foreign country, and an unforgettable age."   —David Goodwillie, author of
                                                Seemed Like a Good Idea at the Time

WORKING STIFF

WORKING
STIFF

THE MISADVENTURES OF
AN ACCIDENTAL SEXPERT

Grant
Stoddard

HARPER PERENNIAL

NEW YORK • LONDON • TORONTO • SYDNEY

HARPER ● PERENNIAL

FIRST EDITION

Designed by Justin Dodd

Library of Congress Cataloging-in-Publication Data
Stoddard, Grant.
    Working stiff / Grant Stoddard. — 1st Harper Perennial ed.
        p. cm.
    ISBN: 978-0-06-087612-8
    ISBN-10: 0-06-087612-3
        1. Stoddard, Grant. 2. Stoddard, Grant — Sexual behavior. 3. Sexologists — New York (State) — New York — Biography. 4. British Americans — New York (State) — New York — Biography. 5. Sex — Miscellanea. 6. Nerve.com (Computer file). I. Title.
    HQ18.32.S76A3 2007
    306.70974'1 — dc22
    [B]   2006043666

07 08 09 10 11 ❖/RRD 10 9 8 7 6 5 4 3 2 1

FOR NEW YORK CITY

The true New Yorker secretly believes that people living anywhere else have to be, in some sense, kidding.

—JOHN UPDIKE

WORKING STIFF

PROLOGUE

I HELD IT IN my hands. Once detached from my body, my genitalia seemed much more impressive. Bouncing it in my left palm and then in my right, I reckoned its weight and volume. I held it closer to my face, closer than hours of stretching, straining, and forcefully curving my spine had ever gotten me before.

"It's perfect," I kept saying to myself in between gulps of supermarket merlot.

With some hesitation I put it to my lips. I immediately grew fearful that Tom Wheeler or one of the cowboys from the ranch would drop by at any moment, and that it's secretly observed private moments like this that give us city folk a bad name in these parts.

"Magnificent!" I concluded as my lengthy inspection continued. I opened another bottle.

I would have been a lot happier about the respectable amount of water my disembodied penis could displace when dunked in a pint glass, or the number of papers it could anchor on a breezy terrace, if I wasn't financially bound and contractually obligated to insert it into my bottom.

Given its ultimate destination, I took solace in the fact that I hadn't immortalized the organ at its absolute largest. This was by circumstance rather than design; maintaining a thumping erection whilst balls-deep in two pints of tepid plaster of Paris for 120 long seconds had proved a task I wasn't equal to, what with my mania, cabin fever, debilitating homesickness, and recent anxiety attacks.

I poured a glass of wine and felt the dip in temperature in the sprawling house. The fire was beginning to die out. There was more cut firewood under the house, but since my next-door neighbor's horse was viciously torn apart by a mountain lion, I was dreading to go rooting around down there after dark. I had self-diagnosed the episodes I'd been having over the past few weeks as anxiety attacks and hoped that I'd seen the last of them. Holing up in a ranch house in the Sierra Nevadas for three months seemed like a fantastic opportunity to get some writing done, but it soon transpired that I really wasn't at all up to the challenge. The weeks of isolation, the paranormal goings-on, the burning to death of a ranch hand, the packs of nocturnal terrors that patrolled the area around the house, and the cessation of my livelihood—the gonzo sex column I wrote for the sex Web site Nerve.com— had all suddenly come to bare and sent me stark raving mad and so very far from home.

Holding an accurate facsimile of my own member in my hands, it's hard to believe how little action the thing actually saw over the course of its first twenty-four years. Since then, of course, it's played a starring role in some of my greatest adventures. I imagined that a cross-section of it would reveal a series of concentric rings, just as one could reckon the harsh winters and long summers from a felled English oak.

Each ring of the member might similarly speak of its own history: the lengthy humiliating dry spells, the blissful monogamous periods, an orgy, a week spent at a BDSM retreat, and, of course, Lisa.

What's really remarkable about the thing is how little wear it seems to have shown for all the miles I've put on it in the name of a half-decent salary and comprehensive health insurance.

"It looks good," said Jamye. "Are you ready to do this?"

"Not yet. In a few minutes," I said.

Jamye had arrived from San Francisco the evening before. I had been counting the days to her arrival since she decided to drive out and keep me company for a while. She's a great friend; I know her from my adopted home, the East Village. Aside from the previous day's grocery run to the comparative metropolis of Oakhurst, I hadn't seen another human being in the week before she arrived. The house's position on the brow of a hill, looking into a steep valley, meant that I could see the headlights of her rental car for the twenty minutes it took her to wind her way around the hill to its apex. I almost hugged her to death when she pulled up to the house.

I'd told Jamye about my latest and ultimate Nerve assignment over the phone and she'd said she'd be more than happy to assist me when she arrived. She's a sex educator and virtually unflappable. After she dropped her bags she mixed the plaster for the mold. We left the plaster cast to dry overnight.

The inherent symbolism of the situation was certainly not lost on me. My leaving Nerve was tinged with acrimony, sour grapes, and bleatings of betrayal and disloyalty. Rufus Griscom, Nerve's CEO, had remained civil, nay *friendly*, toward me, even as his lawyers threatened legal proceedings that would no doubt scupper my eponymous TV pilot. It was his deeds rather than his words that yelled "go fuck yourself." How I allowed it to become a literal instruction, I'm not sure.

"Will you hug me afterward?" I asked.

"Of course! I'll be very gentle. Promise," said Jamye.

She disappeared into the bedroom and reemerged wearing a dildo harness over her pajamas, which were covered in little cartoon penguins.

I tossed the last remaining log and some newspaper on the fire to warm up the room a little, took off my bathrobe, and got on all fours on the shaggy rug.

"It's going to feel strange at first, but it gets better," said Jamye. "I promise."

She took the mold of my penis from the mantel and inserted it through the silver ring in her strap-on harness and ran her hand up and down it, as if she were masturbating. My friend Jamye was sporting my cock. It was strange, but I'd somehow allowed myself to become quite numb to it all. It was work. People talk about becoming their jobs, and for better or worse I'd sort of become mine.

My appointment to the position of Nerve's resident sexual guinea pig was based on my willingness to try things that most people, especially those with legitimate literary aspirations, wouldn't deign to. When, after a few installments, the column became very popular, my desk became a depository for all kinds of sexual toys that companies had sent us to promote vis-à-vis me sticking them up my bum and writing about them. If I didn't intercept mail containing the penis-stretching system, topical arousal cream, or the scrotal augmentation starter kit from a company called Monster Nuts, chances were I'd be spending my weekend test-driving them. It wasn't until I was writing about the intricate workings of my nether regions that I had to devise a way of dealing with the thought of friends and family back home in our dreary little English commuter town reading it.

What would they think? Who was I kidding? I doubt they even remembered me. But what if they did? Would I be publicly shamed if and when they saw me again? And what's more shameful, commuting over three hours a day to be a mortgage broker in the city, only to flop into the doughy arms of a local girl each night for curry and telly, getting legless on the weekends at a franchise theme pub or . . . this?

I'll come back to that.

Being in another country, in an alien job, and surrounded by "sex-positive" Ivy League grads who sang my praises and commended my bravery made it easier, but the fact remained that I didn't even want to think about my own prostate gland, and precisely why I was professing its awesomeness to an international audience of countless strangers was completely beyond explanation.

Jamye rolled a condom over the prosthetic, squirted some lube onto the end of it, then very tenderly applied a squirt to my bum and gently rubbed it in.

"Okay?" she asked.

She placed her hands on my waist.

"Wait!" I said and downed the remaining merlot.

"Okay," I said, acutely aware that I was at the end of something big.

WHEN I MET HER, Beatrix Cecilia Montague was somewhere between seventy-five and eighty-five years old. She was born in colonial India and attended a posh girls' finishing school in Harrogate, Yorkshire. Her hobbies included bridge, golf, and tennis—her mother was the all-India women's tennis champion. She made sure she never missed an episode of *EastEnders*, *Neighbours*, or *Coronation Street*, owned a beige fifteen-year-old Ford Fiesta and a cockatoo named Dippy. She smoked a pack and a half of Lambert and Butler cigarettes per day, washed and reused the half dozen pieces of cling wrap she owned, and seldom arose before eleven. She delivered a right-wing news-letter throughout the neighborhood regardless of inclement weather. Her hair was salt white and pepper gray save for a pompadour, stained the color of egg yolk from cigarette smoke. Her entire wardrobe was polyester and sported all sorts of unclassifiable stains. On any given day she could smell of faintly spicy sweat, pet stores, or musty cupboards. She didn't flinch when using racist, empirical terms like "golliwog" and "pickaninny." Beatrix Cecilia Montague was my college roommate.

Mrs. Montague—I never once addressed her as anything else in three years of living with her, so I won't here either—was above all else a woman of principle. She wasn't in the business of taking advantage of anybody and was vigilant in ensuring that she wasn't being taken advantage of herself. This is what I knew about Mrs. Montague prior to meeting her: in her inconveniently located ground-floor flat in leafy Hanwell, W7, she had a spare room that she rented to students for twenty-five pounds per week. She had one pet, a cockatoo, she was a smoker, and she would not be providing meals.

"Twenty-five quid?" said Sandra, my mum's best and brassiest friend, when I told her about my bargain over a meal from Mandarin Court, an establishment known locally as "the chinky." "Blimey, that's cheap, innit? A cockatoo? Are you sure it doesn't say she's looking for a cock or two?"

Getting a cheap place with no lease was of the utmost importance to me. Here's why: I was not exactly college material. A precocious five-year-old, I had peaked early intellectually. Since then I'd become bone idle and had developed a socially debilitating love of heavy metal and had a D+ average. Undeterred, my dad threatened severe economic sanctions unless I at least *tried* to get into a school.

In the United Kingdom, where until recently education was entirely paid for by the taxpayer, all university places are provisional until the publication of A-level results in the second week of August. A-levels are the equivalent of SATs. Let's suppose your first choice of school was Oxford but you didn't get the grades required there. You would have to opt for another one of the schools you were provisionally accepted to who *would* admit you based on your A-level results. Schools are required to keep these provisional places open until the results are published. This means that after publication a lot of university places suddenly become available and there is a mad scramble to fill them. (On the day the results are published, broadsheet newspapers include supplements made up purely of ads from different schools to entice those still without a place to secure one over the phone!) Places at better schools are snapped up instantly by the most qualified, but the trickle-down effect means that a lot of the shittier universities are practically dragging people in off the street regardless of their academic aptitude. That's how I got in.

Upon getting a place at Thames Valley University my plan was to leave Thames Valley University. I felt by the age of eighteen there was barely any room left in my brain to learn any new stuff—even "Media Studies"—but I *also* knew that my attending university, even for a semester, would make my father a happy man. Nobody in our family had gone to college and it was my father's ambition that I should be the first to go, in spite of me expressing absolutely no interest in furthering my education or even having the grades to get into anything but the most piss-poor of institutions. In our town, going to university was far from expected from a child, and I felt it unfair that I was being randomly singled out to attend. In my graduating class, I would say less than one in twenty kids went on to university, or "uni," as it's known.

All I really wanted to do was play in what I now realize was a dreadful rock band. My plan was a tightrope act: I had to teach my parents a lesson about not overestimating their children, but I knew that if I made that lesson an expensive one, I'd never be able to forget it. That's why when I saw Mrs. Montague's ad in TVU's Accommodations Office, I knew I had found the perfect housemate. TVU had no student housing but instead provided listings of whole houses to rent with other students or rooms to rent within a family home or private residence. In either situation, it was unheard of to pay less than fifty quid a week.

Before my mother and I took a train to London to meet her and see the available bargain room, I hoped that Mrs. Montague was a sexy divorcée, or better yet, an independently wealthy widow in her early forties, yearning for the company of an eager house boy as per the ad's insinuation. The way I saw it, what a sultry Mrs. Montague could teach me in the bedroom would ultimately have a more practical application than anything I'd glean from a patchily attended semester of Media Studies classes at Britain's worst university. The school's only real claim to fame is that it used to be Ealing College of Art and was attended by rock heroes like Queen's Freddie Mercury, The Who's Pete Townsend, and Ron Wood from the Rolling Stones. With such a rock-and-roll precedent, I idly hoped that, if nothing else, a bit of uni might bolster my chances of rock stardom.

After a week spent convincing myself that I'd be spending the autumn at the mercy of a nymphomaniacal Anne Bancroft type, my mother and I pulled up to Golden Court, the grand name given to what looked like a run-down assisted living home. Mrs. Montague opened the door to her dusty little flat. To my utter horror she had about forty years on the Mrs. Robinson character from my sordid imagination.

She ran a wrinkly hand through her thick wild hair and peered at us both from behind her bifocals.

"Hello, you must be Grant," she said with a dark brown voice and a throat that begged in vain to be cleared. "And you must be Grant's mother. Won't you both come in?"

She turned on her heel and we followed her down a narrow hallway. My mother was trying hard not to make eye contact with me. She was finding a lot of amusement in the thought of me shacking up with the old buzzard and was very close to succumbing to a fit of the giggles.

Mrs. Montague showed us in to one of her two living rooms and introduced us to Dippy, who was emitting cranium-splitting squawks at the rate of about two per second. The late-afternoon sun picked up the thick dust that filled the room and gave everything a tangerine aura.

"The bird came from my grandchildren. A gift if you please. Heaven knows what they were thinking."

She turned on her heel to fetch tea and biscuits, both allowing my mother to expel some of the laughter that was threatening to shake her apart and treating us to another rear view of her trademark quick march. I'd never seen a senior citizen walk with so much haste and conviction. Long, quick strides, each foot planted down as if stomping an injured field mouse out of its misery.

"Ain't she posh?" said my mum, and she struggled to regain her composure.

In fact Mrs. Montague was just about the poshest person I had ever met, and in the truest and most literal sense of the word. (Posh is an acronym for Portside Out, Starboard Home, the preferred cabin allocation for the upper classes as they traveled by boat to the far reaches of the British Empire, so as not to subject their faces to any more sunshine than absolutely necessary.) The various knickknacks from Africa and India around the room suggested a colonial past, the dust and tatty furniture suggested a chaotic one. She hurriedly returned with some tea in chipped pastel-colored mugs and an assortment of biscuits arranged on a glass plate.

"Well, you must tell me about your journey."

When you are raised in the borough of Thurrock in Essex, London is often referred to as "town," and a visit to the capital might be signified by saying that you are simply going "up the road." The insinuation of geographical proximity to the nation's mighty capital is of course borne out of the indignity of residing in one of the UK's cultural blind spots. Conversely, to Londoners, Essex is a far distant and unfortunate place. The way Mrs. Montague oohed and aahed through my mother's recounting of the ninety-minute trip, you'd think we'd trekked in from the Congo.

Growing up, I felt incredibly intimidated by and ill at ease in London. All of my family had lived there at one time or another but had all moved east long ago. As a child I would accompany my mother on day trips to Covent Garden, Kensington High Street, and Knightsbridge. I vividly remember the filth, the overtly sexual atmosphere, the punks, seeing the black, the brown, and the Irish for the first time and being frightened and confused by the maelstrom of stimuli. I felt an immense relief when it was time to get back on the train and go home.

As a teen, I'd only go to London to see my favorite bands play, a bittersweet experience. Skid Row at London Docklands Arena, Def Leppard at Earls Court. Heavy metal fans were a rare and unpopular breed of teenager in our town. I had an overwhelming feeling of fraternity as my long-haired and much put upon chums and I drew closer to the venue, the number of virginal, acne-ridden, problem-haired, studded-leather-jacket-wearing brethren growing thicker and more vociferous on the streets. In the leafy commuter villages of semirural England we metal heads scuttled around in the shadows, trying to avoid the thorough beatings our getups so clearly invited. Here in London, far out of arm's reach and earshot of the incensed local "trendies," we strode triumphantly, singing "Youth Gone Wild" at the top of our lungs. In reality, the youth, as wild as we were, had to get back to Fenchurch Street station by 10:56, when the last train to Essex carried us home, drunk, deafened, and temporarily vindicated. The race back home often meant that we had to leave a show halfway through the encore, the strains of our favorite band's greatest hit singles still playing as we made a desperate drunken dash for the tube.

I saw London, and by association any big city, as a big, pulsing, offensively cool, sexual, scary hassle that served only to highlight my virginity, provinciality, and lack of savvy. As I sat there with Mrs. Montague and my mother, I sort of couldn't believe that I would be actually living in the belly of the beast. But Hanwell, in reality, was far from the belly of the beast. Sure it had a metropolitan postal code and was crisscrossed by red double-deckers, but it was too far west to have any urban cred whatsoever.

MRS. MONTAGUE had an abnormally jowly and wrinkly face; in the telling daylight it appeared positively scrotal. I could only count four tombstone teeth on the top of her mouth. A rare wide smile exposed two large gaps on either side of them. She was taller and thinner than most old ladies, although she was always bent at the hip, ensuring her precise height remained shrouded in mystery. Mrs. Montague gave us a quick tour of what would be my room, as well as the kitchen and bathroom we would share. My room was pokey, eight feet by six and a half, only room for a narrow little bed and quite dim, the ground being level with the windowsill. The bathroom contained a tub but no shower. I also couldn't help noticing a threadbare toothbrush whose handle was in the shape of a naked man with an erect penis. The kitchen was painted a weak yellow and boasted thick, dusty cobwebs wherever possible.

The whole afternoon was just a formality; I knew that Mrs. Montague's pad would be perfect for my plan to waste precisely the right amount of my parents' time and money.

The following week, as my parents drove off home after delivering me and my personal effects to Golden Court, I started to wonder why they didn't once ask me if I was sure that I'd be okay living with some wild-eyed old bat. They thought either that living with a relic would be somehow character-building, were agreeable with her bargain asking price, or had gotten wind of my ill-fated plan and were fixing on teaching me a lesson of my own.

My going to college garnered me only pity from my school chums, who couldn't fathom why I had agreed, albeit under duress, to go. They wanted fast cars, sharp clothes, booze-fueled vacations in warm climates, and, a couple of years down the road, enough for a down payment on a house in or around Corringham. Uni would just be putting that all off for another three or four years, slowing down the fags and booze-fueled march to a plot in a local cemetery.

My farewell drinks do at the White Lion Pub was more like a wake.

"Well, looking on the bright side," said John, who, despite being two years younger than me, was already pulling down a good salary at the Bank of England, "you might actually get your balls wet, for once."

My friends were always riding me about my status as a sexual nonstarter. Every Friday night a group of four or five of us would drive to some obnoxious super-club to "pull birds." John, Martin, John, Matt, and the other John would invariably snog a handful of birds and probably get their hands in their knickers on the dance floor, a maneuver we called feeding the pony a sugarlump. I, on the other hand, ended up as the designated eunuch. I would have loved and appreciated an anonymous tug-job in the parking lot of the Pizzazz! nightclub. It seemed that normal sexual experiences like that were being doled out willy-nilly to my crew, while the only visceral pleasure I could count on was rounding out the night with a gyro from Memet's Abra-kebabra.

If any of us could have benefited from three years of undergraduate bacchanalia, it was probably me.

I'LL BE ASKING you to make yourself scarce every second Wednesday," said Mrs. Montague with what I was beginning to realize was a permanent phlegmy rattle.

She watched me stack cans of baked beans and pasta onto my end table, windowsill, and under my bed.

I was told that all of the real estate in the refrigerator was accounted for and that I should also stick to "nonperishables" that I could store in my room.

"You can stay in your room on these occasions if you've nowhere to go but you may not use the bathroom, as movement can be distracting."

She went into the other room to watch the omnibus Sunday screening of EastEnders but carried on talking to me in her haughty, horsey tone. "On those occasions, you ought not to drink a lot of fluids. Bridge tournaments, don't you know. Distractions. We have our home games here. We play Putney next week. Putney! They are awfully good but oftentimes late."

And then, with a drag on her cigarette and a heavy sigh, she added, "To the victors go the spoils, I suppose."

She stopped for a long, loud slurp of tea. When it came to imbibing hot fluids, she had this interesting habit of giving her month a running start, beginning a powerful inhalation before she had even lifted her cup from the coffee table.

"I saw your banjo."

She was referring to my Fender Stratocaster.

"I trust that you won't be playing it while I'm about. I can hear everything. I'm like a hawk."

The theme tune to the UK's most watched nightly soap opera began, and even from the next room I could feel that Mrs. Montague had been placated.

"I say," she shouted from the living room in a softer, sadder tone, "would you care to watch *EastEnders* with me?"

And so began a ritual. Mrs. Montague would knock on my door with exactly enough time for the kettle to boil, the tea to steep, before the opening credits finished.

I always found it interesting how my haughty housemate took such an acute interest in a gritty soap opera about the cockney underclass. I'm sure she saw it as a sociological documentary.

"Would you credit it?" she cried after an unexpected turn of events, her arms gesticulating wildly. "The gall of the man! I don't like him at all, Grant. No, not one bit."

Most nights, Mrs. Montague ate her supper on her lap whilst watching *EastEnders* with me. When I went to the kitchen to make the preshow tea, there was often a singular potato, a diminutive piece of fish, and a solitary sprig of broccoli all cooked to death in single-serving-size cookware. Prior to her tucking in, I routinely caught her eyeing me up in my peripheral vision. Content that I was engrossed in what was on TV, she pulled a Pepto Bismol–colored plate from her mouth that harbored two of her four top teeth, and placed it on the telephone table that sat between our two threadbare chairs. It was at this time that the loud rotary-dial phone would typically ring.

"*God's teeth!* Who is calling me at this time?" she screamed.

This often sent great globs of semi-masticated food flying in my general direction.

"Four-oh-eight-nine?" she'd answer brusquely, her excellent diction compromised by her temporarily toothless mouth.

Mrs. Montague was evidently still living in a world where phone numbers were made up of only four digits; 4089 became a sort of code word for my friends from home to allude to my supposed intergenerational-sex-for-affordable-lodgings trade.

In the rare event that it was somebody worth interrupting her TV program for, she'd noisily rattle and click her plate back into place. If it was what she termed a "nonemergency" call she gummily suggested that they call back after "my *EastEnders*." If it was for me she'd hand the phone to me and angrily jab her index finger at the screen. If I hadn't gotten rid of them within the time it took for a slurp of tea, she raised the TV volume until the sound distorted, sending poor Dippy into a feathery squawking panic.

Over the din she'd yell, "Why on earth they have to call at this time, Dippy, I'll just never comprehend."

At some point within the first few months of my strange new life in west London, I must have decided that I was in no rush to leave Mrs. Montague's flat or Thames Valley University. The nine hours of classes I was expected to attend per week meant that I enjoyed an amount of leisure time I could have only dreamed of before attending college. The classes I took were fairly eclectic, mainly due to the fact that I selected them purely based on the time they took place. My aim was to try to shoehorn everything into one bumper Wednesday. The rest of the week was spent lying in bed and puttering about the flat with my ancient housemate.

I grew to like and admire Mrs. Montague immensely and few were the times that I rued missing the opportunity to shack up with three or four snot-nosed northerners in a damp basement flat closer to campus for three times the price. How I got to TVU and how I lived once I arrived made me feel that I was separate from almost everyone else I met there. I felt like I'd fallen asleep and woken up in somebody else's life, and quite inexplicably I had just gotten on with it. It was the first time in my life that I'd really taken a step out of my comfort zone as well as breaking formation with my own peer group, and I began to find the feeling of being somewhere or doing something I wasn't destined to do somewhat exhilarating. At university, I felt that I infiltrated a whole strange genus of human beings who wanted to learn, grow, aspire to lead interesting, satisfying lives, go on cycling vacations through the south of France, eat salad with every meal out of little wooden bowls, watch less television, read more books, read the *Guardian*, expose themselves to interesting cinema, stage an intervention when they saw a parent smacking his or her child on the street. I would return back to Essex to see the boys at the weekend and noticed myself cringing as everyone else happily watched someone be kicked and punched motionless in a nightclub car park.

I didn't realize it at the time, but through osmosis I must have started to adopt a new mind-set.

At university, there was certainly no one from my part of the world to relate to. In fact, Scousers, Geordies, Mancs, Toffs, Taffs, Brummies, and Slones all found common ground in swapping tired Essex jokes in my presence, asking me what the correct rhyming slang for this or that was, making fun of the way that I spoke! Up until I left for college I was told on an almost daily basis how "properly" I spoke.

"What time are you off to college in the morning?" said Mrs. Montague whenever I retired to my bedroom after an evening's television feast or political debate.

If I told her that I had a class that started before noon she would dramatically place both hands on her head and exclaim, "By Christ, that's the middle of the night! Leave quietly or on your own head be it."

In the colder months she'd request that if I was going to be out early would I mind scraping the ice from the windscreen of her crapped-out Ford Fiesta. Given the pittance that she was charging me in rent, I could hardly say no. To be honest, I rather liked doing things like that for her. On the few occasions I did catch her up before noon she cut a striking figure with her red silk kimono and wild unbrushed hair. For the first ninety minutes of consciousness, the skin of her face seemed to lack any elasticity whatsoever and her features just tended to dangle, swaying to and fro in the morning sunlight. After a few cups of tea she could make enough basic sounds to let me know what on earth she was doing up before the crack of noon.

"I'm having a man in," she'd whisper, defeated, pointing to yet another appliance that she'd completely reduced to a pile of screws and transistors. On an almost weekly basis, Mrs. Montague would become convinced that some other household item was "on the blink" and ruthlessly take it to bits.

With a screwdriver and fifteen minutes of spare time, the woman was a menace.

Every once in a while she'd inform me that she was "having a soak" and that I should "attend to any urgent business sooner rather than later."

I soon noticed that, at bath times, my roommate was walking into the bathroom with a bundle of clothes. It seemed that Mrs. Montague would bathe and wash her clothes in one fell swoop, her loud splish-splashing in the tub a bid to re-create the motions of a washing machine. The only question that remained was whether she was washing her clothes in bath oils or was bathing in detergent. I tended to suspect the latter as her skin did appear considerably tauter after she emerged, though neither she nor her polyester garments seemed any *cleaner* after an hour-long bath. With no dryer, she hung the clothes over three taught lengths of thin white rope above the tub. Bathing meant worrying about gravity getting the better of Mrs. Montague's dripping drawstring bloomers and then depositing them on my face should I dare to close my eyes for the briefest of moments.

MRS. MONTAGUE was a personification of the demise of the British Empire. Born just after its zenith, she enjoyed a privileged childhood spent in India, then dubbed the "Jewel in the Crown of the British Empire." In Hanwell, W7, she lived a mile away from Southall, the highest concentration of Indians in the world outside of New Delhi. But it was the Pakistanis and Bangladeshis living in the neighborhood that proved more irksome for her. Around one particular religious holiday in which fireworks were let off, she would gaze mournfully out the window, shaking her head as rockets lit up the sky.

"I wish those ruddy wogs would shut up, don't you, Grant?" she said as a Roman candle exploded in great blooms of magenta.

I hated it when she asked me a question like that in regards to ethnic minorities, but just didn't have the chutzpah to tell her that she was a crotchety old racist. I often met her halfway.

"I suppose they are being a *bit* noisy. Getting their revenge for Guy Fawkes Night, I expect."

"Wogs," she said gently under her breath.

I began to think that the old woman I lived with had lost her marbles, but it became increasingly clear that Mrs. Montague simply didn't give a shit anymore. The senior ladies I'd ever met had been cheery, house proud, clean, early to bed and early to rise, tolerant and sweet to a fault. These suburban old dears that I'd grown up knowing seemed lobotomized compared to Mrs. Montague, who was becoming noticeably more militant by the day.

A few days after commencing classes I returned home to the flat to see Mrs. Montague surrounded by the innards of yet another electrical appliance that she'd decided to vivisect in order to find the omnipresent "blasted squeaking noise" that could usually be attributed to Dippy.

"I shall have to have a man look at this," she said. She put the screwdriver down and picked a cigarette up. I knew that she didn't mean me.

"What's that? One of your textbooks?" she said and nodded to the thick hardback I had tucked under my arm.

In retrospect the correct answer would have been a simple yes.

"No, a Hare Krishna man made me buy it for ten pounds," I said.

"*Pardon me?*" she screamed with so much gusto that poor Dippy flew into a feathery conniption.

"I mean, he didn't forcibly make me buy it, but he said I really should read it."

My first few months at university were extremely lonely, mostly because I'd chosen to live with a geriatric, almost three miles away from campus, which precluded me from what little university life was on offer at TVU, and I spent my long weekends back in Essex. I was feeling a bit depressed for the first time. The shaven-headed gentleman in the orange robes on Ealing Broadway was very friendly seeming when he jumped into my path and started firing off questions, quickly convincing me that he was interested in the answers I had to offer. He was both a figurative and literal splash of color in a time period that was awfully gray seeming. Pretty soon he'd swung the conversation around to the huge box of books he had nearby, but he didn't do it in a way that seemed at all mercenary. The book, he promised me, was full of answers to finding happiness and enlightenment that were possibly less chafing than my own methods. At that moment it seemed to be just what I needed. Before you could say country cousin, I had made my purchase, finding that suddenly my grinning friend was immediately less interested in continuing our chat.

"Where are my keys?" said Mrs. Montague. "This is a bloody liberty, you've come up from the country and you are being ripped off. This is something I shan't stand for, by Gum."

She shucked herself into her decades-old Marks & Spencer Windbreaker and continued the hunt for the keys.

"Where are you going?" I said. I was worried by her furrowed brow and the ferocity with which she sucked on her cigarette.

"We're going to get your ten bloody pounds back. We're going to teach him a lesson! Shame on him for taking your father's money. You've just come up from the country."

I felt grateful that my elderly landlady had my father's finances at heart, annoyed that she had outed me as a bumpkin, and fearful for whatever she was about to inflict on the unwitting Hare Krishna.

"Please, no!" I cried, doing everything to demonstrate my horror at her guerrilla methods besides physically restraining her as more feathers spewed from poor Dippy's cage.

Nothing's quite as emasculating as having an old lady you hardly know defending your honor on the leafy thoroughfares of Ealing.

"Bloody golliwogs, I've a good mind to call the authorities. Get out of the way!"

"No, he was white!" I said, which immediately seemed to take some of the wind out of her sails. "And I *did* know what I was doing."

"Well, now," she said, slowly unzipping her jacket and pointing a bony finger into my chest. "You really ought to be a lot more careful."

After a cursory leaf through its nonsensical pages, I left the Krishna book on Mrs. Montague's nightstand as a kind of thank-you for looking out for me. It stayed collecting the flat's ample dust for three long years.

Far from the lovefest I'd sort of hoped it to be, university had proved to be a continuation of my invisibility to the opposite sex. That theme had begun so long ago that I wondered if I'd ever successfully shrug it off. I logged countless hours at the student union bar, but in spite or perhaps because of my wounded, lovelorn glares, there was never the slightest danger of a snog.

Being a city school with its students spread all over London, there was no palpable school spirit at TVU. And certainly no pride, given that in my third year a BBC documentary on what a ridiculous institution TVU was had been televised, as well as numerous tabloid articles about the school offering degrees in making curry. In addition there was a self-perpetuated segregation between the mature students and the teens, the southern Asians and the whites, the Sikhs and the Muslims, the Greeks and the Turks, the Americans and the English, which would in some cases escalate to verbal abuse and physical violence. Still, TVU would often take pains to kid its students that the school was as much a university as the red-brick institutions across the land, and an increasingly apathetic student body was coerced into taking part in what was known on bulletin boards as "TVU Life."

To that end, a few times a year the student union bar (called the Dog's Bollocks) would throw jolly traffic light parties. Attendees would be asked to wear green if they were "totally up for it," yellow if they would "consider a shag," and red if they were unavailable or not interested. I took this to be a dress code that everyone would adhere to in the spirit of being young, crazy, and financially subsidized by the government.

It had taken forever to find a pair of forest green pants, but this being my first traffic light party I didn't want to give off any mixed messages. I wore a pastel mint button-down shirt and olive tie and began the three-mile walk to campus.

I saw one of the other new "freshers," who was disconcertingly dressed in normal clothes, standing outside.

"Well, you certainly look the part," he said with a chuckle.

I walked into the Dog's, which was only half full. I ordered a Dog's Bollocks Brew, which only cost a pound a pint, and surveyed the field of battle. It appeared that everyone else had deliberately not worn the slightest hint of green or yellow or red in their outfits.

"Look, it's the jolly green not-so-giant!" said one portly northern girl to her group of field hockey friends, who all had a hearty laugh at my expense.

"Do you think he's trying to tell us something?" she continued.

As innocuously as possible, I took off my tie and fed it into my pocket, but I still looked like a Jehovah's Witness who'd been dunked in chlorophyll.

"You been having a dry spell, mate?" said the hateful ringleader to my face.

"Um . . . I thought this was the traffic light party tonight," I said, hoping for a respite in her brutality.

"Yeah, but no one actually dresses up. That's just fucking"—she looked me up and down—"*really* sad."

She looked over my shoulder.

"Wait, tell a lie," said the girl. "There's a girl in yellow over there. You should go and have a word."

I saw the girl in the corner. Aside from her pin-straight, slightly lank-looking hair, she was not terribly unattractive. But I decided to hedge my bets and wait for some other people who weren't "too cool" to literally wear their hearts on their sleeves. I ordered the undergrad cocktail *de choix*, a snakebite and black: half a pint of lager, half a pint of cider, with a splash of concentrated black currant juice and a shot of Pernod for good measure. The mix is so potent that it was recently banned in a lot of pubs in Essex, where it is known as a catalyst for violence. There it's called Diesel or a row in a glass.

I needed to be drunk enough to be numbed to the smirks and stares being cast at me from every direction, yet lucid enough to be charming and funny with any other earnest soul clad in yellow or, preferably, green.

After a half hour I noticed that no one else was adhering to the dress code aside from the Sissy Spacek look-alike sitting on her own in the corner. The girl noticed that I had been leering at her for the past five minutes and seemed to be looking back, playing with her hair, which I'd heard was a good sign. Everyone else in the bar seemed to be aware of the two of us sizing each other up on either side of the room and surveyed the scene with their heads on swivels, as if they were in the first row at Center Court at Wimbledon.

"Go on then," said the zaftig hockey lezzer, punching me hard in the shoulder.

I was probably imagining it but I swear I heard the volume of the music—"Roll with It" by Oasis—dip considerably.

I put my glass down and started taking confident strides toward her; the throng of undergrads began to part like the Red Sea before me. I was at college, miles from home. A brand-new start.

"No one knew me here," I repeated to myself as a mantra.

No one knew, for example, about the brown stain that was found on my towel in the showers after gym. (As I said at the time, it was the remnants of a melted Kit Kat in my gym bag.) No one knew about when I offered the high school good-time girl a fiver to snog me out of desperation. (She laughed and told everyone. Her hook-nosed cousin said she'd do it for fifteen, but I didn't have the money.) No one here knew that I was sometimes called "the Jew" because I was one of three kids in my grade who was circumcised, and out of the three of us the only one with foreign lineage and, relative to the other fair-skinned, peg-toothed, sandy-haired, blue-eyed, stubby-nosed pupils, had a vaguely international look about me.

Anyway, she, the girl in yellow, didn't know any of these things.

She seemed to quiver with fear as I walked closer to her, the crowd following my progress with their eyes.

"Do it! Do it! Do it!" the hockey girls began chanting as I drew ever closer.

"*Do it! Do it! Do it!*" The chant caught on and grew louder.

The girl looked at me coming closer, shook her head, and mouthed "Fuck off" at me. Without breaking pace, I hooked a sharp right turn and scurried out the double doors and out of the student union building.

She seemed to have known all about the kind of hapless eunuch I was just from my getup. I ran out into the rain and across St. Mary's Road to the kebab shop. The night was a bust. I ordered a doner with salad and chili sauce and a can of Lilt, a fluorescent green tropical fruit soda that tastes disgusting and is wildly popular in the UK.

I began walking back to Mrs. Montague's, when a group of sixteen-year-old girls detected my frailty, which I was learning must be completely apparent to all.

"Oi, mate!" one of them yelled out to me. I ignored her and picked up the pace.

"Oi, mate! I is fucking talkin' to you, innit?"

I turned around.

"What?"

"I'm not being funny, yeah, but does you know that you look like a massive, wet bogie?"

I turned around and resumed walking.

"Oi! I'm fucking talking to you!"

Ridiculed by my peers, humiliated by the girl in yellow, and now victimized by a group of urchins. Only two weeks into further education and I was at a breaking point.

"Fuck off, slag!" I shouted once I was twenty yards ahead.

"You *what*? Does you know who my bruvvah is, you little cunt?"

The language! I couldn't believe it. Reminded me of home.

"Come back 'ere and say you is sorry," she shouted. "I'll 'ave 'im cut you!"

There's only so much humiliation I could take in one evening. It was time to stand up for myself for once.

"*Bollocks!*" I screamed and began defiantly sprinting away up St. Mary's Road, leaving steaming slithers of reconstituted lamb in my wake.

I thought I'd left the girl and her posse behind until I heard the *swoosh swoosh* sound of her arms pumping against the sides of her puffy jacket. She was just a few steps behind. I may have shrieked at this point but I often like to think that I didn't.

The possibility of being kicked to death by a gang of teenage girls for no more a crime than expressing my loneliness in hues of green gave me an added burst of speed that allowed me to break away from her as we headed toward Ealing Broadway, which at nine forty-five was still thick with people.

I dropped the kebab completely in the vain hope that my tormentor would skid to her death on it. I could hear a sudden quick burst of footsteps, which I correctly guessed was the girl stopping herself dead in her tracks.

Victory, I thought as I made for the bright lights.

Victory was tainted by the sharp yet thudding blow I received to my neck two seconds after. The little cow had thrown a full can of Cherry Coke at me. A few inches higher and I would have been knocked out cold.

"*Aaaarrrggghh!*" I screamed, turning heads all around.

"You better fucking watch yourself from now on," she screamed.

Still in a sprint, I turned my head to see her looking at me. Disoriented from the blow, my foot came off the curb and I twisted my ankle.

"*Fuck!*" I screamed.

"*I'll be looking for you!*" she shouted out.

Humiliated, emasculated, injured, and missing a doner kebab, what else could I have to pay for? I limped a few hundred yards down the road until the pain in my foot grew too great and I jumped on an atypically convenient double-decker bus.

I arrived at the flat to see a number of people leave. It was ten fifteen. It was bridge night.

I walked into the flat, which was rank with cigarette smoke, old ladies' perfume, and sweat. There was evidence of some truly manic game play—be-doilyed plates full of cookie crumbs, stained coffee cups, emptied bottles of sherry, and an emotionally spent Mrs. Montague sucking hard on a postmatch luxury-length cigarette, shaking her head and lamenting the terrible hand with which she and her partner, Mrs. Boothroyd, had once again snatched defeat from the jaws of victory.

"Maddening, Grant." She sighed, her eyes still fixed upon an arbitrary patch of her ratty Persian rug. "Years to learn and a lifetime to master. This game is designed to send one completely around the bend."

Bridge, I learned, was not so much a game as a calling.

"And what on earth has happened to you?" she asked.

My wet hair was plastered to my head, my tie hung out of my pocket, and a massive chili stain stretched the width of my chest.

"You look like a sort of weed."

Too emotionally beaten down to explain, I simply smiled.

"What would you say to a nice cup of tea?" she said, making for the kitchen. "I taped *EastEnders* from earlier on."

"That would be lovely," I said.

I meant it. Mrs. Montague was old and I was an old soul on the run from the brutality of the modern world, the indignity of love, and the arrested social development of my hometown. Mrs. Montague was my new best friend, gently easing me into a world I hadn't conceived of living in just a few weeks before.

AMERICAN GIRL

I MET BECKY at the beginning of my third and final year at Thames Valley University at a mutual friend's party. It was the fall of 1997. Reports of university being all sex, drugs, and rock and roll had been greatly exaggerated as far as I could tell. In two and a half years I hadn't gotten so much as a smooch. Surely, living with a racist geriatric some distance from campus hadn't helped matters, but even without that knowledge I felt that girls could somehow detect that there was something vaguely rotten about my person. They could smell the fetid odor of desperation. For some reason, Becky could not. After a shaky start—I accused her of being in cahoots with the large and obnoxious Yankee mob—we got along swimmingly.

The American presence was loud and large at TVU. They were

known collectively as the Septics, septic tank being cockney rhyming slang for Yank. The Septics tended to hang out only with other Americans in groups of twenty or more, overtaking the student bars and generally making a red, white, and blue nuisance of themselves. Subsequently, a few of the more vociferous American guys had been badly beaten up by members of the rugby squad and walked around with black eyes and something to prove.

Becky was smart, funny, engaging, and sexy, with a hint of what I found to be a charming New Jersey accent. She had short and shaggy black hair, a mischievous fun-loving spirit, colorful tattoos, and a tongue piercing. Her breath smelled of Jolly Ranchers. The party ended up with us sleeping on the hard floor, and, after a four-hour conversation, I decided I might love her. There were several points where I might have tried to lay one on her but thought better of it: I had been fitted with braces the previous week and was afraid of lacerating her pink, puffy little lips.

I had a free National Health Service retainer throughout my teens, but it mostly stayed in my pocket and I sat on it a lot. By the time I became self-conscious of my classily English gnashers I was almost twenty-one and no longer eligible for NHS orthodontia. I worked a summer as a credit fraud analyst at HSBC and saved up almost four thousand dollars to have fixed braces, subconsciously paving the way for future Americanization.

IF AN ANGLOPHILE is a lover of all things English and a Francophile is an admirer of the French, I think it's odd that there's no snappy equivalent for people like me: people who are enamored with the people and culture of these United States. As a kid, and I mean a *really* young kid, I understood that if it was bigger, better, louder, or greater, chances were that it came from America.

My earliest vivid memories were of a family vacation to visit my uncle Philip in Texas. Like most of my family and a large proportion of the men in my town, he had worked on the messy end of the crude oil refining process. Unlike the rest of them, however, he had managed to work his way up to being a trader and in 1981 was seconded to work for famed oilman Oscar Wyatt at Coastal Oil in Houston.

It was as a five-year-old, in the hundred-degree Houston heat, that I learned to swim in Uncle Phil's pool. I experienced a world that had more than three TV channels, Wild West–themed restaurants where the mastication of three-inch-thick steaks was summarily interrupted by staged gunfights, and where glamorous oil wives marveled at my accent and comparatively excellent diction.

As a young teen, this translated into a thing for American girls. All the ones I'd met in my youth were confident, bubbly, sexy, outspoken, fearless, and athletic. They were almost always sun-kissed, smelled like tropical fruits, and had perfect white teeth. They were, to me, exotic. Most important, they were much more interested in me and whatever I had to say than were any of their English counterparts.

During a two-week vacation to see family friends in rural South Dakota, these vivacious corn-fed beauties lavished attention on me and referred to me as "cute," which I found most thrilling. These girls may have had considerable trouble pinpointing Europe on a map or have little notion of what Bastille Day was all about, but at fourteen they were legally allowed to drive cars, which made them appear most worldly and in control to me. Though I didn't have the guts to accept what I can now see was an open invitation to French a few of them, those family vacations to the American Midwest were the undisputed highlight of my youth. Not a sexual awakening so much as a realization that I was perceived differently, more favorably, by the opposite sex on the opposite side of the Atlantic. In this respect, I often liken myself to Superman; he would have grown up to be an average guy on his home planet of Krypton, but here on planet Earth, he is comparatively superhuman. It's location, location, location.

THE NEXT DAY, Becky called me at Mrs. Montague's flat and invited me to audition with her for parts in *The War Zone*, Tim Roth's directorial debut.

"I haven't acted before," I said.

"So what?" she said. "Neither have I, really. C'mon, it'll be fun."

That was what was so fresh and exciting about Becky and American girls in general: they seemed ready to fling themselves at anything, and in the same spirit of reckless abandonment I rather hoped that she might throw herself at me.

"Yeah," I said. "I suppose it *will* be fun."

We met early and took the Central Line tube into central London. We were auditioning for the parts of a brother and sister who were fourteen and sixteen respectively.

"Aren't we a bit old?" I said. I saw hundreds of eight-by-ten-clutching debutantes lining up around the block. Becky shrugged.

"What are they going to do, arrest us?"

American Studies was my minor at TVU. In a module entitled "Peopling and Settlement of the United States" we had learned about the "rugged individualism" of the pioneers, but I had little understanding of how that concept seemed to have filtered through to everyone some three hundred years later. Becky's can-do spirit was intoxicating. As different as we seemed to be, I felt that I could understand her fully. Paradoxically, I'd never really had a real connection with the girls I grew up with. They seemed cold, dispassionate, apathetic, and hell-bent on keeping their underwear and myself segregated at all times. Inexplicably, the other boys—even the most feebleminded ones—seemed to know exactly how to break down the icy façade at a young age. It's as if they all had girl decoder rings and I didn't.

Becky and I were photographed out of courtesy, quickly shown the door, and walked around London for the rest of the day. I was officially falling for her.

The last time I saw Becky was at my twenty-first birthday party. There were about a hundred people crammed into our converted bungalow. Twelve friends had chartered a minibus from TVU to my parents' house in Essex. I even managed to kiss one of the girls that came, but it wasn't her.

Becky left Thames Valley University in early December without saying good-bye. I thought that we were close enough to warrant some sort of warning that she was heading back to New Jersey. She purposefully didn't say good-bye to anyone. She thought it was better that way. I've grown to see her point, but at the time I was quite upset by it; I was getting used to my braces and was gearing up to make my move. No one seemed to have her contact information or even knew her last name.

In March of the next year, I began working in the university library for some extra cash. My job was to place the books back in their assigned spots as mandated by the Dewey decimal system. After a few tedious shifts, I figured out that the library had no system for tracking which temp was putting the books back and whether they were being put back correctly. I slotted the books onto random shelves and napped without feeling that guilty about it. As I lay facedown on a desk one blustery damp afternoon, I became aware that someone was asking me a question.

"Are you Grant?" he said. He shook my shoulder.

"Yeah?" I said and wiped the cool drool from my cheek and used my sweater sleeve to wipe more from the graffitied surface. He handed me a crumpled piece of paper.

"Becky is trying to get in touch with you."

The piece of paper had her name, e-mail, and phone number. I wasted no time e-mailing her. Over the next few weeks the e-mails between us became long, complex, and, if I was reading them right, mildly flirtatious.

After two weeks and dozens of communiqués, I'd invited myself to stay with her for two weeks. Three thousand miles of ocean seemed to relieve me of my usual backwardness in coming forward. I arrived at Newark Airport on Independence Day 1998. I funded the trip with money I'd borrowed from my dad. That money was intended for a suit, a pair of dress shoes, some shirts, ties, and anything else I'd need to fluff up a BA in media studies from a university that had become a national joke during my tenure there.

With rejection a dead certainty throughout my life, I wasn't in the habit of putting myself out there in any sense, but especially with regards to the romantic. Turning up in another country to woo a platonic friend then was completely anathematic to my character, but I couldn't shake this strange gut feeling that the endeavor was worth the emotional and financial risk.

As luck would have it, the feeling was correct. Becky felt the same way.

We spent the duration of the two-week stay having sex, making out, and making googley eyes at each other. I took great satisfaction in the idea of imposing my will and getting the girl I had a crush on; rugged individualism at work.

Upon leaving, I promised that I would come back just as soon as I could. We said that we loved each other and hashed out a crude plan: she would begin cosmetology school so that she could become a licensed hairstylist, I would live with her in her parents' basement until she had her license, and then we would both move to London, a place for which Becky had an affinity. At the time, I just wanted to be with Becky and didn't care where we ended up. She and she alone was my purpose in life.

To that end I got a temp job at Blue Star Engineering, a metal fabrication plant in the rough little town of South Ockendon. I worked the night shift from 10:00 p.m. until 6:00 a.m. The pay was eight pounds and fifty pence an hour and I saved practically every penny I earned to get back to Becky and New Jersey as soon as I could.

Being met by Becky at the airport remains one of the top three greatest feelings I have ever experienced. Three months of separation in which I worked high-paying but labor-intensive jobs, made and received hugely expensive international phone calls, sent and received thoughtful care packages of photographs, mix-tapes, and dirty underwear (hers) and sweated through a nerve-racking conversation with increasingly suspicious U.S. immigration officials ended here, in the arrivals hall of what was once known as Newark International Airport.

Becky's parents were presented with somewhat of a fait accompli when they arrived back from a vacation in the Carolinas to find that a foreigner had taken up residence under their house, though they quickly and unreservedly embraced me as if I were one of their own.

Becky's mother, Angela, was an Italian-American women whose joyous hospitality knew no bounds. The usual number of the house's inhabitants was often augmented by random foreign businessmen, teens with speech impediments, adult illiterates, and people with various cognitive challenges. These people were students from the various specialist English classes that she'd taught over the years. Angela liked to delegate her hospitality throughout the family, once going as far as setting an eighteen-year-old Becky up on a date with a juvenile delinquent student who'd just been charged with arson. She also famously offered her older daughter Beth's apartment as a safe house for a foreign student who hinted at being beaten by her husband.

For the first month of my stowing away in their basement, the Schumachers were also playing host to a snake-hipped six-foot-seven German grad student named Reiner, who would unleash a shrieking, effeminate laugh at the slightest provocation. The petting-zoo atmosphere in the three-bedroom Colonial made it fairly easy for me to fade into the background.

"It's like the freaking UN in here!" wheezed Angela cheerfully, rustling up yet another stack of blueberry pancakes and a fresh pot of coffee. It was more like the cafeteria at the Tower of Babel.

Becky's father, David, though also an educator, could not have been more different from his wife. A literature professor at a nearby university, he was stoic and Germanic, tall, blond, and mustachioed. He looked like Robert Redford, handsome and weather-worn in a manner that a man in his sixties deserves to be. Whatever he had to say was measured, thoughtful, entertaining, and always worth listening to. This wasn't lost on the hooting, shrieking, stammering linguistic misfits, who fell to reverent silence when he spoke.

Understandably, Mr. Schumacher spent a lot of his free time in his wood shop, where he made hand-carved and extremely ornate scale models of schooners, model airplanes, and once got to work on refurbishing an impossibly long marimba from Central America.

Becky, her parents and I lived in Madison, New Jersey, which is also known as the Rose City. It's a really charming, tidy little town about thirty miles west of New York City. It has an old-style movie theater with a marquee, an impressive white stone town hall, a picturesque main street with a town clock, and its lampposts have these spherical glass enclosures atop them, giving the town the appearance of being gaslit.

Without a work visa I couldn't work legally in the United States, so I would have to find under-the-table work. The favorable exchange rate plus living at the Schumachers meant that the money I'd saved from my work at the factory would go a long way. Yet I felt that I needed to hustle for the sake of my incredibly generous adopted family. Becky had begun attending cosmetology school in Denville, leaving me to putter around the house all day. Some weeks passed and I grew self-conscious of my disheveled omnipresence in the Schumacher residence. Mr. Schumacher was on a yearlong sabbatical; we were always bumping into each other around the house and soon I was sufficiently embarrassed to at least *appear* to earn my keep in some capacity.

At Becky's suggestion and with his permission, I took Mr. Schumacher's steel-strung acoustic guitar and auditioned for a gig at a local coffeehouse. They were impressed enough by my performance of "Ziggy Stardust" to offer me a half-hour slot three months down the line, on the condition that I provide my own PA system and a large crowd of fans with a penchant for overpriced lattes and biscotti.

In the meantime, Becky began to keep me busy by having me attend cosmetology school with her four nights a week and using me as her model. I would bring a book to read while Becky quickly honed her styling of finger waves, application of eye shadow, manicures, pedicures, and paraffin hand wax treatments. There were around twelve other girls in the class, who would bring their friends, sisters, mothers, aunts. Half of them, Becky explained, were "royal guidettes"; the other half, near-destitute white trash. Only one other boyfriend was repeatedly subjected to the nightly makeovers. Chip had buck teeth, a dirt-lip mustache, and a thinning flat-top hairstyle. He looked to be around thirty and was incredibly scrawny. He wore a holey, blue New York Yankees sweater with a cream-colored dickey underneath and acid-wash jeans that had an elasticized waistband. By the end of each night, however, his eye shadow was fierce, his skin rid of superficial blemishes, and his hands baby soft. Despite the dark rings around her eyes and missing bicuspid, his girlfriend, Tiffany, was a stunning-looking twenty-year-old, though far too poor to realize it and too luckless to do anything about her situation. She was carrying Chip's child. On a couple of occasions they hopped into their rusty pickup truck after class and met us at the nearby Applebee's, blasting Def Leppard all the way. Across the table, Chip and I embarrassingly batted our thick and lustrous eyelashes at each other.

Through a friend of Becky's I began interning at a tiny independent record company on the Lower East Side of Manhattan, about an hour-and-twenty-minute commute from Madison. Becky and I had gone into the city a handful of times, though my first commute alone was incredibly daunting. Due to my childhood experiences with London, I was still unsettled by the very idea of the city, and felt much more at home slinking around the Mall at Short Hills than the mania of New York City. As I walked down to the platform at 34th Street, I couldn't quite believe that I had summoned up the courage to actually be riding the New York subway system. The perception of the New York subway in England was around ten years out of date. I had been led to believe that being mugged, stabbed, or shot was virtually assured, and despite Becky's insistence to the contrary, I was practically shaking as I inserted a token into the turnstile, and I nervously chuckled at the ridiculousness of the situation.

Becky had given me a crib sheet of exactly how to get to the Orchard Records office:

Midtown Direct train from Madison to Penn Station.
Take the A, C, or E downtown to West 4th St.
Walk down a level and catch a B, D, F, or Q train to
    Grand St.
Walk four blocks east to Orchard St., turn south.
45 Orchard Street is between Grand and Hester.

I'd asked Becky if New Yorkers carried compasses, as they always seemed to talk about things being north, south, east, and west; it's very alien to the English ear as an urban navigational tool.

"If the street numbers are getting higher you are headed north, if the avenues are getting higher you are headed west. Get it?"

I looked at her blankly.

"Look, if you can see the Chrysler Building or the Empire State Building, that's probably going to be north. If you can see the World Trade Center, that's almost definitely south."

I wasn't confident that I'd get to my destination without incident, so I brought a pocketful of quarters in case I needed Becky to talk me in remotely. Despite the alphanumeric subway lines making little sense, I managed to make it.

The Lower East Side, south of Delancey, looked exactly how the huddled masses had left it. Everything about it was decrepit, musty, and narrow. I'd been to Times Square, midtown, and the West Village, but this was a part of the city I immediately felt a strong affinity for.

Orchard Records was headed up by a gentleman named Richard "Richie" Gottehrer. His name came with the garish and unwieldy prefix of "music industry legend." Richard cowrote a host of hits in the sixties, including "My Boyfriend's Back," "In the Night Time," "Sorrow," and "I Want Candy." He produced "Hang on Sloopy" by the McCoys, cofounded Sire Records with Seymour Stein, had produced the first Blondie records and albums by the Go-Gos.

Chris Apostolou managed almost everything in the office, including the staff of interns, which at the time was really just me. With petty cash, Chris paid for my commute and lunches, and usually found an extra fifty bucks for me at the end of the week. My work was mostly helping with tour support for the seven or eight groups on the label. This meant preparing and sending tour posters, press releases, and CDs to radio stations and venues, plus runs to the bank, post office, print shops, and so on. While running errands around the Lower East Side, I never ceased to be amazed by the insular urban neighborhood feel where Jewish, Chinese, and Hispanic neighborhoods had converged, how their boundaries were constantly being redrawn month to month, with Chinatown encroaching from the west and the hipster contingent pushing down from the north. Yet in this state of flux, many shopkeepers of a bygone era stayed put.

Orchard Records rented half a shop front from Irving and Beatrice Salwen, who sold wholesale umbrellas in the other half. Irving was a ninety-five-year-old man who was as much a fixture of the neighborhood as Gus's Pickles, Katz's Deli, and Yonah Schimmel's Knishes. Irving would sit in a plastic chair outside the store and play his fiddle to the rapidly diminishing number of customers who walked by. Bea, being twenty-five years his junior, ran the store, ran their home, and increasingly ran Irving as he lived out the last years of his long life.

The block was still full of Hasidic men who sold men's suits or women's hosiery. I always thought it was odd that though even shaking a woman's hand was forbidden by their religion, they would spend all day displaying thongs and fishnet stockings in their dusty windows. Every day, five times a day, Israel would try to talk me into a "nice suit." With the changes on the block, business looked to be waning and everyone was getting the hard sell.

After a surprisingly short period of time, I found myself falling in love with the life I'd fallen into by accident, feeling more at home in a foreign country, in an alien situation, than I ever had done in my hometown. Since arriving in America, I'd been humbled by the hospitality showed to me and found myself wondering what it was about being in New York that made me feel like the "real" me. There seemed, for the first time, to be nothing to stand in the way between me and being truly happy.

THE TIME
DIFFERENCE

AFTER BEING AWAY from home for three months, I started to get a different perspective on where I'd come from. The threat of random acts of violence was suddenly palpable to me. In New York, I haven't even *heard* of anyone having a pint glass smashed into their face, a pool ball in a sock swung into their teeth, or being thrown through the window of a kebab shop. Not only could you see all this on any given night at a chain wine bar in Essex, you could set your watch to the opening salvos of verbal abuse at chucking-out time. These places require "gentlemen" to wear a dress shirt, formal leather shoes, and dark trousers, purportedly to keep out the riffraff, harkening back to a time when the local shit-kickers couldn't afford to look presentable.

Whatever the feeling is that makes someone want to beat another person until they stop moving, it's contagious and intoxicating in towns that sprang out of the countryside surrounding London after the Second World War. I spent my late teens wary of being its victim and frightened at how easily I could be swept away in the exhilaration of a "good kicking," albeit from the sidelines. Along with my dress shirt and dress shoes, I slapped on enough of the aftershave I got for Christmas to mask the fear.

The town I grew up in is the perfect petri dish for arbitrary vandalism and senseless violence. Corringham manages to combine the humdrum existence of a country village with all the trappings of urban decay, making the place look like a vandalized Teletubby land. The glass bus shelter at the bottom of our street is shattered, replaced and shattered again every week, the red phone box stinks of stale piss, and the iconic red pillar boxes have all had the word "cunt" painstakingly etched into the paintwork with a school's compass needle. I still get embarrassed just thinking about the white-haired and russet-faced old ladies who have to read it every time they post a letter. You can divide the town's populace neatly in two: those who have come to the town in the past fifty-five years and their descendants are the majority, initially from heavily bombed parts of east London; and then a small and overwhelmed minority of hobbitlike country folk who were there before, presumably from the beginning of time.

Initially a distinction was made between the areas where the original village folk lived and where the interlopers had moved into new housing estates and blocks of flats half a mile away. Now Old Corringham and New Corringham run into each other and are much less distinguishable in both look and feel.

Corringham has changed more in the past fifty years than at any time in its fifteen-hundred-year history. A thousand-year-old church stands next to a centuries-old pub, all adjacent to a farm. A hundred and fifty yards up the road is a parade of around a dozen shops that in my lifetime included an old-fashioned barbershop, a butcher's, a bakery, a place that sold local fruit and vegetables, a fish and chip shop, a fishmongers, a post office, a betting shop, an old-fashioned druggist, an electrical repair shop, a bank, a bicycle repair shop, and a doctor's office. Lampits Hill now encompasses a tanning salon, a hair and nail parlor, a kebab shop, two Chinese restaurants, an Indian restaurant, a disco and party supplies store (run by my uncle's brother-in-law, a.k.a. Dennis the DJ), a "continental-style" café, and at the very top of the hill, the office of a rather eccentric New Age reflexologist and Reiki healer, who also doubles as my mother.

Whatever it was that possessed her to become the town's shaman took hold shortly after I left for college. I was extremely skeptical about the demand for black magic in a town like ours, but apparently business is booming. My mother's clientele is elderly and plentiful around Christmastime, thanks to her brilliant introduction of gift certificates. I always imagine the look on a dignified yet provincial older lady's face as she steps into a room filled with the sounds of the panpipes and the alien stink of frankincense. The poor old girl had probably expected a pair of slippers.

The town stands in the shadows of a huge oil refinery complex on the mouth of the river Thames, thirty miles downstream from central London. Local people like to stop and speculate on how a major explosion at the refineries would blow Corringham "sky high," then cheerfully go back to whatever it was they were doing. Several members of my family had long careers there, though I only managed to clock up two months at the refinery. This was one of the many jobs I took between ninety-day stays in New Jersey, the maximum time a U.S. tourist visa allows for EU citizens.

A portion of the refinery was cleared for maintenance, creating a glut of extra jobs that BP rushed to fill. From Monday to Friday, I drove an eighteen-passenger bus around a three-mile circuit of the BP plant, obeying the speed limit of fifteen miles per hour under threat of dismissal. One of my coworkers was Kevin, a forty-year-old man who had lived in Corringham all his life, though, to my ear, he had a strong Afrikaans accent. On my first day, a grease monkey I'd struck up a conversation with told me that Kevin "shits in a bag." It sounded at first like some perverse compulsion, but it became apparent days later that this was just his colorful way of saying that Kevin had received a colostomy. I took over his rounds as he recovered from the operation by sitting in the subcontractor's oil-spattered garage, drinking sugary tea.

Dave was Kevin's brother-in-law and was about ten years older, with eyes that went in markedly different directions. He worked on the refinery's broken vehicles. Dave had worked all his life in a slaughterhouse that had recently gone under, which he bitterly blamed on the rise of vegetarianism. I'd only see Dave and Kevin every few days if they happened to catch me driving around at lunchtime.

I started at 5:45 each morning and finished a little after 8:00 at night. My passengers were engineers, surveyors, grease monkeys, jetty pilots, and Philippine crew members coming ashore to spend their wages on booze, whores, and electrical items in nearby towns.

Almost half of my shift was spent in total darkness, the remainder under low, heavy, charcoal-gray snowy skies as large, foul-smelling steam clouds belched forth from every nook and cranny of the plant. I'd only have people in the van for a tiny fraction of my countless daily laps, meaning I could listen to the thoughtful mix-tapes Becky was sending me at the rate of one a week. I could pull over and compose letters to her expressing my longing for her and my new American life and, as the weak winter light began to fade, furiously masturbate.

On Saturday and Sunday I worked twelve- to fourteen-hour shifts in the refinery's canteen, scrubbing industrial-sized pots and serving up food that would repulse foreign oilmen who hadn't built up a tolerance to British cuisine. The "chefs" were a posse of hard-drinking, chain-smoking, pink-faced Scots who had spent most of their careers cooking for large numbers of working men on rigs, refineries, or tankers. I spent the latter half of the shift in the pot wash area. My only company at the sinks was a thirty-year-old beanpole of a man named Gazza, working to fund his seventh trip to Thailand for the purpose of having sex with young prostitutes. Over the course of five weekends, I had become an unwitting expert on backpacking, youth hostels, and the Thai skin trade.

It was during my last weekend that the siren signaling an imminent catastrophe sounded. We were all rushed into a lead-lined, underground shelter, which I overheard a fellow evacuee saying would be "fucking useless" in the event of an explosion. The Scots, who looked, sounded, and acted like latter-day pirates, didn't seem to care, taking great pleasure that they were being paid to stand around. Other people joined us and busied each other with gallows humor, cheerfully resigned to our imminent death. I, however, was petrified with fear. Of death itself, sure, but more that I would die here, the place I was escaping by inches and under the doomsday circumstances that every local had contemplated so many times. I had kept my imminent escape to America to myself up until I was forced to confront my mortality. Kevin had taken a dislike to me after I mentioned that I had been to college, and I didn't want to incur anyone else's hatred for what is known locally as having "ideas above your station." I longed for Becky and the Garden State. Something no one else here could understand.

"America?" spat George, the middle-aged and effeminate catering supervisor huddled next to me in the shelter. He wrinkled his nose in disgust.

"They say everything's so much bigger over there, don't they? No, I'm quite happy here, thank you very much."

George had somehow interpreted my plan of a new life as an invitation for him to join me and had declined point-blank. He represented a commonly held view that almost everything about life in America was grossly out of proportion. The cars people drive, the food they eat, their disposable income, the energy they consumed, the volume at which they talked, the number of TV channels they had, the distance between any two places. It's all sort of valid, but while others took offense at America, I found myself drawn to its bigness, hungry for a heaving slice of it.

My leaving Corringham happened in gentle increments over a period of almost four years, which helped dull any pangs of homesickness. First there was college: my mother cried when they left me in the care and tutelage of Mrs. Montague, but I soon found myself coming home every weekend. Then, a yearlong period of spending three months in America followed by two or three months at home, working like a dog to fund another ninety-day stint in New Jersey. I'd heard stories of people not being allowed back into the States after overstaying their visas, if only by a day or two. I wanted to make sure there was no reason for being kept out, or worse, deported.

The contrast between these seasons at home and abroad was brought into sharper focus by how I was spending my time in each. Being at home meant full shifts of manual labor and grabbing as much overtime as I could: unclogging wet cement from turbines at the breeze block factory; pressing shapes or drilling holes into sheet metal on the night shift; saving every penny while my peers were suddenly commuting, buying cars and homes, and getting two-hundred-dollar haircuts.

In the comparative affluence of Morris County, New Jersey, life felt like an extended vacation: dining out twice a day, trips to the beach, camping, sailing, strolling around the city, making new friends with just my accent, watching art-house movies, all with a vivacious, outspoken American girl whom I loved and who loved me back.

HOMELAND INSECURITIES

WHAT ARE YOU planning to do with that guitar?" asked the immigration official.

"Play it," I said.

"For money?"

"No, just for fun."

This was my third entry into the United States in seven months and the immigration questions were getting tougher.

"Mr. Stoddard, you have already spent a lot of time in the United States in the past few months. What are you doing here and how are you funding these trips?"

"I'm taking my time seeing the country and my parents are rich."

He looked up at me sternly.

"Then you are a very lucky man," he said and handed my passport back to me. "Have a nice day."

Any residual homesickness had been flushed out of me on this last gray, cold, depressing trip back to England. I knew that I had to somehow find a way to live and work legally in the United States, though the obstacles to that end seemed to be insurmountable. I had no skill set, no specialist training, and no prior work experience. Becky had repeatedly offered to marry me, though I saw it as a last resort, not least because our relationship was beginning to show signs of cooling.

While I was away in England, I'd been trying to reckon how I would get my immigrant status straightened out. It had become abundantly clear that I wanted to be legally allowed to live and work in New York; I was in the pursuit of happiness and was gaining some serious ground. Another ninety-day visa waiver period would soon elapse and it was likely that immigration officials would not let me into the country easily after two consecutive ninety-day visits.

Everyone else in the office was dumfounded by the obstacles in the way of obtaining a work visa for me. Pre-9/11 New Yorkers looked at the people bussing their tables, delivering their lo mein, folding their laundry, messengering their documents, driving their taxis, cleaning their offices, serving their cocktails and assumed that the gateway to America was still flung wide open. The number of illegal immigrants in the United States is more than seven million. These men and women serve to do the jobs that Americans don't deign to and as a result are largely unhindered by the authorities. Conversely, the INS is well aware that white, college-educated Europeans are not coming to America to scrub toilets and are in fact vying for positions coveted by their own blue-eyed boys and girls.

While Becky was originally more than prepared to go to City Hall with me and quietly tie the knot, her motivation was becoming more romantic than practical. As a marriage of convenience became a more distinct possibility by the minute, she began leaking our plans to her mother, who started sketching out an elaborate summer wedding with all the trimmings, which had helped fire Becky's imagination, and the two of them created this feedback loop of flowers, wedding dresses, wedding songs, prime rib, seven-tier cakes, and so on and so forth.

As I weighed a marriage of convenience against the risk of deportation, Richard Gottehrer came to my rescue. Richard offered to produce a demo tape for me and sign me to a developing artist deal with Orchard Records. Richard's business partner called in a favor with a family friend in Washington, and within a week I had an approval form for an O-type working visa, which was good for three years. It arrived immediately prior to my ninety-day visa waiver was about to expire.

Becky was happy to hear my news despite having gotten carried away with the idea of a lavish summer wedding. She had just graduated from beauty school and had been accepted as a trainee at Bumble and Bumble, a trendy midtown hair salon where countless stars came to be coiffed. I returned home for two months to finalize my visa status, tie up some loose ends, and convince my friends that I really was going to live in America for good. I was an émigré.

"So you're really going to live out there, are you?"

Everybody asked me this, having regarded my previous stays in the United States as little more than extended vacations. When I told people of my intentions I unleashed a tidal wave of resentment. When you leave England, people sort of take it very personally.

I recently read an article in a British daily paper about Kate Moss buying a place in LA that was headlined "Drug-Troubled Model Turns Her Back on Britain," as if she'd left the rainy little island out of spite.

Having the visa in hand made it official in my mind as well as everybody else's.

While I was at home Becky began searching for a place for us to live in Manhattan, now that we would both be working there. She eventually signed a one-year lease on a tiny, newly refurbished one-bedroom on Attorney Street between Houston and Stanton. Attorney Street had been a one-stop shop for heroin just a few years earlier, but by 1999 represented the easternmost reach of gentrification on the Lower East Side. Until I moved in there with her I had never been east of Essex Street. Because she was still in education of sorts, her parents agreed to pay a third of her $1,400 rent, meaning that Becky and I only had to find a little over $460 a month apiece, which was quite doable, even on my starting salary of $20,000 at The Orchard. Though my official job description for visa purposes was "recording artiste," I was, in actuality, just a general office assistant, continuing with the same duties I'd always had.

"What do you do for . . . The Orchard, Mr. Stoddard?"

At Newark Airport, I could now answer the immigration official's questions with confidence and candor.

"I'm in a rock band."

For the first time Becky wasn't in the arrivals lounge to meet me after I collected my baggage. She eventually turned up after about ten minutes or so. The e-mails and phone calls between us had been shorter and less frequent on this separation. For my part, the approval of my visa meant that living and working in America was no longer bundled together with holy matrimony. Becky had been working at Bumble and Bumble for almost three months and had found a new slew of friends and distractions. My sudden abandonment of our marriage plans upon getting the visa had hurt her.

Over the phone, Becky had said that the fourth-floor walk-up apartment at 161 Attorney Street was small, but I wasn't really prepared for quite how tiny it was. The bedroom was big enough for a double bed and about a foot-wide space down one side. The living room was only six feet wide, the kitchen appliances were in miniature, and I'd seen bigger bathrooms on airplanes.

"Don't freak out!" said Becky as I looked around. "It'll seem bigger once everything is in it."

"No, it's . . . nice," I said.

It was certainly not a suitable dwelling for more than one normal-sized person, and I immediately felt trapped. I took Becky's word that some hastily purchased IKEA furniture would give us a better perspective on the place and went downstairs to unload the truck.

The location certainly made for an easy commute to work. I experimented with a few routes but would usually walk west along Stanton, south down Clinton, west along Delancey, and south down Orchard; a walk of about eight minutes or so.

For me, having a relationship *period* was exciting. Having a *long-distance* relationship was extremely exhilarating. The separation engenders an incredible longing, the distance sparks creativity in communication, the time difference forces you to shift your perceptions of days, and the day's date is simply a tally toward seeing one another again, the clear and present danger of being refused entry to the country a nail-biting climax. The time you end up spending together is so precious, the arrivals and departures so fraught with emotion, the days and weeks of togetherness so fleeting. It was like having a protracted holiday romance. I had allowed the romantic drama of our transatlantic love connection to drive our relationship, and I hadn't realized it until it aged and suddenly ceased to exist, and, instead of our relationship being demarcated by ninety-day periods of togetherness and separation, it was now just us in 250 square feet, time stretching out infinitely before us. We got down to the day-to-day business of living normal lives and it suddenly became clear, to me at least, that the easy, breezy vacation part of our relationship was over.

It became apparent that Becky liked to hover within the margins of untidy and downright filthy, whereas I was coming out of the closet as a neat freak. At about the same time, she developed a stupefying habit of smoking large quantities of weed. Although I originally thought I might have been imagining it, other girls were beginning to take an interest in me and part of me began to resent that I'd gone from virgin to a cohabitating malcontent with none of the fun, casual, reckless part in between.

It seemed a terrible shame to be this unhappy with my relationship situation when so much else seemed to be going well. Though it was I who sought out a relationship between us, Becky had subsequently put much more into it, even scrapping our original plan to move back to England on my behalf. Her family had taken me in unconditionally, and as awful as splitting with Becky would be, prying myself away from my adopted family would be even more difficult.

We spent Christmas back in Madison, and on New Year's Eve I told Becky that it was over. She cried and then her parents took us to dinner at Benihana on the way back to the city. Becky was inconsolable at the hibachi table, even though the chef pulled out his best shrimp-tail flicking tricks and making the little volcano with slices of onion.

A week later I moved in with my friend Frank, who lived off the Ditmas Avenue stop, about halfway out to Coney Island. I was there through January and half of a frigid February before Becky called to tell me that she still expected me to pay my third of the rent until the lease ran out in August.

"I can't afford to pay two lots of rent money!" I screamed.

"Well, you agreed to live with me for a year, and it's sort of not fair on me or my parents," she said.

Though I had sort of agreed to it, my name was not on the lease. Out of respect for Becky's wonderful parents I felt I had no choice but to move back in with Becky, though this was part of her plan to reconcile. She was going to be spending two weeks visiting her sister in California, then I found an outrageously cheap round-trip fare back to England, so that took care of March. The month of April proved to both of us that there was no way either of us could endure the rest of the summer in 250 square feet of hell and so finally, begrudgingly, she let me go.

HASIDS AND
HAYSEEDS

IT SEEMED THAT by the late summer of 2000 my allotted quota of American hospitality had been almost entirely cashed. My employer, The Orchard, now owed me almost six thousand dollars in back wages, and seven weeks had passed since I'd last received a full paycheck. It had become apparent that leaving the company meant kissing that cash good-bye for the foreseeable future. In addition, my nefariously acquired work visa allowed me to work *only* for The Orchard. There was part-time under-the-table work to be had, but I lacked the gumption, confidence, and wherewithal to effectively hunt it down. Plus, the thought of washing dishes nights and weekends while my employer owed me more than I'd paid in rent the previous year made my blood boil. My father had wired me money before but had recently lost his job. He said that he could only give me more money if it was going toward a one-way ticket home. Friends from home were buying property, two-week vacations in the Greek islands, cars, and luxury goods, and it seemed that I would have to go back and, after a good helping of humble pie, play catch-up in a race I didn't care to run. I was flat broke, but unlike the *genuinely* poverty-stricken, I was safe in the knowledge that the struggle, the discomfort, the heartache, the occasional hunger could be ended with one collect phone call. Imagining the phone call, the good-byes to my new friends, to the city I loved, the return to my old bedroom, the rain-sodden search for an arbitrary profession kept me from making that phone call prematurely.

As terrible as things seemed to be going, I felt that being poor in New York City was preferable to being rich anywhere else, especially Corringham. I adopted the sentiment as my mantra when my stomach rumbled or I found myself walking miles home from Manhattan in near hundred-degree weather. I was becoming ill, looking drawn and beaten down. I thought I'd been doing a good job at concealing my run of bad luck but realized it permeated my being as homeless people gradually stopped asking me for change.

I was now single and renting the open kitchen/living room of my friend Lizzy's dilapidated Brooklyn apartment as a crash pad, answering phones and shrink-wrapping CDs at The Orchard in the hope of being paid and living off of bagels that sandwich franchise threw out at the end of the day. They were hardly stale, and if you froze them immediately a bag might last you ten days or more. Occasionally I could stop being angry at what had become of my existence long enough to revel in my penny-pinching ingenuity. I often felt a very real sense of pride as I marched cheerfully across the Williamsburg Bridge with yet another week's starchy sustenance slung over my shoulder. Being incredibly thrifty was a game I was getting better at and even enjoyed at times. I began to amass a catalog of money-saving techniques that I'd either invent or adapt to suit my own situation. The leanest times gave me some surprising perspective on how I could make do with so little. I let this thinking inform my lifestyle further.

I always carried an empty to-go cup. I'd spot friends brunching at a diner and siphon off a cup of their bottomless coffee. I'd bring a mason jar to house parties and pilfer a few fingers of gin, then dump in the remainder of an abandoned screwdriver or rusty nail. I'd go home and put the jar in the freezer, then take it out to the next night's party and repeat the process. Some combinations were vile, but in general the resulting mixture was not unlike a Long Island Iced Tea and improved by the mouthful. I scaled back this practice after nearly choking to death on a rogue cigarette butt at a friend of a friend's movie screening.

If the universe was offering something, I'd gladly accept and decide whether or not I could use it later. One weekend's bumper harvest included a copy of the previous week's *New Yorker*, a shoe box full of well-thumbed paperbacks in Spanish, twenty-five square feet of plastic grass, a superficially damaged lawn chair, a cup of Baskin-Robbins's Rum Raisin, a ratty-looking videotape of *Moonstruck* (with the last third taped over with music videos), over a dozen assorted gourmet olives, a three-foot-tall Frosty the Snowman lawn ornament, several bite-sized panini samples, a comped entry to a local band's "showcase" gig, and a floor lamp.

Luckily, the lean times coincided with the summer months. When the weather was nice I stayed outside as much as possible. The sunshine was a great leveler and made me feel human again. I borrowed one of Lizzy's books and sat in McCarran Park or strolled around the East Village for hours on end. Three dollars would get me to the beach at Coney Island and back. On more unpleasant days, I trained myself in the art of appreciating vegetating under the covers. Many of my contemporaries had a reverence for sleep, but I had only known it as a necessity. I would while away hours listening to Lizzy's Stereolab albums and drift in and out of consciousness, willing myself back into beautiful dreams.

Lizzy and our other roommate, Albert, eventually confronted me with regards to my being habitually late with rent money and the cold cuts I'd taken from the fridge without asking. It took several minutes for me to realize they were actually asking me to leave. I was being evicted.

"You're chucking me out?" I said upon the realization.

"Well, we can't afford to cover your end anymore," said Albert. "Plus, you're sort of a thief."

Silently, Lizzy looked at the floor.

"It was a few slices of cheese!" I pleaded.

"Look, someone else has offered me a lot more for the space than you're paying and things aren't working out with us, so here's your two weeks' notice."

"Where am I going to go?" I said.

"Sorry, dude," said Albert.

The phone call home had practically become assured in an instant. I ran out of the house in a vain attempt to get some sort of grip on the situation. Aside from the beautiful people languidly criss-crossing it, Bedford Avenue—Williamsburg's main drag—is incredibly dull. When you're hungry and your clothes are out of style, it's down-right depressing. I decided I would wander the Lower East Side until I had hashed out an action plan regarding somewhere to go.

The L train wasn't running so I walked over to the Marcy Avenue stop, a part of Williamsburg where gentrification hadn't dared to encroach. From Grand Avenue southward, the neighborhood was strewn with crude graffiti slogans.

"*Gentrification = Death!*" "*Kill Borzois Oppressors!*" and "*Stop Gentrification Now!*"

By the late nineties it had become resoundingly obvious that a plea to stop gentrification was as ineffectual as a motion to stop plate tecton-ics or signing a petition opposing photosynthesis. It was a natural pro-cess beyond anyone's control. Furthermore, I'm certain that the call to arms was sprayed not by the Dominicans, Poles, or Hasidic Jews but by distraught members of the first few waves of blue-eyed immigrants who had arrived over the previous decade, people desperately aware of how more affluent later waves would surely unseat them from their cheap and behemoth loft spaces.

Before I got my first cell phone in late 2001, I had the mental agil-ity to hold and recall fifteen of my friend's phone numbers. I had about

ten more written down in miniature on the back of a business card
that I'd wrapped in Scotch tape. As I got off the train, I counted seven
dimes in my pocket, meaning I was able to make two brief phone calls
at best. Who I decided to call was often based more on the likelihood
of them picking up the phone than on whether we had anything to say
to each other, something I reckoned as I walked south down Essex in
the muggy August air.

Chris Apostolou could often be found at the Orchard during the
weekend; I decided I would walk across Hester Street to see him and
guiltlessly make my personal phone calls on the company's tab. Aside
from being the company's de facto accountant, Chris was its handy-
man, using his weekends to build shelves to hold more CDs, painting
the walls, squeezing in yet another workstation.

"I have something for you," he shouted over the dying din of his
circular saw. Chris ran to his desk and returned with a check for three
hundred dollars paid to cash. "I'd run to the bank now if I were you.
I'll keep chipping away at it for you," he promised. "Things are looking
a little better. I'll have another five hundred dollars for you late next
week."

My ego bolstered by the unexpected three-hundred-dollar windfall
and the promise of more cash on the horizon, I walked tall up Orchard
Street and up into the East Village. I picked up a copy of the *Voice*
and commandeered a booth for myself at the Odessa diner on Avenue
A, ordering pork chops, mashed potatoes with gravy, and sweet corn,
despite the late August heat outside. With a full belly and wallet, I
even felt good enough about myself to casually flirt with the strawberry-
blonde, apple-bottomed waitress and let her talk me into a slice of pie
and some coffee. I toyed with the idea of asking for her number but
became deterred as she frowned, watching me fill my to-go cup to the
brim. The practice had become deeply ingrained.

I took my ratty-looking to-go cup across the street to Tompkins
Square Park and had myself a think in the shade. I thought mostly about
my imminent eviction and subsequent relegation to homeless-person
status. My friend Mike had told me about a possible room opening up

in his place in Washington Heights on October first. I'd not realistically considered it before, as I always wanted to live within a somewhat reasonable walking radius of the East Village, but these were desperate times and he told me the place was large, clean, cheap, a block from the A express train, and I would have my own door. I pulled out my laminated business card and squinted to make out Mike's number.

I eventually found a working pay phone that didn't have blood and/or fecal matter smeared all over the receiver and told Mike I would take the room sight unseen.

With the sun setting and some semblance of an action plan coming together in my mind, I walked back to Williamsburg, across the bridge.

The apartment was hot and stuffy. It had been for weeks. The iron bars encasing the windows of our street-level part of the house meant that it was impossible to install an air-conditioning unit. Hershel the landlord had promised the bars would be removed though warned that we would certainly be burgled. Lizzy and Albert had each brought two huge air conditioners to the house, but they sat hulking and redundant on the floor under the windows waiting for Rico the superintendent to remove the bars. It never ceases to amuse me that the apathetic alcoholics employed to keep a group of apartments in good working order are—without the merest trace of irony—typically referred to as "Super." In the ten New York City addresses I've called home, these men have been anything but. We had a ninety-degree heat wave that lasted for two weeks in May 2000. Rico still had the central heating on full blast until June.

Driven to distraction by the heat, I turned on one of the dormant air conditioners despite its just sitting on the floor. The unit noisily coughed out some blue smoke before blowing the house's main fuse, which happened to be located in a closet only Rico had the key to. We were without electricity for twelve hours. Since then we had all been using cheap fans and misting bottles to abate the summer heat.

I decided that even though I had two weeks in Williamsburg, I would spend as little time there as possible. I started immediately and took the now-running L train back over to First Avenue and treated myself to a late movie in the icy cool of Cinema Village East on Second Avenue. The first time I had ever been to the movies on my own. It made me melancholy but I felt that I had grown some in the process, though I can't remember what film I saw. It was after two by the time it was over, too late to ask friends to crash. I decided to pull an all-nighter.

I emerged and walked back to Odessa. A different waitress was on. She was older, harder, colder. Though it was largely unoccupied she said that I could only sit at the counter if I was just going to have coffee. I drank coffee to the point of itchiness and nausea. Five reluctantly refilled cups later, I twitched out of the diner. It had become chilly outside. It was after four and the only people around were heading to 7A, a twenty-four-hour diner, for food to soak up the booze. I did a lap of the twenty-four-hour Key Foods supermarket before I succumbed fully to fatigue. I had $270 on me—most of my first rent check at my new digs—and didn't want to sleep in the open elements. I stumbled into the Citibank ATM vestibule next door, shoving the roll of cash into my underpants. I got two hours of restless sleep under the fluorescent lights before getting turfed out at around seven. A bright Sunday morning.

In the relative safety of daylight, I laid in the park until I registered the sun burning into my face some twenty minutes later. I looked around. Crack whores sat expectantly by the chess boards, junky couples argued about ripping each other's shit off. Old Ukrainian and Polish men sipped booze and mumbled to each other, their big red noses making them resemble proboscis monkeys. I was merely playing at being homeless. I thought about who would step in to save me if I let myself descend further.

In actual fact there were plenty. But surely *these* poor pricks had friends, girlfriends, boyfriends, families. They'd gone to high school, some had attended college. I had been seeing these same bums in the two years since I'd moved to New York. They had been left to their own devices for so long that they had become living folk heroes and villains replete with colorful creation myths, nicknames, and accompanying lore.

That morning I felt sure that I would never realistically be allowed to become feral. I had great friends and I wasn't addicted to meth. I knew that if I recaptured some of the hope and optimism I had when I came to America to be with Becky, I was leaving myself open to something good. I lay back down and let the sunshine warm my face some more.

LIVE FREE OR DIE

FRIENDS OFTEN PUT TO ME that I hadn't really taken full advantage of my time in America, but none more succinctly than my friend Mark.

"Y'know, you've been here for two years and you've only fucked one girl."

His calculation was both smarting and accurate, but didn't take into account that for eighteen months I was living with Becky, the girl I had come to America to win over.

"So?" I said, feeling incredibly defensive.

"I'm just sayin' is all. You're twenty-three years old, you play guitar, living in New York City. You ain't *that* bad-lookin', *and* you've got that stupid fuckin' accent. Girls love that, don't they?"

"Well, some do . . . I suppose."

"Well, you should be livin' the life, balls-deep in strange ass every fuckin' night of the week."

While I'm sure that my accent has enabled me to make time with more pretty women than I've really deserved to over the years, its aphrodisiacal value—at least in my experience—is infinitely more subtle than one might think. In addition, there's nothing like being penniless to negate the charm of a foreign accent. I couldn't afford meeting a girl for drinks or a movie, let alone dinner. In theory, gallery openings could mean free wine, cheese-based snacks, and entertainment, but this was only worth attempting if they happened to take place within walking distance of my tumbledown part of Williamsburg, Brooklyn. Even then, I doubt I'd have the gall to invite them into the space I called my own, just a ratty mattress on a scuffed linoleum floor in a common kitchen and living room area that inexplicably smelled strongly of gasoline. As is the case for many men, my ego inflates and deflates in concert with my cash flow, and consequently, this was a near all-time low. I craved to hold a naked female but I was in no state to court women in the time-honored tradition. I needed a sure thing; no drinks, dinner, or pretending to be interested in them or pretending to be anything more than a foreign drifter.

That I was prepared to travel three hundred miles for sex I'd won in an online trivia contest surprised me.

I stuffed a bottle of tap water and two frozen bagels in my backpack with some clean underwear and a toothbrush. The bus ride to Portsmouth, New Hampshire, was a long one. I walked north from my squat behind the Domino Sugar factory. The area was largely untouched by gentrification and still pretty colorful: a biker's hangout was stationed opposite the ramshackle building I was calling home, its denizens always revving their hogs and doing wheelies through the potholed streets. Hasids in giant hockey-puck-shaped fur hats poured through the streets at sundown on Fridays, followed by wave after wave of well-scrubbed Poles en route to the Warsaw Social Club an hour later. Dominicans made full recreational use of the sidewalks, with the sound of meringue music filling the air all day and the smell of burnt sugar hanging thick at night. The sugar factory workers were in a running dispute with their British parent company and had taken to defacing the Union Jack and images of the Queen in protest on Kent Avenue. It never failed to stoke the few dying embers of patriotism that I still had in me.

It was 9:30 a.m., hours before the Saturday brunch rush on the more genteel and gentile stretch of Bedford Avenue. Trembling pretty people with preposterous cockatoo haircuts were still getting home. They had been drinking, drugging, and having sex and generally making the most of both their early twenties and the beautiful Indian summer. I had not. I was broke. In fact, I was quasi-homeless, hungry, ill, lonely, and a bad month away from going back to England a broken man, provided I could scare up the airfare. I took the L train from Bedford Avenue, changed to an uptown C train at Eighth Avenue and waited for the Greyhound to Boston at gate 71 of the Port Authority Bus Terminal at 42nd Street. I had just over an hour to sit and think about what was waiting for me on the other end of my journey.

Two weeks prior, with my reluctant repatriation seemingly inevitable, I decided that I would have a stab at doing something that took me out of my malaise, if only for a few hours. As I opened my mind beyond what I could scrounge up to eat, an opportunity plopped neatly into my lap: a friend suggested that I enter a competition, a general knowledge quiz that took place in an Internet chat room. The prize was sexual intercourse with Lisa Carver, a former teen prostitute, performance artist, and writer at her home in Dover, New Hampshire. She lived up there with her husband and six-year-old son, who was sired by a prominent member of the Church of Satan.

Up until this point my experience with women other than Becky was next to nil. By the age of twenty-three, the opportunity to engage in casual sex had not presented itself, and I remain clueless as to how to effectively go about it to this day. Free, transactional sex was the perfect sexual adventure for a socially awkward and downwardly mobile man.

Lisa, bless her restless, reckless heart, was giving me that opportunity, and in doing so the opportunity to resurrect my American dream.

Lisa wrote a biweekly column for Nerve.com in which she reported on the intimate details of her long, rich, and tumultuous sex life. She had recently gotten married and decided that she would keep things interesting for herself and her fanatical following by having sex with the winner of a random trivia contest. I hadn't heard of Nerve.com or Lisa Carver before entering the competition; being preoccupied with my life's downward spiral I had reverted to a hunter-gatherer existence, oblivious to popular culture. A coworker at The Orchard sat me down at the computer to answer trivia questions at work. It was only after the competition that she filled me in on who Lisa was, what Nerve was all about.

By the time the decrepit bus willed itself past Hartford, Connecticut, I noticed that the reds and golds of autumn had arrived here weeks sooner than in Manhattan and that my bagels had thawed just enough to eat. I tore off bite-sized hunks of the cinnamon-raisin and popped them into my mouth despite being nauseated with fear. I found that the only way to abate the nausea was by telling myself that Lisa would understand if I backed out.

We pulled into Boston, where I ran to catch my connecting ride to New Hampshire. I got the last available seat, which was behind the driver, and asked him to tell me when we got to Portsmouth. I didn't have a particularly clear idea of what Lisa looked like. There were a handful of pictures that existed online, but she looked dramatically different in each one. They spanned a period of almost fifteen years, a spectrum of hair color, and a marked difference in breast size. In one picture she was holding a puppy, in another she was peeing in a litter box in front of a large crowd of cheering Frenchmen. I *could* gather that she was pretty, tall, wiry, and feral, but little else. I hardly told anyone about my trip up north in the two-week period between winning and collecting the prize. Every day I woke up thinking that I should probably bail out, but somehow I kept forgetting to make the call. I wanted adventure, I wanted to have sex with somebody I probably wasn't going

to marry, and I didn't want to pay for it. As the bus drew closer to Lisa
and the sun began to sink, I could barely recognize my behavior as
my own. I felt I was choosing darkness. Filiz (pronounced Felice), the
college friend who had introduced Becky and me, was visiting from
London, splitting her time between us both like some overgrown love
child. Though it was inconvenient for both of them, I sent Filiz to
Becky's new apartment in Newark so that I could have loveless sex with
a stranger. I told them that I had a job interview in Boston. I was desperate, deceitful, and a terrible friend.

From the other side of the window, New Hampshire was telling
me it was tough, that it was the Granite State, that its residents live free
or die, that its motorcyclists don't wear helmets. Dover, Portsmouth,
Durham—as the situation I had put myself in became more alien, the
place names on the road signs became more familiar; they were all
English place names. No one at home would believe this.

Lisa and I had talked on the phone the night before. It was my last
out, but I'd solemnly vowed that I would be on the bus.

"I'm exited to meet you!" she said. "Dave's excited to meet you,
too!"

Dave is Lisa's husband. Dave had told Lisa that he was cool with
the competition but had second thoughts about it all a few days before.
Lisa appeased him by having a second trivia competition that yielded
a female winner for Dave to have sex with. Dave was the gentle foil to
Lisa's wildness in her columns and had quite the following himself.

"Dave's winner backed out last-minute. Can you believe that?"

"No." I could *definitely* believe that.

"So I have this other woman on standby. So she's coming by. She'll
take care of Dave while we, y'know."

"I know."

I felt calmed that I would have another outsider there, someone
else who would probably be feeling similar emotions, somebody to
absorb the oddness of the situation along with me. I had told Lisa that
I was broke. She said that I should borrow the bus fare and she would
reimburse me.

The bus driver told me that we'd reached my stop. I got out and noticed the twenty-degree dip in temperature throughout my body. Because of its size, weather in the UK is rather uniform. The idea of hopping on a bus to change the weather continues to startle and fascinate me after years in the United States. I hadn't brought a decent jacket. The stop was in the middle of a parking lot off the highway. This didn't look at all like the stop Lisa had described. I walked into a glass terminal structure and made four fruitless calls to Lisa's house on a pay phone.

"Please check the number and try again," said the infuriating voice each time.

I became scared that I had written her number down wrong and would be left here to freeze overnight. I've grown to feel helpless, disoriented, and uneasy once I leave Manhattan, and being broke, cold, and hungry in the middle of nowhere was the actualization of my worst fears. I considered crying, and then considered having a temper tantrum, then considered leaving out the area code, as this was probably a local call, and immediately got through. I described my surroundings and Lisa said that they'd be there as soon as possible, although I was an hour early and several miles away. I had half an hour to wait and erroneously pegged three different women as being Lisa, giving them goofy and unrequited smiles before she strode into the empty terminal.

"Hey." She smiled politely but didn't look at me for more than a second, which surprised me and made me feel on edge. I feared that she could not stand to look at me and was asking herself why she'd gone through with this. Lisa spun around and marched out to the parking lot.

"Dave's in the car," she said over her shoulder without looking back at me.

She walked fast and I had to break into a canter every few steps to try to keep up with her, but only saw her from the back all the way to the car. She wore high-heeled black leather boots, which when coupled with her foal-like gait made an incredible noise. She wore black woolly stockings over her equine legs and a black corduroy miniskirt. A cream-colored angora turtleneck clung tightly to her fake breasts, making them look conspicuous even as I viewed her from behind.

Lisa opened the car door and folded the front passenger seat down for me and looked above my head and over yonder, nixing another opportunity for a proper greeting. The back of their compact car was full of trash and magazines, for which Lisa apologized, then added that she was buying a new car next week anyway, so there was no point in cleaning it up.

"Hello," said Dave without looking at me, and put his foot on the gas before Lisa had closed her door. It was immediately evident from their conversation about the best way to drive to dinner that Dave was gentle and passive and Lisa was odd and spasmodic.

"Do you like Pacific Islander food?" asked Lisa, facing forward.

"I am not sure that I've ever had it," I said, relieved that the ice was broken. I stuck my head in the gap between their headrests, prompting Lisa to look out her window. I wondered if she was autistic.

"We are meeting them at the Tiki Hut. I think the food is very good there," she said.

I gathered that Lisa was talking about Dave's contest winner but wasn't aware she was coming with someone. Lisa answered my question before I asked it.

"She doesn't drive, so her husband is with her," she said. Dave shook his head and blushed. Lisa looked at his embarrassed expression and pointed, giggling at him.

"Aw, Leese," he said. Everything about Dave had an "aw shucks" feel about it, which I found acutely endearing.

We soon arrived in downtown Portsmouth and parked by a life-sized fresco of a blue whale. Any initial standoffishness dissipated as Lisa shook my hand in exaggerated fashion that jarred my shoulder. She looked me up and down. She had a kind face that protruded forward, longish brown hair, and excited blue eyes that looked younger than the rest of her.

"Ha ha ha! You look like Dave!" she said, pointing at me then him to illustrate her point. Bashful Dave was strolling around the car and I agreed that we could be related.

Lisa and I talked on the way to the restaurant as Dave shuffled on a few steps ahead of us, and by the time we arrived at the restaurant I'd concluded that she wasn't the lunatic that her life story suggested she might be. An attractive Waspy girl in leis and a grass skirt showed us to the table Lisa had reserved.

"It's on me, so please order whatever you'd like," she said, eyeing the menu up and down. "I am starving!"

"*Oh my God, Lisa!*" screamed a shrill voice as we pondered the menu.

I spun around along with the rest of the restaurant's patrons to see a short Filipina in a cocktail dress, tiara, and a purple feather boa around her neck. She teetered through the tables, unwittingly trawling the end of her boa through an elderly gentleman's Lobster Rangoon, though he seemed too amused to mind. She fell into Lisa's lap and gave her a loud smooch on the lips that three younger guys at the next table applauded. Dave looked mortified and almost disappeared under the table, causing Lisa to again point and laugh at him. This was the stranger Dave would be having sex with, a concept he had apparently refused to think about until she was standing in front of him, larger than life. Lilly looked at Dave and me with a quizzical look on her face.

"*This* one's Dave," Lisa said and patted my knee under the table. Lilly ruffled his hair, then held his chin between her forefinger and thumb and shook it from left to right, causing his teeth to clatter together, and took the chair next to him. Dave looked like he was about to cry as Lisa clapped her hands in excitement. Dave's shyness and good nature amused Lisa to no end, and she seemed to live to affectionately tease him for his blushes. Behind the ostentatious diversion of Lilly was her unassuming husband, Paul.

"Hi, everyone," he said before plonking himself down next to me. Lisa made the introductions. Paul was originally Lilly's chauffeur when she was an exotic dancer and sometime porn star in Las Vegas. Around forty and sporting a paunch, Paul looked like any suburban workaday Joe, which is exactly what he became after he and Lilly moved back to Peabody, Massachusetts.

"So you're the bloody bloke, are ya?" he asked, slapping me on the back.

"Er . . . yes. Yes, I am."

"Well, I traveled a lot to Jersey and Guernsey for work and I tell ya, you guys can put down a few pints."

"Yeah!" I said, though typically drinking a few pints makes me feel bloated and in need of a nappy nap.

"They have Boddingtons here," he said as the waitress delivered the tropical cocktail I'd ordered in a hollowed-out pineapple. She set it between us and lit the sparkler that had been thrust through the lid. I gave Paul an apologetic look through the plume of leaves at the top.

"Oh," he said and turned quickly to Dave, terrorizing him with frank statements about his wife's genitalia. "She's got a great little pussy, Dave, just you wait." Every facet of Dave's body language screamed that he wanted out, right now. I said something that I found hilarious and Paul announced to the restaurant that my British sense of humor was too dry and "needed a big squirt of lube," horrifying a redheaded hula girl.

Dinner conversation was propelled along by Lilly and the revelations of her sex life, which she delivered in the most Anglo-Saxon terms, embarrassing Dave, arousing Paul, entertaining Lisa, and leaving me wondering how on earth I got to be sitting there in the first place. Lilly, it transpired, was a squirter—a woman who can ejaculate. Paul, fittingly, was adept at facilitating this phenomenon.

"Paul can make anyone squirt," said Lilly, looking lovingly across the table at her husband. "I've seen him do it a bunch of times."

Lisa, being the celebrity and usual instigator of this kind of weirdness, looked out of place as the beta female. I looked over at her as a single tear ran down her cheek.

"Are you okay?"

"I'll be fine in a second," she said, beginning to gently weep. "It's *this*." Lisa pointed skyward and I followed her finger to whatever was upsetting her.

"It's the music."

Though it was barely audible, Lisa had been moved by the guitar solo in "Brothers in Arms" by Dire Straits. They were playing the whole album and I struggled with how it fit in with the overall theme of the South Pacific.

"It's just so . . . soulful," she said, wiping her tears with her napkin and returning to what I imagined to be her normal self. From what I'd read, and from what I'd seen prior to Lilly and Paul's arrival, Lisa was usually the person doing the dumbfounding with her uninhibited antics. Lisa was now the reactor and not the instigator. As Lilly took full control of the conversation, Lisa shot me looks that said, "Can you believe this shit?" I couldn't.

Lisa decided that we'd all go bowling after dinner and we split into two cars, Dave with Lilly and Paul, me with Lisa. Lisa's driving was an extension of her reckless spirit, and a thankfully short white-knuckle ride toward the bowling alley ensued. We reached a bridge and Lisa skidded over to an off-ramp and told me that she wanted to show me something.

We walked down some steep steps to where a grandfather and his grandson were fishing off a dock in the moonlight.

"Caught anything?" Lisa asked them, seeming genuinely interested.

"Not yet," said the older man.

Lisa sat on the end of the dock, dangled her legs over the edge, and motioned for me to sit down next to her. We watched a cloud of silverfish tumble around in the water below us for about a minute. I thought Lisa was going to mention something about the reason I was here, the competition, sex or backing out. So I waited, saying nothing.

"My mom's here," Lisa said eventually, looking up at the moon. "This is where I scattered her ashes. Do you like it here?"

"I do."

We looked on as the younger fisherman felt a nibble on his line and reeled in fast, but it got away. He recast his line and we peered at where it had sunk for a minute or so.

"When did she . . ."

"We should get back now," she said, then turned to the men. "Good luck, guys!"

They waved and I chased her up the hill and into the car.

We checked our shoes at the bowling alley, where Lisa suggested that we do candlepin bowling and not tenpin. Paul and Dave went to get drinks and Lilly didn't want to play. Lisa was first up. She took a ten-step run, her gangly limbs flailing, and launched the ball across three lanes before almost falling on her ass. I couldn't figure whether she'd meant to do that or not. Then her second ball sailed four lanes over and she hit the deck laughing. People from the third and fourth lanes over glanced in our direction but said nothing.

"The bar here is closed," said Paul, who was ruthlessly intent on drinking a lot more. "The bartender got wicked sick and went home."

We all agreed that if tonight was going to happen the booze needed to flow and swapped our bowling shoes back at no charge. Lisa and Dave conferred about a suitable venue and we split into our same groups and rendezvoused at Carabella's, a charming dive bar that was holding a karaoke night, hosted by DJ Jazzy Jeff. Whether it was *the* DJ Jazzy Jeff remained unclear as a huge rubber alien Mardi Gras mask enveloped his constantly bopping head.

Lisa gave me a twenty and asked me to get a round of drinks while she went to the bathroom. To my horror, Lilly asked for a sex on the beach, a drink the flannel-shirted barkeep was completely unfamiliar with. Lilly shouted the list of ingredients as a woman missing some fairly important teeth sang "Livin' La Vida Loca" to the best of her smoker's lung's abilities. I talked the bartender through the process and he seemed eager to learn. He washed the dust off a seldom-used cocktail shaker and pressed an upturned glass inside it. He had somehow applied too much pressure and broke the delicate cocktail tumbler, forcing a shard of glass into the artery where the palm meets the wrist, shooting an arc of blood through the air and into the ice trough. The stools around the bar all noisily scooted back as loyal patrons helped to the best of their inebriated abilities.

"Hold it above your head, Jack!" slurred one.

"Somebody wrap a towel around it!" offered another.

"Oh my sweet Lord!" wheezed the woman through the karaoke speakers.

One drunk sobered up enough to improvise a tourniquet and helped the poor man into his car and swerved off toward the emergency room as a wizened regular dutifully took over behind the bar. Oblivious to the pandemonium she'd unleashed, Lilly had cornered Dave and was stroking his inner thighs to his extreme discomfort. Lisa arrived back in the bar, also unaware of the carnage, and helped me deliver the drinks to our unlikely fellowship. The karaoke had become too loud to talk over so we mostly just listened to the performances and swapped a few words in the relative calm between songs.

"Let's go fuck!" said Lilly during one of the respites, causing Lisa to spit a mouthful of gin and tonic back into the glass. I was filled with trepidation and was trembling before I stepped into the forty-degree night in my inadequate jacket.

Lisa's lemon yellow house was in the center of a thickly wooded cul-de-sac.

Dave, Lisa, and Lisa's son, Wolf, had not been living there long. There were still unpacked boxes, vast expanses of unbroken white wall space, and a new squeak to the slick blond wood floors. It was very cold in the new house, though I seemed to be the only person registering discomfort. My teeth were chattering as Lisa gave us all a perfunctory tour. We returned to the living room, and while Lisa made drinks, Paul went outside and came back in with two boxes, which he set down in the middle of the living room.

"Now I want you all to sit down," said Lilly with the inflection of a petulant eight-year-old. "I've got something to show you."

Dave and I sandwiched Lisa on a small pullout sofa as Paul leaned against the dining table, smiling. Lisa noticed my shivering and produced a crocheted blanket for me to wrap myself in.

Lilly took a videotape from the first box and inserted it into the VCR. It was one of the porno flicks in which she had recently starred. It was queued to a scene featuring Lilly and an unfamiliar actress in a

69 position. Lilly's head spun back and forth between the TV and the shocked audience on the sofa.

"Hee hee, that's me!" she said.

"It's beautiful!" her loving husband chimed in.

Lisa spied the growing bulge in Dave's jeans and playfully flicked it, laughing.

"That other girl is dead now," she deadpanned. "Drugs."

Silence. We watched Lilly's celluloid orgasm in reverent silence.

"What does that tattoo on your ass say?" asked Lisa, finally breaching the stillness.

Preferring to show rather than tell, Lilly immediately stripped down to underwear no bigger than an eye patch and jutted her round posterior into Lisa's face. Lisa laughed and squeezed it like a melon at the supermarket, Paul smiled proudly, Dave's erection became more pronounced as his face reddened, and I was unable to stop shaking. Lilly then dropped to her hands and knees and opened the second box and produced about fifteen Ziploc bags, each containing a sex toy. I'd seen a vibrator before, but not the spectrum of butt plugs, ball-gags, strap-on harnesses, riding crops, handcuffs, and mammoth dildos that she neatly laid out before us.

"My goodness!" said Lisa.

"They're all washed and ready to go," Lilly professed.

"Good to go," confirmed Paul.

"Where can I fuck your husband, Lisa?" asked Lilly, grabbing an appalled-looking Dave by the scruff of the neck.

"Uh . . . in our bedroom. Grant and I will stay down here."

"Do you have somewhere I can sit and read?" asked Paul, a dog-eared issue of *Guns & Ammo* rolled up in his hand.

"In my office," she said. "At the top of the stairs."

With the three of them gone, Lisa centered her full attention on me.

"Are you still cold?" she asked.

"I'm shivering all over."

Lisa produced a comforter and asked me to lie on the rug. She laid next to me and we wrapped each other up in our arms for warmth.

"Is that better?" she asked, moving every part of her frame to create maximum friction.

"Much better, thanks."

We held each other until our combined body heat had filled the space under the puffy comforter.

"Lisa!" Dave whined from upstairs. "I need you!"

Silence.

"Perhaps we should have married sex," said Lisa.

"What's that?"

"That's when you do it like you've got someplace to be in a hurry. It sounds like Dave needs me. Just lie on me and put it in."

I froze momentarily before deciding that I would do something bold and fearless—something that was very unlike me. I reached into Lisa's miniskirt and pulled her tights and underwear off in one motion, causing her to exclaim "wow," and shoved my face between her legs. My intent was to impress her with unabashed enthusiasm. Seemingly enraptured, she tugged at my hair, moaning and giggling. She said wow a few more times. After a few minutes, Lisa shoved me to the floor and returned the favor with equal vim and relish. I reached for Lisa's breasts and helped them free of her sweater. I'd read in her diary that she'd had implants and was taken aback at how alien they felt. Very solid and hard but not unpleasant. Unlike real breasts, they seemed attached to her rib cage, and I found that I couldn't push them together very far.

The comforter suddenly disappeared and there above us stood Lilly, buck naked and brandishing a leather paddle, greedily feasting her eyes on what was happening.

"What are you doing, you bad girl!"

"Um . . . I'm sucking Grant's cock," Lisa said matter-of-factly. It shocked me.

"Can you stop for a sec and come upstairs? Dave is sort of having a meltdown."

"We'll be up in a minute," Lisa said as I began to feel the cold air around us and my penis soften.

Lilly gamely bounded back up the stairs. We shrugged off the rest of our clothes and Lisa warmed me up again with her windmill limbs.

"Are you okay?" she asked.

"Yeah. It's just, this is really nuts!"

"I know."

"I've spent the last two weeks reading practically everything you've written!"

She seemed stunned.

"I told you not to! I don't break into your house and read your diary!"

"*Lisa!*" came a desperate scream from Dave.

"We'd better go and help him," said Lisa, grabbing my hand and pulling me up the stairs.

I saw Lisa's body for the first time in the ambient light coming in from the porch and it was like nothing I had seen before or since. She was incredibly lean; I doubt she'd float in water. She had a long musculature, her breathtaking legs and ass were those of a Kenyan boy, her pinched waist slowly curved out to elegant, squarish shoulders, off of which swung graceful arms. Her torso seemed incredibly long, and despite her never deliberately exercising she could probably muster up a six-pack while you wait. In spite of her nudity she walked proudly up to the door of the master bedroom. Because of mine, I cowered behind, doughy, slouched, and shielding my private area from view. We waited outside the door and listened as Lilly—we *hoped* it was Lilly—emitted little squeals.

Paul was feet from Lisa and me as we hovered outside the bedroom door. He read his magazine in the study. We locked eyes with him as he looked up from his magazine. He acknowledged our presence with a nod and nonchalantly went back to an editorial concerning either guns or ammo.

"Are you ready?" Lisa asked.

"Let's do it."

We fell into the bedroom to see Dave taking Lilly from behind on the bed.

"Thank God," said an exasperated Lilly. "I think he could do with some moral support."

"Leese!" he cried. "Hold me."

Giggling at her bashful husband, Lisa wrapped herself around Dave and whispered encouragement into his ear.

"It's working. He's getting bigger!" reported Lilly.

With the three of them in a strange chain, I paced along the side of the bed, cupping my bits and pieces with both hands.

Paul, I noticed, now leaned on the doorjamb, taking in the scene.

"Hey, honey!" said Lilly sweetly as Dave thrust into her with a renewed vigor.

"Hey, beautiful," Paul replied and blew his wife a kiss.

"C'mere!" she beckoned.

Paul took a few steps closer before Lilly grabbed him by his belt and hauled him toward her, unzipped his Dockers and popped his chubby penis into her mouth, creating a lascivious human chain that I hovered around, feeling very much like a fifth wheel.

Paul walked around the bed and slid a hand up Lisa's thigh, inserting a finger in her vagina before she knew who it belonged to.

"What's happening?" she screamed, closing her eyes tight.

"Let him do it, Lisa," pleaded Lilly. "It's awesome."

"Oh my God. Don't you dare make me squirt!"

Paul began using his fingers with the speed and dexterity of a flamenco guitarist.

"What are you *doing* in there?" she screamed.

"Do you want me to stop?" asked Paul.

"Are you going to make me squirt?" she said, almost crying.

"Some other time, then," he said, and removed his stubby magic hand from her groin.

I had been largely ignored for the past several minutes as I hovered, stark naked, some feet from the scene.

"Lisa, do you mind if I suck Grant's cock?" asked Lilly as sweetly as if she was asking if she could use the bathroom or have a glass of water.

"Be my guest," she replied. I wasn't asked and I sort of liked that fact. I liked the idea of being a piece of sexual property to be traded and swapped so much that I birthed a thumping erection and lost my usual modesty.

"What a nice-looking penis!" screamed Lilly. "Lisa, doesn't he have a nice-looking penis?"

"It sure is," she agreed.

"Yeah," mumbled Dave, prompting an amused look from Lisa.

"Thanks!" I said, basking in the positive attention my penis was finally getting.

The number of people who had seen my erection in my life had doubled in an instant.

"I didn't think he'd be circumcised," added Paul, detracting slightly from my moment in the sun. "Are you Jewish? I didn't think you'd be circumcised."

Neither did I.

Inexplicably, I had the surgery somewhere around my fourth birthday, I can remember that time clearly. An overwhelming majority of European males are uncircumcised. I didn't know that I was different from everyone else until my first swimming class as a five-year-old, when one of my schoolmates screamed, "There's sumfink wrong wiv Grant's willy!"

The thing that made me male also made me different from everyone else I knew.

Originally it was a curiosity to the other boys when we went swimming. In the locker room at high school it further supported the theory that I was Jewish: I had a largish nose by Anglo-Saxon standards, my father was raised in Highbury, North London, and I was disinterested in (read rubbish at) football.

When undressing in front of more worldly American girls, they often nod toward it and say:

"Oh, I thought you wouldn't be . . ."

And I'll say, "No, I *have* been . . ."

What's nice about it is that they seem relieved that they don't have to "deal" with something different. In fact, when they match up my circumcision scar, my straight, white teeth, and not terribly pale complexion, my ethnicity is once again under scrutiny.

"Are you *really* English?" they ask.

Arousing suspicion for being "normal" is a lot less harrowing than being scrutinized for being different. I don't mind it at all.

Lilly was much less interested in my heritage. Before I could answer Paul's question I was up to the hilt in his good lady wife's mouth as she reached for both of the married men's joints, serving the three of us simultaneously as Lisa looked on in awe. Paul became a sort of commentator, saying what he saw as if for a radio audience.

"The Brit's in her mouth, she's got the man of the house in one hand and me in the other. Lisa loves it . . . it's a wicked good time."

"He's really good at going down," said Lisa, who was temporarily unattached to anyone and free to instigate.

"Oh yeah?" said Lilly, and without missing a stroke offered up some real estate between her thighs. I decided to give Lilly the same bionic tongue-lashing that all five of my sexual partners—six including Lisa—had endorsed.

I received a reflexive donkey kick from Lilly to the sternum that knocked me on my backside.

"Oooofff!" I wheezed.

"Arrrghhh!" she squealed.

"Hey! Fuckin' take it easy, pal," said Paul, understandably protective of his wife's vagina. I'd never had an unclothed confrontation before and it unnerved me greatly. "She's wicked sensitive. You gotta go super slow and work up to that shit, man."

I regained my composure and tried to make up for my overexuberance.

"Do you wanna put it in?" she invited after several uneventful minutes.

I stood up; Paul handed me a condom, which I rolled on before fucking the love of his life.

"How'd ya like them apples?" he said.

"Wicked awesome," I said.

Paul again began rearranging Lisa's vagina, and in a short period of time she had succumbed to his mysterious tricks, crying, whinnying, and apparently on the cusp of drenching anything in a three-foot radius. It all proved too much for Dave, who came all over himself, Lilly's hair, and Lisa's fake boobs before curling up into a ball on the edge of the bed.

"Thataboy!" commented Paul, embarrassing poor Dave further.

I had an ultimately unsatisfying orgasm and then stood there, a used condom hanging off me and wondering what to do next.

"Well, *we're* going to fuck," Paul announced, and shepherded Lilly down to the pullout sofa in the living room and their arsenal of sex toys. Dave disappeared into the en suite bathroom. Lisa said that I could take the spare room. My clothes were downstairs, which was now filled with the sounds of Paul and Lilly's boisterous monkey sex, and were therefore irretrievable. I snapped off the dangling rubber and threw it in the bathroom garbage and went into the spare room, feeling around for the light switch in vain. I stumbled into the single bed and got under a thin comforter and shivered. I was worried I would wake up frozen but was too tired and shell-shocked to do anything but curl into a tight ball and tough it out until morning. I could make out the hands of a wall clock in the moonlight. It was 12:45 a.m. Far too respectable an hour for the unbridled debauchery that I had just witnessed, I thought.

I had been trying to ignore the cold for a half hour before I heard a faint knock on the door.

"Grant?" Lisa whispered.

"Yeah."

"Can I come in?"

"Sure," I said. "I'm freezing."

Lisa dived under the comforter and I spooned her warm, tight, hard body.

"So I was just about to drift off to sleep and I remembered that we were supposed to have sex. I mean that's the reason you're here, right?"

It was. In the process of helping Dave and the impromptu five in a bed sex romp, we'd somehow neglected to go all the way. In fact Lisa, who had put this gala evening together, hadn't had sex at all.

"Can we talk for a bit first?" I asked.

At the age of twenty-three I had just had sex for having sex's sake for the first time and I had decided that it made me feel funny. I told Lisa and she reached a long arm around to touch me in a comforting way. We told each other that we were fond of each other. We talked for an hour about ourselves before the conversation had swung back around to sex, specifically that we both really wanted to fuck each other.

"Shit. I have condoms but they're in my car."

"I'll get them," I said, gamely forgetting that I was without a stitch of clothing.

"It's after two," explained Lisa. "We are the only people awake for miles around."

I crept down the stairs and passed the "hooligans," as Dave had dubbed them. I donned a pair of waiting galoshes at the door and rooted around the car bare-assed until I found a solitary rubber. It was freezing out. I darted back inside, knocking over a broom, which broke the hooligans' postcoital slumber with a loud bang.

"What the eff?" Paul said and got up to see for himself. I hoped that his interest in both guns and ammo was largely theoretical.

"It's okay, it's just me, Grant," I said.

Paul was looking at me from behind as I groped around in the dark to set the broom upright. He scratched his head at the sight of a moonlit naked man bent double and wearing knee-high boots and fell back into bed.

I felt my way back up to the bedroom and beside Lisa. She had put on some sort of recording of train noise that was both strange and soothing. After warming back up we had sex like two people who had become really fond of each other. When it was over I was immediately aware that I was having sex with someone that I had no degree of ownership over. She was someone else's in a big house with a big yard and two cars and a kid and I would be going home stealing bagels and willing myself to stay in the country in the face of common sense.

"Did I see a tattoo on your bum?" I asked. I knew how to work my Britishness when I was trying to charm somebody.

"Yeah. I'm not proud of it."

"It says something, what does it say?"

"You can't look at it!"

Now I was intrigued. My eyes had adjusted to the light enough to pinpoint a lamp on the end table. I flicked in on.

Lisa was squirming, covering her tattoo with her hand, but I had forgotten all about it as I scanned the room. She turned the lamp off. We hugged for another ten minutes before she went back to her room and her husband, and I made a concerted effort to fall asleep, for Lisa's residual body heat had dissipated entirely.

Lisa woke me up the next morning good and early. Paul and Lilly were attending a funeral—Paul's grandmother's—in Boston and offered to drive me there. I only had time for a much appreciated hot shower, a few swigs of coffee, and a slice of toast and jam before Paul took their sex paraphernalia out to their SUV. I hugged Lisa and easily refused her when she tried to give me some cash for my bus ticket.

"You know, I think there is a customer service job at Nerve going," she said. "I could put in a phone call and you can say that you know me. And in the biblical sense! The money would be good and steady."

I barely had time to thank her before the hooligans were rushing us all out the door. I hugged Lisa again. I didn't want to let go, but she squirmed in my arms like I'd already had quite enough. I didn't want to leave. I didn't have sex with people then just leave. I was already attached to her. I could envision myself falling for her. I teared up a little, surprising the both of us.

"You don't want to make the hooligans late!" she said once they were safely out of earshot. She ruffled my hair. I shook hands with Dave and almost hugged Lisa a third time before stopping myself.

We had to make a pit stop at Paul and Lilly's apartment on the way to Boston. They needed to shower and dress appropriately. Lilly was still wearing her boa. On the way to Peabody, Massachusetts, Paul explained the mechanics behind female ejaculation and I struggled to make sense of it all.

"We have a video at home," Paul said immediately before placing a drive-through order at their local Dunkin' Donuts.

"Gimme three large coffees, all light and sweet . . . she squirts so hard . . . a sausage egg and cheese on a toasted everything . . . I mean in this one bit it comes out with so much force . . . an apple and spice and a Bavarian crème . . . that it knocks the camera right off the tripod . . . okay, you have a good day too."

Paul sat me on their couch and found the right cassette from their extensive home video library and popped it in the machine. It was queued to the right spot.

From across the room Paul and Lilly were pictured on a bed covered with rose petals. Sade's "Sweetest Taboo" was blasting in the background. The scene was prefaced with some light making out but deteriorated to a battery of tormented monkey noises facilitated by a range of large and unwieldy sex toys.

"This bit's great," said Lilly as she walked naked from the bathroom to the bedroom, a towel wrapped around her head. I started to eat my bagel.

The monkey noises grew louder and more violent-sounding as an unwitting Sade crooned sweetly "You're givin' me the sweetest taboo." From the bedroom, Lilly sung along, and it became apparent that she thought the song was entitled "Swedish Taboo." I wondered if she'd stopped to ponder what a Swedish taboo might actually consist of.

"Wait, this is it," said Paul, running out of the bedroom. Paul was wearing a white shirt, black tie, black socks with sock garters, patent leather shoes. No trousers, no underpants.

"You ready for this?" he asked, as a jet of fluid appeared over Paul's shoulder and toward the camera, knocking off its target. He grabbed the remote and rewound.

"Check that shit out!" He chuckled and replayed the moment ten times, marking the moment of ejaculation with a *"Bam!"* or a *"Pow!"* every time.

Squirt.

Paul: *"Bam!"*

Me: "Wow!"

Sade: "Sweetest taboo."

Lilly: "Swedish taboo."

Squirt.

Paul: *"Boom!"*

Me: "Wow!"

Sade: "Sweetest taboo."

Lilly: "Swedish taboo."

Back and to the left, back and to the left.

Back in the SUV we made a beeline for Boston and arrived at the Quincy T stop sooner than I had expected.

"You should come visit us and Paul can show you how to make me squirt," said Lilly from underneath a black mourning veil, which she lifted to give me a peck on the cheek.

"That'd be great," I said. I sort of meant it.

"Okay, champ. We'll see you around," Paul said and shook my hand, and then sped off to grieve his loss.

I took the T to downtown Boston. My friend Fatty was up there for the weekend and said he could give me a ride back to New York with him. Seeing one of my best friends was a relief, as I felt that I'd somehow been altered beyond recognition by my experience.

"Dude!" he said after I gave the tale its first telling. "I just can't believe you *did* that!"

Fatty and all of my other friends knew me as a sort of sweet, scrawny little kid. The kind of wide-eyed rube who gets addressed "sport," "champ," or "li'l buddy," who has his cheeks pinched, his hair ruffled, his leg pulled, his chops busted. Certainly the least likely candidate to travel across New England seeking sexual adventure. I'd told my friends about the trip before I went. It seemed that no one really believed I would go through with it, and until I was actually on the bus, I don't suppose I did either. Because of my difficulty talking to girls, and later, women, I'd always fantasized about some sort of emotionally void sexual transaction and I thought that this might have been an experience like that. But I liked Paul, Lilly, and Dave, and grew particularly attached to Lisa, and so even in this most bizarre sexual scenario, my nature had prevented me from being the sort of person who could have sex willy-nilly. The evening seemed to have a profound effect on me. For the days and weeks afterward I'd replay the night's events over and over in my mind, trying to retrace my steps from the debauchery I'd inexplicably gotten myself involved with back across the ocean to the person I used to be. I was never a thrill seeker, a bad seed, a drifter—how did I even get myself into this? I liked cups of tea, watching telly, saying no to drugs (they were never really offered), talking with old people about the Blitz. Outside of what I know, I become terribly nervous and unsure. I like routine; growing up I'd become accustomed to it. Yet somehow, pushing further away from my comfort zone left me feeling alive, proving that I had some semblance of control over the outcome of my life, after all. Where I grew up, one's life seemed largely predetermined. By fourteen everyone seemed to know if they'd be working at the Ford plant in Dagenham, at the BP refinery in Coryton, in the mall at Lakeside, at a mortgage brokerage, insurers, or multinational financial institution in the City. We knew when and where we would likely meet our husbands and wives, how attractive they'd be, and in which neighboring town they'd be looking to buy a starter home. Beyond that, at home, life choices are reduced to where you vacation, what you drive, where you drink, the team you support, and whether you spend Christmas Day with *her* family, Boxing Day with yours, or vice versa. Needing to make any decisions beyond these binary ones is seen as a complete imposition and most undesirable. Unless you have some sort of inner conflict, ambition, or restlessness, it really pays to move only within the channels provided.

With the end of my American excursion almost inevitable, I'd been perversely looking forward to marching in step with everyone else. Contenting myself with the beautiful simplicity of it all. I'd have some catching up to do, though; most of the people I knew from back home were either married, home owners, parents, or all three.

But somehow, meeting Lisa under those extenuating circumstances had been the point of no return. I'd changed forever. At home everybody was busy getting their lives on track, but I was suddenly and inexplicably off-roading; living on someone's couch, dirt poor, lamming it from the INS, unable to earn a living wage, leaving my very existence entirely to chance for the first time and wondering how I could live any other way.

SLEEPING MY WAY
TO THE MIDDLE

MY TRIP TO NEW HAMPSHIRE immediately prefaced a general upswing in my living situation. The combined effects of getting laid by two married women in one night, a slightly improved cash flow, and a bedroom with a door had me feeling like I had the world on a string.

The week after meeting Lisa and Dave I moved uptown. In the fall of 2000 you didn't see that many young white kids in Washington Heights. I took some pride in being among the first groups of rent refugees establishing a beachhead at the top of the island, eschewing the trendy hairstyle set, like some sort of grown-up.

The place was a gem. Large, cozy, and fairly clean, like Mike had said, the apartment had astonishing views of the George Washington

Bridge, the mighty Hudson River, and the deliberately unblemished New Jersey Palisades on the opposite bank. From our roof, the long strip of Manhattan was laid out before us. The topography of the area meant we were at eye level with the top floors of the World Trade Center and the Empire State Building. The commute downtown was 185 blocks long. The location fostered a drive to make the most of the neighborhood. This meant trips to nearby Ft. Tryon Park, dining at the grimy but charming Hillside Diner, and generally reading books I'd been meaning to read and watching movies I'd never gotten around to renting. Being a ne'er-do-well made moving easy. I arrived at 436 Fort Washington Avenue with a mattress, box spring, and a Hefty bag full of clothes and bedding. I painted my yellow and blue bedroom walls a deep scarlet and felt fully satisfied that I finally had a place I could rightfully call my home.

LISA CALLED ME to ask if there were any details I would like her to omit or otherwise obscure before she handed her account of the previous weekend to Nerve for publication.

"Um . . . I don't know, should I?"

"Well, I'm not going to say anything bad," she said. "I'm very fond of you. You don't mind if I use your real first name?"

"Are you going to say I was . . . y'know, good in bed?" I asked.

"I *might* do."

"Then, yeah. Go ahead."

Since being back in New York, I had read almost all of the writing Lisa had on Nerve.com and I rather loved the way she described the characters in her life. I decided that if I was going to be immortalized in her prose, using a pseudonym would remove me from the experience and somehow read untrue. More important, it would make it harder to convince the lads back home that the shy English wife-defiler in this crazy woman's online diary was actually me, "Grunt" Stoddard. I had planned to e-mail them the story when it came out.

Reading a public account of your sexual mannerisms is an extremely surreal experience, especially when you are as sexually inexperienced as I was. Nerve, Lisa told me, was attracting over a million unique visitors a month. My heart was beating its way out of my chest as I began reading the first line of Lisa's diary at my desk at The Orchard.

Grant comes from Manhattan via London . . .

I tried to read about the details of our weekend as if I were disconnected from the experience entirely. Lisa had indeed portrayed me in a very flattering and touching light. Most of what I'd said had appeared verbatim. This made me cringe at first, then be thankful that I didn't say anything worse. It's like that awful realization of how you actually sound when you hear your voice on a home movie or a tape recorder, but many thousands of times worse.

At Lisa's suggestion, I contacted Nerve about the Customer Service Rep position she'd mentioned. Lorelei Sharkey promptly returned my e-mail and invited me to Nerve's offices for my interview that Friday afternoon. The elevator opened up into a large open loft space and almost total silence. Aside from the tapping of keyboards, there was a pronounced public library feel to the place. If it wasn't for the huge neon Nerve logo on the back wall, I would have thought I'd gotten off at the wrong floor. I'd researched the company ahead of time and learned this:

It was in 2000 that Nerve made the leap from a small Internet magazine about sex started by a couple in their studio apartment to producing a glossy print magazine, groundbreaking online personals database, and HBO show. The Web site featured contributions from writers like Norman Mailer, Spalding Gray, Yusef Komunyakaa, and Erica Jong, and was being translated into several different languages. Copublisher Rufus Griscom was the self-styled Hugh Heffner of the twenty-first century, his staff a collection of beautiful, brilliant libertines, the work atmosphere a cocaine-dusted bacchanal at the nexus of business and pleasure, all in a sunny loft on Broadway and Spring.

"Hi," whispered the young blonde girl at the front desk.

"I have a meeting with Lorelei and Julia."

Lorelei was the head of the Nerve Center, the name given to their online community. Julia was handling customer service. The successful candidate would be her assistant.

Lorelei skipped over to meet me and gave my hand a firm shake. The blonde girl offered me some coffee and a seat in the open lounge area, and I accepted both.

"You come highly recommended from Lisa Carver," said Lorelei, without so much as a smirk.

"Oh, that's nice to hear."

I had no idea whether Lorelei knew the capacity in which Lisa and I were acquainted. The recommendation as an asset to the company could only have been grounded in cunnilingus.

Julia ran me through what I'd be dealing with should I get the job: answering e-mails, sending out back issues of magazines, sending people forgotten password information, and helping people with their online personal profiles. No one would be baying for my blood over a ten-dollar payment and I was told that the phone hardly rang.

Lorelei suggested that I create a personal ad myself so that I could get a better idea of the type of problems people might experience. We shook hands and she told me that the job was as good as mine.

What made the Nerve online personals head and shoulders above any other dating site's in 2000 was that its constituents were first and foremost fans of the content of the Web site, a smart, hip magazine about sex that had a fairly even gender split in its readership. One could safely assume then that a Nerve "date" would be literate, liberal, college-educated, and not morally opposed to some reciprocal oral on the first date.

While waiting for a confirmation that I'd gotten the gig, I spent most of my workday at The Orchard creating and tweaking my ad and contacting other personals users. I got my first response from Sonya, a thirty-year-old woman, who stated that she was five feet four and 120 pounds, smoked, drank, and drugged often. Her ad did not include a picture, and so in my first message to her I requested one.

"Don't worry, I'm not ugly," she wrote back. "I look like Brigitte Bardot."

Her personal ad said that she was a huge fan of Lisa Carver, so I promptly told her that I was the gentleman she'd been writing about in her last two columns. Her response was just her phone number and the instruction to call her ASAP. On the phone, Sonya sounded sassy and/or drunk.

"Lisa wrote that you are good at eating pussy," she said. "That true?"

"Well, I don't know. She seemed to think so."

"I love you fucking Brits, man. Such modesty, such fucking bullshit." She took a long drag on a cigarette. "How do you like to fuck?"

This was a neat segue into phone sex. Despite never doing it before, let alone with a stranger, I found myself getting over the initial embarrassment and running with it.

"That was really great!" I realized that I sounded a little too precious as the words left my mouth.

"Yeah, yeah. Call me over the weekend, maybe I'll let you lick my cunt."

Could it really be this easy? I couldn't get my mind around how available casual sex could be in the right circles. I waited until Sunday afternoon, took a train to the East Village, and called her from a pay phone.

"Hello?"

"Um, hi, Sonya? It's Grant from the other night."

"Oh, yeah, right. Where are you?"

"I'm at St. Mark's and A."

"Oh, I'm at the Gap on St. Mark's. Meet me at the southwest corner of St. Mark's and Second in fifteen minutes. Goddamn, I need a drink."

Sonya had seen the picture of me I'd included as part of my personals profile, but I only had her own description to work with. Brigitte Bardot, indeed. This could only mean gap-toothed and blonde.

I stood behind a group of midwesterners under the *STOMP* awning and peered across the avenue. Standing across from me was a blonde woman in cowboy boots, gray single-ply sweatpants, a tan leather jacket, and a pair of sunglasses that ensconced the top half of her face. Her description wasn't entirely accurate, but she certainly looked attractive from across four lanes of traffic. She smoked a cigarette like a fisherman and looked around expectantly. Could it be her? Did women this attractive make a habit of taking scrawny boys home on Sunday afternoons?

I crossed to the northeast corner, then across to the northwest so that I could come in from behind. I wondered if she'd registered my presence across the pedestrians and the traffic. I looked at her from behind. She checked the time on her cell phone. Six p.m. I knew it was time to make contact or lose her. I felt nauseated with anticipation as the thought of her rejecting me entered my mind. It could really go one way or the other. We'd already chatted each other to orgasm on the phone, surely that would count for something. It was do or die.

Fuck it!

"Sonya?" I said.

"Did you get a good look?" she said, still looking toward the *STOMP* marquee.

"Yeah, sorry, it's just that . . . I wasn't sure if it was you, but I mean . . . you're really hot."

No Brigitte Bardot, but certainly upward of a Renée Zellweger.

"I told you, didn't I?"

She flicked her cigarette into the street, hitting a Chinese delivery guy on his bike, and reacted as if he was the intended target.

"There's only one place you can drink in the daylight and that's an Irish bar." She linked her arm in mine. "Let's go, Ringo."

We walked into an empty Irish pub on 14th Street. She ordered a Bloody Mary. I got a Budweiser.

"I'm still hungover from last night," she groaned before regaling me with how she'd hooked up with a girl on the hood of a Trans Am after attending a Nashville Pussy concert. She talked, I listened. The more I listened the more I thought that sleeping with her meant risking an STD.

"There's this video of me getting fisted floating around on the Internet," she threw out casually.

Another drink, another three cigarettes. She still hadn't taken off her shades.

"Okay, sport," she said. "Wanna come back to my place?"

I was totally out of my depth and nowhere near manly enough to be in the same room as this woman. I'm what they call a two-beer lightweight; I can't stand to kiss a smoker; and at the time my drug experience was limited to the time I'd eaten hash and thought I was a piece of paper for the next six hours. But the one and only time I'd slept with a crazy thirty-year-old stranger had turned out to be sort of life-affirming and magical, so I looked her in the eye and said,

"Sure."

Sonya's place was a very large one-bedroom across the street from Irving Plaza. She told me what she paid and it seemed astronomical to me at the time. She worked in retail and I couldn't figure out how she could afford it. She told me to take a seat on her sofa, put out some food for her molting Persian cat, and stood in front of me. She pulled on the drawstring of her sweatpants and, with a shimmy, they fell about her ankles, exposing a freshly waxed vagina, the first I'd ever seen in real life. Sonya stepped out of the pants, and finally exposed her eyes, which were deep set and ringed with purple.

"Eat it, bitch," she said.

I put up little resistance and had been giving Sonya oral sex for almost forty minutes when she rapped me hard on the head with her ringed knuckles.

"Shit, stop!" She frantically searched the couch for the remote control. "My show is on."

She'd stopped me for appointment television, which hadn't happened before then.

"I love *Sex and the City!*" she said, pushing me to the other end of the couch with her feet.

I patiently watched the show with her as she howled with laughter. When it was over she jumped up and led me into the bedroom.

"Fucking cat!" she screamed as we entered, making me jump.

A large cat turd sat in the exact center of the bed.

"I don't think he likes you," she said, picking it up and flushing it down the toilet. She threw the soiled comforter in the laundry basket, washed her hands, laid down on the bed, and spread her legs.

"You may continue," she said. I obligingly did until she came once again.

"Your turn," she said, unbuttoning my jeans, and went at it with similar aplomb.

She stopped after a few minutes.

"Are you holding back or something?" she said confrontationally. "I only ask because I'm *really* good at this."

She was. I had been gripping the edge of the bed, white-knuckled, knees locked, toes curled since she began. Having not gotten any play in high school, a blow job was never a self-contained event for me but rather a warm-up to sex. Sonya, however, had other plans.

"Don't think I'm gonna let you fuck me, I have someone coming over in twenty minutes. Hurry the fuck up."

The very notion that I was just an hors d'oeuvre in a grander feast did the trick almost immediately and I was finished.

Time for afterglow.

"Okay, now get the fuck out."

Sonya scooped up all of my clothes, ran out of the bedroom, and threw me out the front door.

"What the fuck are you doing?" I screamed.

"Oh, be nice, and I'll let you go down on me again," she said, shoving me out into the hall. "I might even let you fuck me."

I managed to get into my underpants and T-shirt before an Orthodox Jewish woman walked down the hallway pushing a baby carriage. Sonya was looking through the spy hole. I could hear her laughing. The woman pretended not to notice as I shrugged my pants on and made a run for the elevator.

I'd been used for sex, and although I found it exciting, I found myself struggling with the emotions it wrenched up.

CHRIS APOSTOLOU was making more progress at chopping away at my back wages, meaning that I could afford a ticket back home for Christmas.

Christmas for me is an odd time to go home. Compared to spending the "holidays" in America, a British Yule is a bit of a sad, tawdry, and drunken affair, demarcated by what's on telly. In the morning, it's carols in cathedrals, then perhaps a program in which terminally ill children have their Christmas wishes granted by C-list celebrities. At three o'clock it's the Queen's speech, followed by a wrist-splittingly depressing episode of *EastEnders*, then a host of blockbuster movies that saw their theatrical releases several years ago. People sit around half conscious with paper party hats from their Christmas crackers perched on top of their heads. The weather in England at this time is approaching its bleakest. Everyone I see asks when I'll be coming home to live, as if I'm still on some extended vacation or being held in America against my will.

"But don't you *miss* it 'ere?" they all ask.

I miss *them* and I tell them so. But gone are the years in which I'll humor relatives and friends by professing to an unrelenting homesickness. Understandably, people can take it to heart when you tell them that you never again want to be where they'll surely never leave, but by 2000 my leaving Corringham had begun to define me in some very significant way. Aside from my immediate family, people at home seemed to take it as a slight against them. In working- and lower-middle-class Britain, I feel that there's an unwritten rule to not do or say anything that would make you seem dissatisfied enough with your lot to actually do something about it. It's the antithesis of the American way.

I'll have a chance to be put in my place when I'll accidentally use an American turn of phrase and be ridiculed for it.

"*Use the bathroom!* 'Ark at 'im! Bleedin' Yankee-doodle."

IN THE NEW YEAR, The Orchard had again fallen way behind with back wages and I found myself in real trouble once again. I called Lorelei to see if there was any chance of the Nerve job becoming available.

"The position has been put on ice indefinitely," she said apologetically. "But we do have a customer service internship available."

I was now twenty-four and felt a little too long in the tooth to be a gofer to a twenty-one-year-old customer service rep, but I was running out of options and money. I quit The Orchard in the knowledge that I might never see the forty-five hundred dollars they owed me.

I began working at Nerve Mondays, Wednesdays, and Fridays at five dollars an hour in January 2001. Technically, my work visa meant that I could only work as a recording artiste and only for The Orchard, but I spoke to some other people on similar visas who said that everyone moonlighted and that the IRS and INS didn't cross-reference data and consequently it shouldn't be a problem. My intern's wages almost covered the cost of my rent and monthly subway costs.

Unlike me, the other interns were almost all in college; they were predominantly female and similarly desperate to get their writing under the noses of the editorial team, and were fully prepared to bend over backward to that end. Nerve had published four issues of their print magazine, and this was the main thrust of the energy in the office.

Though my days were primarily taken up with customer service inquiries, I would also be asked to fetch coffee or water for visitors, run out to Staples or the post office, and deliver everybody's mail to them at their desks. Being on the lowest rung of the company, I found that no one, save my fellow interns, gave me the time of day. I quickly became infatuated with another intern, Abigail. Abigail was from Belfast and, like me, too old and wise to be fetching coffee for peanuts. Unlike the other interns, Abigail had had her writing published in many esteemed British and Irish papers, including *The Independent*, *The Guardian*, and *The Times*, and had also written for a lot of travel guides.

Though she'd hardly set foot in England and I'd never crossed the Irish Sea, we had enough shared cultural reference points to chat about while being dissimilar enough to not steal one another's thunder. Abby was about three inches taller than me at five feet eleven, was long-bodied and swan-necked with incredible blue eyes and snowy white, almost translucent-looking skin. She dyed her hair jet black and her teeth were typically crooked, but in a sort of charming way that reminded me of home. I fell for her quicker and harder than any other girl before or since, and after a month of unrequited advances, persuaded her to finally sleep with me.

Abby was very conscious of presenting a free-and-easy sexual persona, and even before the afterglow of our first time had subsided, she took great pains to tell me that we owed each other nothing and that we should keep things "cool."

"Seriously," she continued, "you should absolutely see who you want, when you want. Because, y'know, I will be."

No one had ever said anything remotely like that to me before, my past four infatuations being traditionally romantic and conventional. I wanted the same thing for Abby and me, but she seemed convinced that we would have the most fleeting of affairs.

Trading on the Lisa Carver connection I'd casually dated several women over the winter, meaning that I was in a position to take Abby's words at face value.

"What did you do last night?" she asked in Des Moines, a coffee shop on Avenue A.

I sort of resented that Abby didn't care enough to want to keep me for her own and decided to pull no punches in my response.

"I fucked a hot med student at her dorm in the Bronx."

Her jaw dropped but no words came out of her mouth.

"You said that we should see who we wanted, when we wanted," I reminded her.

"Well . . . I know but . . . I mean, talk about a blow to the ego."

"Well, if it's any consolation, you're *much* funnier."

Abby stormed out of the café and didn't talk to me for a week.

The following week, Abigail went home to Belfast and was denied entry back into the United States for some sort of visa infraction, effectively drawing a line through our quasi-relationship.

After six weeks as an intern, it was discovered that I was capable of doing Julia's job for less money and she was promptly let go. This meant that for the first time during my almost three-year tenure in the States, I would be paid a half-decent salary with health benefits as regular as clockwork. I couldn't have been happier.

To celebrate, I took Anna out to lunch. Anna Braunschweiger was another intern and a student at Sarah Lawrence College in Bronxville. She had a longtime boyfriend but our conversations became increasingly flirtatious.

With the new job and the exponentially accelerating rate at which I was sleeping with pretty girls, my confidence was hitting hitherto uncharted territory. This enabled me to do things I'd never dared to before.

After a Nerve work function about twenty of us ended up at the Lakeside Lounge on Avenue B. Anna, flanked by her boyfriend, Zach, and myself, was poring through the songs on the jukebox when I started running my hands up her thighs. I was atypically smashed and so was she. She parted her legs enough for me to slip my hand up her denim miniskirt and finger her for a good five minutes, with poor Zach blissfully unaware of what was going on. He ended up selecting a track by the Doors. He was kind of queer like that.

The following weekend, in the middle of May, Anna borrowed Zach's car and drove us a little ways upstate to Bear Mountain. It was nice to get off the island, something I hadn't managed to do in almost four months.

Anna was oddly beautiful, with strong Germanic features, blonde hair, and ice-blue eyes. Though I'd publicly fingered her days earlier, the fact that she had a boyfriend prevented me from making a bona fide move. It took three more dates and her inviting herself over to my place at one a.m. on a Tuesday night for me to get the message. Even then the action was prefaced by her exasperatedly saying, "So, are we just gonna talk all night or what?"

It was four thirty a.m. and we'd been lying on my bed for the past three hours.

I'd been a late starter with women but in the past six months had more than made up for lost time, and now, a year and a half after Becky, I was ready for a girlfriend.

Anna and I were polar opposites. She had designs on becoming a writer, made her own clothes and accessories, chain-smoked Marlboro Lights, and was as cool, calm, dispassionate, and distant as I was nervy, spasmodic, highly strung, and emotional.

It was the end of the school year and Anna was resigned to spending the summer at her parents' house in Maryland for financial reasons.

"Break up with Zach and live with me for the summer," I said, surprising myself.

"Okay," she said.

There's no greater catalyst to cohabitation with a sexual partner than the tantalizing proposition of slashing your rent clean in half. It didn't hurt that Anna was a pretty yet ruthless-looking Aryan, whose every body part jutted aggressively outward, implying ownership over everything in her twenty-one-year-old path.

We took Zach's car and loaded it up with her personal effects from her dorm room, unloaded it at my house, and then she drove down to TriBeCa and returned the car to Zach and broke up with him.

She arrived back at my place and I erroneously told her that she'd done the right thing. My roommate, Mike, was on an extended vacation in the Philippines, so I couldn't ask him if Anna living with us was kosher or not. Something to figure out when he got back, I thought. The plan was for Anna to get a summer job and kick in a few hundred dollars when she could. He'd go for that, right?

In a whopping oversight, Intern Coordinator was added to my job description in June. My first hire was a sexy and incredibly charming California girl named Jenny. Jenny was far too smart and qualified for the likes of me to be telling her what to do, but must have needed the credits for a postgrad course or something. I can't remember.

What I *can* remember was that her first day on the job happened to be an incredibly special day in Nerve's history. Part of the forthcoming Nerve HBO show was a party scene. A huge TriBeCa party venue was rented for the night, naked waiters and waitresses were brought on, hundreds of gallons of free booze were acquired, and in the center of the twelve-thousand-square-foot space an "exhibitionist booth" had been erected. This was a structure that looked like a little cottage and was full of cameras that fed images to the room through a twenty-foot LCD display on the room's far wall.

Anna and I were getting touchy-feely in the exhibitionist booth when new girl Jenny ran in and started sucking her boyfriend's positively ginormous cock. I stepped outside the booth to see a large group of revelers looking at the action and cheering them on.

"I love the new girl," said Ross.

Ross was already sort of in the doghouse with Rufus. Earlier in the evening, Rufus had been in rapt conversation with a millionaire venture capitalist and potential investor in Nerve. Rufus had been chatting with the investor with his hands behind his back. On a dare from his wife, Jordana, Ross had unzipped his pants and placed his testicles in Rufus's hand. Rufus was far too engrossed in conversation to pay too much attention to what he was holding and for the next thirty seconds simply rolled them around in his palm like Chinese stress balls. The penny finally dropped just as the investor offered his hand for Rufus to shake.

I'd now slept with two of the four Nerve interns and each time it had coincided with them leaving the company. It was enough cause for concern for Rufus to pull me aside and have a chat about it.

"The gallivanting Mr. Stoddard," he began in his typically verbose manner. "It seems that yet another fine young mind has fallen foul of your old-world charm and scruffy demeanor."

"I know how it looks, Rufus, but really, Anna is the one. We're living together and everything."

"Well, I hope that this curtails your intra-office carousing, because I cannot let this continue in good conscience. You *do* understand?"

"I do."

I'd never dreamt that it would be my carousing that would get me in hot water at a job. Just a few months prior, the idea would have been quite inconceivable.

"Good, because you are in serious danger of becoming this company's talisman."

"Understood."

"Oh, by the way, congratulations on Anna; she is certainly the employee *de choix*."

It was in mid-July when the print magazine's editor in chief, Susan Dominus, strode up to my desk, her high-heeled boots clicking against the parquet floor. It startled me chiefly because she had never deigned to utter a word to me before now.

"You're Grant?" said Susan.

We'd been sitting two desks apart for four months.

"Er . . . yes."

"You are from England?"

"I am, yeah."

Then, in a hushed tone, Susan said, "Did you win that competition to have sex with Lisa Carver?"

"That was me, yes."

"What made you decide to do it?"

I gave Susan an abridged version of my downward mobility, possible deportation, and quest to have at least one story worthy of telling to the proverbial grandkids.

"Oh my God! And that's why you are working *here*?"

"Yeah, Lisa hooked me up."

Susan walked back to her desk, sat down, got up, and walked back to my desk.

"Okay, well, do you think you'd do anything?"

I'd been saying yes to everything recently and it appeared to have set me on a winning streak. Besides, I was now out of college for almost three years and had little to show for it. Anything seemed more interesting than fielding customer service calls.

"I don't see why not," I said, giving little thought to *exactly* what she had in mind.

"Can you write?"

"Well, to be honest, I haven't before."

Susan asked Ross Martin and me to work out a concept for an item in which I would be inserted into a sexual situation, then write a play-by-play account of my experience. I would be a proxy, an everyman, who, if the bit was made a regular feature, would be ticking off items on a sexual to-do list.

Either Ross or new hire Brian Battjer suggested that the prospective column would really be a series of sexual experiments, that the format would be based on a high school lab report with headings equating to: hypothesis, apparatus, method, results, and conclusions. I wanted to call the column "Lab Rat," but it was decided that it would be called "I Did It for Science."

BABY STEPS

HAVING ME WRITE about sex was like having Steven Hawking write about tap dancing.

Despite the recent spike in sexual activity thanks to Lisa, I was still hopelessly inexperienced and apparently largely misinformed. One particularly brusque partner informed me that I had the "lovemaking skills of a demented muskrat." In addition, I had absolutely zero experience with regard to creative writing. This made the other interns—all creative writing majors—bristle with envy.

Despite having no literary experience, the actual writing part didn't faze me, but I hadn't quite gotten over how disgusting and undesirable I felt throughout high school and college, and the idea that someone could read about my sexploits and not bring up their lunch seemed terribly far-fetched. My first stab at describing a sexual encounter on the page made *me* want to wretch, which left me wondering how I could ever sell it to anyone else. I certainly couldn't have done it without Anna, who was absolutely ready, willing, and able to do anything to help me. Having a hot girlfriend to share these experiences with made them much less scary and enabled me to write without feeling like some sort of disgusting little perv.

Actually *doing* the first few "experiments" wasn't really a problem either. It was writing about my bits 'n' pieces that was scary. I was always aware that recounting a sexual encounter without lashings of self-deprecation, humility, and compassion can result in something that reads like a *Penthouse* "Forum" letter.

The subject matter for the experiments were to be things that are purported to enhance the sexual experience, be it an activity, like having sex outside, a product or device, such as a cock ring, or a fetish, like bondage or dressing up like a sports team's mascot. The beauty of me writing it, I was told, was that my relative inexperience would provide a "vanilla" everyman's perspective that could be accessible to a larger audience.

A large part of my agreeing to write about my sexual adventures for a large audience was that the very idea of it was so incredibly ludicrous. Would my friends commuting to the city or working at the oil refinery even be able to get their heads around the concept? Many of them, I'm quite sure, would question whether I'd had sex at all, let alone being paid to do so. Regardless of who got their pubes first or who went from tenor to baritone the quickest, the true measure of when one becomes a man is his first knickers-off experience with a female. By that token, at age fourteen, I was a boy among men.

What really drove me crazy back then was how nonchalant the popular boys could be about it all.

At fourteen, Joanne Davis had suddenly blossomed into a living goddess. I could barely speak around her, felt I didn't deserve to be in the same *dimension* as her. And there's greasy-haired Mark Wilson, regaling the back row of the biology class with how he absentmindedly fingered her behind the music department, waving his middle finger around as olfactory evidence. I couldn't get a girl to look at me and Wilson was two knuckles deep in my dream girl before recess.

"Smell Joanne Davis!" he said to anyone who'd listen. He didn't even curtail his piggish behavior as Joanne glided into biology and took the seat next to mine, yielding an immediate stirring in my loins.

I looked at her apologetically on behalf of fourteen-year-old boys everywhere. With that look, I wanted her to know that should I be given the opportunity to put my hand in her knickers, I would make it ever so special. I'd probably go the whole hog and tell her that I loved her. I smiled gamely at her and to my complete surprise she smiled back. I was so caught up in the moment that I barely noticed Wilson walk around behind me, where he released something both silent and deadly between my dream girl and myself.

"*Uurrhh*, Stoddard! That fucking reeks!" he shrieked.

A truly awful fart cloud completely enveloped Joanne and me.

"That wasn't me, it was Wilson!" I blurted out as the true perpetrator sought sanctuary on the other side of the biology lab, still reassigning me the blame.

"Oi, Stoddard's just dropped his guts!" he announced to the group he'd been defaming Joanne to just thirty seconds earlier.

"I swear it wasn't me!" I pleaded.

Joanne looked at me with utter contempt.

"You're fucking disgusting," she spat and excused herself from the offending area.

Whether it was my pimply face, buckteeth, wispy frame, or the supposed culprit of a noxious fart, I grew to feel more and more disgusting by the minute.

Humiliation in the eyes of girls had somehow become a daily occurrence for me. Every day at school, it became more apparent that I was a permanent member of a dwindling group of boys who girls wanted nothing to do with. By the time I was eighteen and still hadn't convinced a female to lock lips with me for the briefest moment, I'd grown to accept that I'd be one of the unfortunate creatures that shuffled around Corringham town center smelling of urine and muttering to himself. By age twenty, I was almost looking forward to it.

Yet here I was, a fledgling sex writer, on the platform of the 207th Street A train stop in New York City with my blonde, knockout American live-in girlfriend, who was more than happy to let me fuck her on public transport; my first assignment was to have sex on the subway. My girl's only conditions were that her face or real name not appear in the column, which I thought was more than fair.

It was almost one in the morning, and as I'd suspected, the platform looked deserted. I'd never had sex in public before. We would be able to commandeer an empty subway car for our purposes. It was the height of a particularly steamy New York summer, when the temperature didn't seem to dip with the sun at night. Anna was wearing a tight T-shirt, short denim miniskirt with no underwear underneath, and, at my request, a pair of good running sneakers should we need to flee. Getting caught in the throes of passion was not an option for either of us. Her parents would have been unable to withstand the double whammy of shock and shame at their only child's indiscretions. My precarious visa situation meant being caught with my pants around my ankles could have been good grounds for deportation. Being kicked out of a country that was suddenly granting my every wet dream would have been more than I could take.

Being late at night, there was hardly a soul in the station. As it was after 11:00 p.m., however, the A train was now running a local service and we only had the time it takes for the train to speed from one station to the next, and the risk of onlookers increased with every stop headed downtown.

"You'd better be ready to go once the doors close," said Anna, shoving a hand into my skivvies.

It wasn't until then that it occurred to me that I was really in no mood to have sex at that moment, under the harsh fluorescent lights of a chilly, Brooklyn-bound A train. This was the first time I would be engaging in sexual activity under obligation to a third party, but it certainly wouldn't be the last.

Bing bong.

The doors slid shut and the train lurched forth into the tunnel, before stalling, allowing Anna some extra time to kiss some life into my atypically hesitant penis.

"Come on!" she said and pulled her T-shirt over her implausibly large and perfect twenty-one-year-old's breasts.

Ladies and Gentlemen: we apologize for the delay, we will be moving momentarily.

The PA system in the car was way too loud and the crackly, Bronx-accented announcement hurt my ears and jangled my nerves, causing Anna to work harder than a hard-bodied college senior should ever have to. As the train slowly crawled forward toward the Dyckman Street stop, Anna spun around, hiked up her skirt, and put a foot up on the seat. The train was still moving at a snail's pace but that didn't quell her sense of urgency.

"Fucking put it in!" she screamed at me.

Anna's vim for the assignment far outstripped my own, which sort of surprised me. I did as I was told as the train started speeding toward the next stop.

I grabbed Anna's hips for balance as the train violently shook back and forth on the tracks and tried to center my thoughts on my objectives.

Susan had said that we should go as far as we could. Wanting to exceed my employer's expectations, I was insistent on going to completion. I knew that we only had another few blocks to play with, though it was incredibly difficult to gauge precisely where we were, and so I banged away at my inexplicably willing assistant with everything I could muster. Fortuitously the train slowed to a sudden stop once again. Although I very nearly fell over, the stop bought us a little more time. Anna looked over her shoulder at me.

"Are you nearly done?" she asked.

"Nearly there."

I was close.

The train sped up and then began to slow as we neared the next station.

"Oh no!" I cried, aware that I needed a few more seconds. Anna then inserted a finger into her bum and said something as raunchy as it was considerate.

"You'd better come in my mouth. I don't wanna leave a mess."

Her vocalized civic responsibility was exactly what I needed to bring things to a head, seemingly nanoseconds before the train pulled into Dyckman Street. With a minimum of fuss or mess, Anna pulled her skirt down over her bottom just as a heavyset woman in a Wendy's uniform stomped aboard.

"Are you okay?" said Anna upon noticing that I was clearly not okay.

"I'm fine," I said, visibly shell-shocked. "I can't believe we just did that!"

Anna made the noise that would usually accompany a shrug. She was unflappable to the point of utter disinterest. I felt that at twenty-four, I'd skipped the bit where young people were supposed to have sex partially clothed, outside of the bedroom, high on drugs, and with people they didn't necessarily know or even like that much. Arbitrary, casual, distasteful sex: screwing for screwing's sake. After going so long without any at all, I sort of gave it a reverence my contemporaries didn't. I only fooled around with people I could imagine going on picnics with, people I would look after should they catch the flu. People I—and I shudder to say this—would not fuck, but make love to. I could barely pull myself away from Lisa the night after I met her. I am, or at least I *was*, old-fashioned in that regard. Writing a column about new sexual experiences would provide me with a novel but valid excuse for catching up on something I felt I shouldn't have missed—a free pass to engage in the mischief I felt I'd been precluded from having thus far.

TWO DAYS
IN THE VALLEY

MY LIFE SEEMED LIKE it had been suddenly accelerated as I sat in the back of the empty Boeing 747. Ten days after the 9/11 attacks, I was atypically plastered and flying toward California on my first ever business trip. My brief was to travel to the town of Chatsworth, where I would be appearing as an extra in a porno flick. I would then write about it as, in the past six weeks, I had unwittingly become a writer.

The trip had been arranged a few weeks earlier, but what with the seemingly apocalyptic goings-on in Manhattan, I found myself and my surroundings too discombobulated to sufficiently prepare for my trip.

Nerve's SoHo offices are about a mile from the World Trade Center. The first plane had already hit by the time I boarded the A train at 181st Street. Typically the A rockets through its uninterrupted sixty-six-block run between 125th and 59th streets. It was running incredibly slow that morning, finally crawling into the 59th Street station at 9:25. During one five-minute standstill around 77th Street the conductor announced that there were delays due to an incident downtown. Before September 11th, an "incident" in the context of the subway system meant that someone had jumped onto the tracks. As a subway commuter in New York, one quickly loses compassion for people who choose the morning rush to end it all. It's extremely inconsiderate.

The doors opened. A heavyset Dominican girl jumped in the car and scanned the other passengers' faces for acknowledgment of what was happening downtown and didn't get it. The doors closed behind her.

"Ahm gettin' da fuck offa Manha-en," she said and shook her head in disbelief.

No one looked up from their papers. People are always exclaiming their intent to no one in particular and commuters have learned to ignore them, along with the prepubescent break-dancing crews, Patagonian guitar players, and the women who place the crumpled photocopied sign language cards on their laps.

"Yo, I said I needs ta get da fuck offa dis island, stat! Go ta Jersey or some shit."

Not an eyebrow was raised. The train stood still in the station. Frustrated, she cupped her hands around her mouth for a makeshift megaphone.

"*Yo! Dey blew up da World Trade and da damn White House, people!*"

Now she was beginning to get some people interested enough to look up. The train doors opened.

The woman's shouts were validated by the conductor's announcement that A train service was being suspended and that passengers needed to evacuate the station immediately. I felt sick with the thought that what the loudmouthed girl was bellowing was an actual fact. We quietly disembarked, all of us no doubt thinking about how accurate the Dominican girl had been. Columbus Circle was always frantic at rush hour, but walking up to street level it was clear that something was amiss. It was bedlam outside.

Long lines of people stood in front of pay phones. Cell phones appeared to not be working. People were crying, screaming. I walked into a Laundromat and stared up at the TV screens with a crowd. The image of the second plane hitting the building was being replayed over and over as the crawl confirmed that it was the Pentagon and not the White House that had been hit. The subways weren't running. The buses were nowhere to be seen.

I didn't know whether to walk the three miles to work or the eight miles home. Anna was probably safe, I decided. She had set off to embark on her final semester at Sarah Lawrence College in Bronxville before I'd even left the house that morning. As the enormity of the situation became increasingly apparent, I headed west then turned north up Riverside Park, getting home at around noon. The large smoke and dust cloud was clearly visible from the northern tip of the island. There were four messages on the answering machine: Mike's father, Anna's father, my panicked ex-girlfriend Becky, and my sister. My parents were en route home from Spain.

It was difficult to make outgoing calls. I e-mailed my family, told them I was fine, and made a cup of tea. Anna's father called again.

"Where's Anna?"

It seems inconceivable now, but at the time my girlfriend and I didn't have cell phones. Where anybody was then was reduced to a best guess based on what they told you when you last saw them.

"I'm sure that she's okay, she's up at school." It was probably true.

I sat and waited. I wanted to fall asleep for a month, to be woken up when it had blown over some.

Anna strolled in at around three. I held her close and thought about sobbing into the nape of her neck. After a few seconds she wriggled free of my bear hug and shrugged laconically.

"I'm already kind of over it," she said.

Anna was raised by Germans. I didn't know whether to admire or rail against her steely stoicism, but over the next hours and days, being with her was a welcome relief from the unchecked flow of raw emotion pouring out of everybody else.

By the afternoon, the awful burning stink had made its way up the avenues to the north end of the island. I managed to get in touch with Becky at around five. I could barely make out what she was saying through her wails.

"I thought you were dead," she said over and over.

I wasn't dead.

An e-mail arrived saying that Nerve was closed for the rest of the week. As soon as the bridges were reopened the next day, Brian drove Anna and me out to his parents' house in Jersey, where we watched movies, read, ate in empty restaurants, and got drunk in their hot tub. No one *we* knew had died, but we were each one friend removed from the grave reality of the event.

I'D NEVER BEEN OUT west before. When I met Anna she was creating an art installation inspired by the six-month stint she'd spent in Southern California. I went to see it at Sarah Lawrence and was wholly impressed with my twenty-one-year-old girlfriend's powerful summation of that period in her life; the floor of the art space was covered with sand. Bleached-out transparencies of palm-tree-flanked highways, scrubby hillsides, and concrete structures were mounted in glass cases and hung by fishing wire from the ceiling. The bare halogen lights were far too bright and positioned so that they were always in one's eyes. A scaled-down approximation of the LA River bisected the room. The walls were peppered with appropriate quotes about California from books by Joan Didion and Douglas Copeland. It didn't look like the Hollywood version of Hollywood.

The flight attendants on National Air didn't wear a uniform as such, but rather a purple polo shirt with jeans and sneakers. They looked like waitresses in some godforsaken sports bar, which sort of terrified me. One gave the safety demonstration as if there was more than one person in her section of the cabin, but I was alone. I'd already downed some NyQuil and one and a half Jack Daniel's miniatures before I'd boarded, which had taken the edge off a little.

Ross Martin had arranged to send me to the set of *Hard Evidence 2* but could only scare up enough money for a $175 round-trip ticket and $100 in petty cash. I was still an unknown quantity as a writer: my first installment of "I Did It for Science" had just been published and had gotten a warm yet modest response. I had made out with Anna's friend Luis and had written about the experience of kissing another guy. Two more installments, "Cock Ring" and "Sex on the Subway," had been written and were ready to go.

Ross had made sending me to a porn set a reality, but accommodations and transport were something I had to deal with myself. My Orchard coworker Daryl Berg was the only person I knew in Los Angeles. He gladly let me crash at his Hollywood apartment, though he told me he'd be at temple when I arrived. It was Yom Kippur.

At the age of twenty-four, I was still too young to rent a car, so I took a cab to Daryl's place at Melrose and Spaulding. The ride over looked just like Anna's installation: dusty, arid, spread out, and surrounded by scrubby mountains. The journey from the airport had eaten over half of my cash.

I found the key under the mat and let myself in. The phone rang. It was Daryl; he sounded panicked.

"Dude! Put some water in a pot and boil it. There's pasta in the cupboard, marinara sauce in the fridge. I gotta eat before sundown. *Shit! Shit!*"

I looked outside: the sun had already dipped low in the sky.

"I'm five minutes away!"

Twenty minutes later Daryl burst through the door and into the bowl of hastily prepared rigatoni, scarfing it down with one eye on the setting sun.

"Thank fucking Christ!" he said, exhausted from the speed eating. "I'm going to be fasting all day tomorrow."

After his first year in Hollywood, Daryl had a multitude of sins to atone for. I didn't realize just how pious Daryl could be until I asked him for a ride to Chatsworth the next morning.

"Okay, (A) that's like a fucking million miles away in the Valley somewhere and (B) this is the day of fucking atonement. I can't be hanging out at a porno."

Usually Daryl would be the first in line to attend the shooting of a porno movie.

"Well, how much would a cab fare be?" I asked.

"Dude, this isn't New York. It'd cost you, like, eighty bucks."

"Well, couldn't you just drop me off?"

"Holy shit, dude!" He stomped around the apartment and shook his head incredulously. "Okay, but you have to figure out your own way back."

Daryl mentioned that he was friends with Matt Zane, rocker, pornographer, and self-proclaimed pioneer of the rock-porn crossover. At my request he invited him over so we could talk about porn.

"Maybe you can write about him," said Daryl.

Zane's main claim to fame is that he "invented" the idea of throwing luncheon meat at naked girls. He was about to turn twenty-seven. He arrived at Daryl's looking like a teenage goth kid: hip-length hair and all-black ensemble. His face looked like it had experienced a lifetime of seediness.

"After three or four years," reflected Zane as he stroked his chin, his eyes cast skyward, "one tires of the flesh."

I had hoped that meeting with Zane would heighten my excitement about the upcoming Vivid shoot even further, but over the course of an hour he spoke only of his boredom with the genre, his accidental incarnation as a pornographer, and how being pigeonholed as a pornographer was strangling his creativity.

"If I cannot be free to realize my artistic visions outside of porn, I must welcome death with open arms," he said.

Zane then told me he had "banged almost a thousand chicks," but then six months ago he decided to refrain from sexual relations with girls in the categories of groupies, strippers, or porn sluts.

"It certainly makes it a lot harder to get laid," he added ruefully.

I have been an enthusiast of porn for most of my young life. In Corringham a curious preteen needn't suffer the embarrassment of trying to buy a girlie mag from a newsstand. Instead, my friends and I would ride our bicycles to the nearby woods, where copies of *Readers' Wives*, *Shaven Ravers*, and *Razzle* were inexplicably strewn about the trees and bushes along with soda cans, cigarette butts, traffic cones, an upturned shopping cart, and an old mattress. We surveyed the scattered contraband in silence, our ten-year-old minds trying to piece together the evidence of what had taken place there. What really fired our imaginations was that the scene was in a constant state of flux. The mattress and cones would change position and there would always be a new magazine or two that kept us coming back. The content of the magazines was typically vile and the magazines themselves were putrid: rain-soaked, earth-sodden, and stuck together in places. We were both intrigued and disgusted by them.

With Daryl bemoaning the affront to his fair-weather religiosity the whole way, we arrived at a soundstage in an industrial park in Chatsworth, about thirty miles from Hollywood. I entered a large hangar-type structure, where a rotund woman in her fifties told me that the man I was looking for, stage manager Jay Shanahan, was downstairs. I'd sort of imagined that there would be some sort of security detail at the entrance of the lot, but I took a few steps along a dark corridor and practically stumbled into the middle of the action.

I heard voices and walked carefully toward them. A dim blue glow from a TV monitor gave me a vague clue to my orientation as my eyes were beginning to adjust from the harsh California sunshine. The voices were now surrounding me.

"Cut, house lights!" screamed director Robby D., who wore his head shaved, sleeves of tattoos, and a tuft of wiry red whiskers jutting out from his chin. Half soccer hooligan, half King Tutankhamen.

The cast and crew of about ten people spun around to look at me. I had arrived, silently under cover of darkness, and I seemed to have appeared from nowhere.

"Hello, I'm looking for Jay Shanahan," I said to no one in particular.

"I'm Shanahan," said a man, stepping forward. Thick ivory hair in a crew cut, white socks pulled halfway up his shins, shorts, and a green polo shirt.

"So, you must be Grant Stoddard from Nerve," he said.

He shook my hand while making sure not to make direct eye contact with me.

"I must be!" I said.

"What?"

"I said, yes, I must be Grant Stoddard."

"Well, aren't you?"

Shanahan looked confused as he made a hand gesture to the wardrobe assistant.

"I am."

Nuance and wit, the cornerstone of my interpersonal skills, are largely wasted in Los Angeles, or any place where people seem to never really be listening.

"Okay, well, this is all very exciting, very exciting."

Shanahan left the room as everyone else eyed me with suspicion. "Can you please move? You're in our way," grunted a crew member.

I'd imagined the topsy-turvy world of hard-core pornography to be many things, but not quite this brusque and unwelcoming.

Shanahan returned to the set in a beige suit and orange faux-fur hat. He had a cameo as a sort of psychedelic pimp in the next scene.

The male talent, Kyle, was dressed in a ridiculous superhero outfit, pacing and reciting his lines in a varied array of styles for the amusement of himself and the twenty-year-old runner. Kyle is about five feet seven inches tall, and in his early forties. Not an ugly man, but not a person you'd characterize as classically handsome.

Shanahan was visibly frustrated by the late arrival of the girl in the first sex scene of the day.

"Where's the goddamn girl?" he shouted at no one in particular.

Chelsea Sinclaire (née Ebony Sinclaire) arrived on set at that very moment dressed in a glittery rainbow tube top and miniskirt. Aside from the huge breasts squeezed into her top, Chelsea didn't look like a porn star. She was petite, naturally pretty with flawless dark brown skin. With her broad north England accent, she didn't sound like a porn star either.

All the porn I'd seen growing up had come from the United States, Germany, or the Netherlands and featured American, German, and Dutch performers. Though the country's most popular paper, the *Sun*, featured topless "page three" girls daily, legislature from 1968 made it illegal to produce, buy, or sell images that depicted XXX material in Britain. An older friend of mine used to buy this contraband that a gentleman called Bazza would drive in from London. He would buy a copy of *Backdoor Madchens* from the trunk of Bazza's car in the parking lot of a large home-improvement chain, risking prosecution. He would then run off copies for me.

Consequently, I had no idea that there were English girls *in* porn. Hearing that thick Yorkshire accent come out of a porn starlet was both arousing and thought-provoking. What was her story? I had to find out.

"Oh, beautiful tits, Chels!" said Robby D.

She took her place on set. "You just get those done?"

"Yeah, seven weeks old," she called from the other end of the set.

This was the first time they were captured on tape.

"They look real good, like real natural black titties," Robby shouted back before turning to the crew. "I'm thirsty for chocolate milk!"

Someone in the crew muttered the name of a prominent surgeon.

"Gordo do those for ya?" Robby asked Chelsea.

"Gordo," she reported back.

The crew members nodded their heads in unison. They'd seen his work before and held it in high regard.

In this scene, Shanahan, as the pimp, is physically disciplining his ho, played by Chelsea, when Harry P (Kyle) comes to the rescue, beats up the pimp, and is rewarded by Chelsea with sex.

Shanahan left the set to change back into his suburbanite attire.

"Okay, suck his dick, Chels," said Robby D. "Look grateful, he just flew in to save your life. Get nasty with it. Spit on it, Chels, don't be shy. Great, now say something real nasty."

Chelsea took Kyle's penis out of her mouth, and in that heavy accent breathed, "I love your cock."

Robby rolled his eyes and looked at the crew.

"'I love your cock,'" he said, mocking her. "Jesus."

"Okay, let's see some soft shots," said Robby, clapping his hands together. In order for a film to increase its revenue, all of the scenes in a movie are shot twice, with the second version not showing any penetration or erect penises. That way it can be sold to a soft-core market that includes cable stations like Spice and the Playboy channels.

Kyle and Chelsea dry-humped in a few positions before Robby asked for an FIP, which is their shorthand for Fake Internal Pop. Kyle banged his flaccid cock against Chelsea's behind and finished with a theatrical bellow.

"Okay, let's fuck!" shouted Robby as Ross the runner handed him Chelsea's discarded thong. He held it to his nose and sniffed.

"Mmmm, want some?" he asked, offering the scrap of material to the morbidly obese boom mic operator.

"No, thanks, man," he said. "I'm trying to cut down."

Jay appeared briefly to complain about how slowly things were moving and walked out swearing under his breath. Kyle and Chelsea sat across from each other, making small talk while she applied lube to her vagina and he slapped and vainly tried to rub some life into his penis.

Kyle said something to Chelsea that I couldn't hear, but her answer was "Sure."

Chelsea got on all fours with her head down and bulbous derrière thrust skyward. Kyle drilled his tongue into Chelsea's ass, which garnered an instantaneous erection.

"Well, whatever works, man!" Robby called out to Kyle.

Kyle put on a condom, their use now mandatory on most porn sets.

"Let's have a nice slow insertion," called the thuggish and strangely likeable D.

The actors churned out a carbon copy of the pretend scene, which was somehow no more convincing despite everything slotting into its natural place. The "pop shot" was conducted on Chelsea's breasts. Still photos were taken and the crew took a lunch break.

A woman everyone on the set referred to as Mom was cooking catfish in the kitchen-hospitality area upstairs. An enormous buffet was laid out on the counter as she buzzed around and took orders. A couple of scantily clad girls talked about makeup and shopping.

"I got these jeans at the mall that make my ass look totally fucking amazing," said April Flowers, who has since become a notable star in the adult industry.

The men talked about their recent purchases of gas masks, water filters, and automatic weapons in response to the September 11th attacks.

"I was there," I offered as a point of interest. The room fell silent.

They were all very intrigued at Nerve's proximity to the site of the World Trade Center.

"Aren't people freaked out there?" asked one crew member.

"Kind of," I said. "Everyone's wearing flags."

They swapped glances and chuckled.

"You'll need more than that!"

Two of them revealed that they had bought biochemical suits.

"Maybe we should videotape girls' ankles and sell it to those Afghan fuckers!" said a potbellied cameraman. "Seriously, that's porn to them!"

I caught Chelsea's eye and asked if I could talk to her.

"Be with you in a minute!" she said, wiping Kyle's semen from her chest with a towel.

"You know that we're next, right," said the boom mic operator. "The porn industry . . . biochem attack in Van Nuys, man. You can bet on it. They hate freedom, bro."

Everyone nodded their heads.

I sat down with Chelsea on an empty set. Chelsea was twenty-two and had recently graduated from Bradford University with a degree in management. She told me that her sister got her into the porn industry by putting her in touch with an adult film agent in England. An American affiliate then invited Chelsea to come work in the United States.

"Porn's a lot different here," she said, dressed in track pants and a baggy white T-shirt. "A lot more professional. In England, there will be a couple of guys and a video camera. A lot of money goes into films over here, and the people are . . . well, they're just really nice."

Chelsea had just become a Vivid girl, a handful of elite women who are the de facto superstars of the adult entertainment world. Vivid girls only have to make seven movies and seven special appearances per year for their decent salary. Typically, noncontract girls earn money per scene and per activity. Facial come shots, anal scenes, and D.P. (double penetration, anal and vaginal) all carry a higher price tag.

"What's it like to have no choice over who you get to have sex with?"

"If I don't find him or her attractive, it really puts me in a bad mood, but once we get down to it, it's fine."

Chelsea said her boyfriend was from Louisiana and that she met him on Venice Beach. They planned to get married.

"How does he feel about what you do?" I said. I couldn't imagine that this demure little English girl was studying business just a year ago.

"It hurts him . . . here," she said, dramatically placing both hands on her heart. "He hates the industry, but he loves and respects me enough to get past it. I was doing this before we met. It's me job, d'ya know what I mean?"

I saw Shanahan and asked him about my scene.

"You'll be playing a convict," he said over his shoulder while striding away.

"Well, did Ross Martin at Nerve tell you what I wanted to—"

"Ross Martin didn't tell me a goddamn thing."

Shanahan walked into a room and closed the door behind him.

I walked up to the kitchen area, where I found Kyle reading a book.

"If you're gonna be in porn, you'd better like reading novels," he said.

I had already made up my mind that I was not going to be in porn.

"I've done this for about fifteen years, but lately the calls have been getting fewer and farther between," he said.

He explained that, up until two years ago, when Viagra came on the market, only a handful of men could maintain a successful career in hard-core pornography. Kyle was relatively short, positively nerdy, and his penis was within the normal size range. His real value lay in his ability to keep his penis hard for extended periods of time. "It's harder than you'd think!" he said. "Pun intended."

Kyle refused to use Viagra or penis injections, a physical crutch many other porn stars rely upon.

"I'm pretty convinced that those guys are going to have serious health problems in the years to come," he said. "But in the meantime, they're making a living and I'm not doing so well—but we'll see. People ask me why I don't use pills or shoot up to keep wood and I say, 'Hey, I'm old-fashioned. I like girls!'"

Kyle told me that he has never had a serious relationship with a woman.

"It's really too much to ask of anyone," he said. Yet conversely, all of the female actors seem to be attached.

I began asking around if anyone was headed back to the city after the shoot, but it transpired that everyone lived nearby and talked about LA as if it were light-years away. This was the Essex to LA's London.

A quick comedy vignette in a jail cell was taking place downstairs. Shanahan had another brief walk-on as a prison guard. The nonsex scenes are wrapped up quickly, and the dialogue sounds like it was written in an equally rapid fashion. The scene involved the three young male protagonists commiserating after being brutally sodomized by a fellow inmate.

On the next set, Robby was shooting a girl-girl scene starring April Flowers and Krystal. The set was all black, giving the actors the appearance of floating around in space. Despite looking like the archetypal porn star with her massive breasts, heavy makeup, and permed, bleached mane, Krystal was a newcomer to porn and was still a little coy.

April is a pro and was going through the motions with a bored look on her face. It was insinuated that April and Robby D. have more than just a working relationship.

"Okay, fucker," April said under her breath as D. gave stage direction.

The girls flashed lusty pouts at the camera while they made out and fingered each other. The highlight of the scene was when both girls wrapped their lips around a fifteen-inch double dong and slipped it farther and farther down their throats until their lips met. Robby went crazy.

"This is fucking amazing!" he said.

April gagged and her eyes teared, ruining her makeup. She was not pleased, not least because Robby kept getting her name wrong. No one was looking forward to shooting the next scene. I heard the crew discussing it: "It's a boy-boy-boy-girl. Three cocks to get hard, three pop shots, and the kicker is that the guys in the scene are going to be passing around a handheld camera. The shadows are going to be murder."

The three guys in the scene were short, ugly, and bereft of any body hair. They looked like shaved carnies. The woman in the scene, Kelsey, looked a little older than the other girls. Before the scene, she ran outside to smoke some weed with one of the crew.

Jay was the most seasoned member of the entourage aside from "Mom," so during quieter moments he was often quizzed by the crew about the old days. "Ahh, the good ol' days," he said, "when pornography was our friend. It looked better and felt better. Maybe that was just the coke!"

After a quick shower, the three guys took their places on the set, made to look like a college frat house, and ran through their dialogue. A bit later, Kelsey undressed while the guys attempted to get their dicks hard off-camera. This girl was the only one I'd seen who looked as though she was enjoying shooting a scene. She was also the only one who got high beforehand.

When she had a penis in each hand and one in her "cookie," Robby commanded the girl to commit to the moment.

"Come on, babe, get real fuckin' nasty with it!" he shouted.

"If we really wanna get nasty, why aren't we doing anal?" inquired Kelsey.

Laughter erupted throughout the crew.

"'Cause we can't fucking afford it, that's why!" yelled Jay from another room. Anal sex is an extra two to four hundred dollars; this figure is then multiplied by the number of men in the scene. The guys estimated that going anal would put the production over budget to the tune of a thousand dollars. "We'll do it if you want to do it for free," shouted an optimistic Robby.

Kelsey started laughing. It was getting late; I had dinner reservations in Hollywood at eight with Daryl and had no idea how I was going to be getting there. There were no busses. I started to get that nightmarish feeling of being trapped in the wilderness, penniless, miles from civilization.

My scene, of course, was the last one to be shot.

"What's this movie called, anyway?" I asked the PA, Sam, as we got into orange jumpsuits.

"Hard Evidence," he said. "No, wait, Hard Evidence Two. I think."

Sam had a busy day: he fetched water and lube when the girls asked for it, removed discarded clothing from the set with the speed and skill of a ball boy at Wimbledon, and had driven to the local pharmacy on several occasions to buy douche kits, home enema sets, and condoms. Sam couldn't believe that I'd flown in from New York. "You came all this way for this?" he said. "You must be disappointed."

Jay is a friend of Sam's family and offered him some work on his movies while he looks for PA work in mainstream pictures.

"I thought I was going to get laid," he said. "My friends are all jealous of me. In fact, Jay had me round up a bunch of them to be extras in a scene tomorrow. Then they'll see."

We took our places on a set made to look like a prison rec room.

"I've spent half my fucking life in prison and it looks just like this!" said Robby.

Kyle sat at a table with Sam as they shuffled through a pack of Vivid playing cards, each featuring a porn starlet.

"Fucked her, fucked her, I'd like to fuck her, I'm fucking her next week . . . ," said Kyle.

"Take your medication and get in the fucking shower!" Jay screamed into his cell phone. "I fucking mean it!"

He continued pacing up and down, waving his free arm around.

"I . . . I don't care, Marcy is in charge now. Do what Marcy says. Take your medication. I'm going to throw you in the fucking shower when I get home. I mean it. Get Marcy on the goddamn phone."

He strode out of the room. No one else batted an eyelash. I became unsettled and uncomfortable. I signed a release form.

I was sitting next to a four-hundred-pound black man who was stroking my shoulder. It appeared that I was playing his prison bitch. "Okay . . . er . . . what's your name?" shouted Robby.

"It's Grant," I said.

"Okay, Grahhnt," he said, aping my accent. "Now, he's going to put his arm around you and I want you to look really fucking terrified, okay, Grahhnt? Action!"

The camera panned across the scene as the big guy stroked me like a lap dog. I looked terrified and it wasn't acting.

"And . . . cut!" yelled Robby. The scene was over and I was free to go.

"Okay, Grahhnt, you're all set," he said and then looked at me quizzically. "Uh, why are you here, anyway?"

"I'm writing a piece for Nerve in New York," I explained, realizing that Jay had kept everyone else in the dark as to what I was doing—which incidentally seemed to have worked to my advantage.

"Oh," said Robby. "I thought that you just walked in off the street, and you weren't getting in the way so I didn't say anything."

He shook my hand warmly and I ran outside.

"Walked in off the street?" I said to myself as I walked out into the warm California evening. There is no street—the studio was on a lot in the middle of the fucking desert!

I called Daryl and pleaded with him to come and pick me up.

"What the fuck?" he screamed. "It's still Yom Kippur!"

"The sun's going down. It'll be dark by the time you get here."

"This is re-goddamn-diculous!" he said. I could hear him rattle his car keys in the background.

I felt awful dragging poor Daryl out again, and I swore I would do anything, anything if he helped me out. He said that if I should ever write about him, I should portray him as tall, dark, and handsome.

The desert scenery put me in mind of Anna's installation. I couldn't wait to get back to New York. I leaned up against a truck, watching the porn stars leave the set one by one and drive home elsewhere in the San Fernando Valley. Daryl arrived forty minutes later and took us back to Hollywood for a "breaking the fast" dinner.

An empty plane ride home.

Back in New York I began to have breathing problems, as were a lot of people at the time. I saw my doctor, who suggested that I had posttraumatic stress syndrome and prescribed the antianxiety medication Klonopin. I suppose the 9/11 attacks had affected me more than I'd allowed myself to believe. I'd tried to take Anna's icy position on the situation and it didn't take. Anna gently made fun of me for it, then offered that my malady was more likely linked to what I'd experienced in California.

■ **HOW WAS YOUR TRIP** to Los Angeles?"

My mother's question during our biweekly phone conversation took me aback.

"Um . . . it was good."

I backtracked to our previous conversation and thought about how I'd framed my business trip to my family. Only one installment of "I Did It for Science" had been published and I was waiting to hear whether it would be ongoing before telling my parents about it. I felt that with my family getting high-speed Internet service, they would soon be on the cusp of discovering Google, and, seconds later, would be rocked by the revelation that their only son had left the continent to become a sex worker. I needed them to hear the sordid facts from me.

"You were going to a film set, weren't you?" she said.

The events of September 11 had provided enough background chatter for me to leave the details extremely vague, but now my family were back in the business of finding out what was going on in my life.

"Yeah, I went to a movie set and wrote about it," I said.

"What's the name of the Internet company you're working for?" she said. "I keep forgetting it."

I didn't even tell my family I'd left Orchard Records until months after I made the move. They were temporarily satiated when I told them I'd become an admin assistant at an Internet company, but now that I was being flown across the country, they were on an incessant quest for fresh information.

"It's called Nerve," I said. "What's the weather been like?"

"And I can find it . . . y'know . . . on the computer?" she asked.

"In theory," I said. My mother was so afraid of the laptop my dad had given her when she started her business that she'd only logged a few hours using it. Her technological incompetence had only infuriated me before, though now it seemed it might actually pay dividends.

"So it's double-u, double-u, double-u, dot, N, E , R . . ."

"Wait!" I said upon hearing a slow clicking sound far away in the background. "Are you at your computer?"

"No," she said. "Dad is. So, Brad, it's N, E . . ."

The idea of my parents being confronted with what they would almost instantly gather was a Web site devoted entirely to the flesh was too much. They were mere seconds from discovering what the theme of my first business trip was all about and I didn't need to hand-hold them for that revelation.

"Mum, I have to go, right now."

"But . . ."

"Love to Dad." Click.

Since I began writing "I Did It for Science," the most common question among my friends had been, "What do your parents think about this?" It was a question I hadn't wished to ruminate on for more than a nanosecond. The last time I'd visited them and something vaguely risqué or sexual had come on the telly, I had to run out of the room. My sister could happily sit there in the midst of a sex scene or a graphic joke, while the sight of a nipple sent me scurrying into the kitchen yelling, "Would anyone like a cup of tea?" They were no doubt aware that I didn't have a girlfriend throughout high school and college, and, consequently, I'm quite sure the idea that I was gay had crossed their minds.

After hanging up I sat on my bed and imagined the Web site in all its Dionysian glory flickering before their eyes, three thousand miles away, before instinctively running into the kitchen asking Anna if she'd like a cup of tea.

FREE FOOD

BECAUSE of the cheese-and-wine parties, the book readings, the movie premieres, and prerequisite cocaine use, Nerve had a fairly liberal attitude toward the official commencement of the working day. CEO Rufus Griscom couldn't let a militant stance toward timekeeping detract from Nerve's hard-won image as the online home of literate hedonism, but somewhere between the bleary-eyed start, slow warm-up, two-hour lunch, the much ballyhooed thirty-minute catnap, heated set of Ping-Pong, and the evening's next round of comped drinks to quaff and swag bags to collect, there was apparently work to be done. Pre-dot-com crash, employees were pretty much golden provided they managed to stagger in by 11:00 a.m. or so. Rufus gradually coaxed the staff into a less decadent work schedule, via the cunning use of complimentary doughnuts, which appeared on the conference table between 9:45 and 10:15, a window of time we called the sugar rush. Without ruffling anybody's feathers, Rufus squeezed an extra hour of productivity out of twenty-five people—many Ivy League graduates—at the cost of just sixty cents a head. It remains his most astute business accomplishment to this day.

As we shuffled around two boxes of Krispy Kreme doughnuts one bone-chilling February morning, Emma Taylor, Nerve's other Brit, told me about a conversation she'd had at a mixer at the Tribeca Grand the night before. Emma (Em) was one-half of Nerve's irreverent sex advice columnists, Em amd Lo, Lo being Lorelei Sharkey. It was at the beginning of a gold-rush period, in which the opportunities of ceweb-rities seemed suddenly lucrative and limitless. Book, TV, and movie deals were dangled in front of everybody's faces—as evidenced by what you currently hold in your hands—and Em and Lo were in the midst of the feeding frenzy. Introduced as straight-shooting sex columnists, Em and Lo were received with relish as they glad-handed and double air-kissed their way through the trendy hotel bar. Toward the end of the boozy evening they were introduced to a particularly enthusiastic agent named Peter, who proceeded to treat them to an anomalous sexual encounter he'd had around the holidays. Sex advice columnists are often expected to ply their trade at the drop of a hat, and four martinis in the ladies were happy to oblige.

"This guy we met, Peter, had a date with this other guy, Jonathan," said Emma.

"Go on."

"Apparently the nicest guy, well dressed, whatever. So they go back to his place and he asks if Peter wants a beer. He says no, but Jonathan insists that he have one. He asks Peter to take a swig and spit it out all over him. So he does and he sort of just moaned. Then he stripped off—"

"Who strips off?" I said, still half asleep.

"Jonathan," said Emma, annoyed that my confusion was interrupting the flow of her story. "So *Jonathan* asks him to go to the fridge and throw all the food at him."

"Sploshing." A copy of *Splosh!* magazine had recently arrived at the office and the staff had become acquainted with the kink.

"It's called sploshing. When all the food was gone he asks Peter to leave. The next day Peter gets an e-mail saying that he'd had a fantastic time, that it had taken him four hours to clean up, and that they should 'do it again sometime.' And he wants Peter to bring a friend."

UP UNTIL NOW the "new things" I had tried included having sex with my girlfriend on the subway, product testing a cock ring, Frenching a guy, being an extra in a porn movie, and competing in an amateur stripping contest in front of two hundred drunk and very aggressive women. Six months earlier, I was the perennial virgin, a shy, inexperienced, terribly self-conscious immigrant nerd, destitute and a gnat's eyelash from throwing in the towel on my American excursion and fleeing home with my tail between my legs. Now my name was synonymous with being a willing participant in perverse sex acts throughout the tristate area. Unbeknownst to me, it became my calling.

"He said he'd love to have you along, if you'd like," Emma said, washing down her second free doughnut with a swing of free black coffee. Before I had a chance to compute how my life was rapidly spinning out of control and beyond recognition, the sploshing idea was floated at the next editorial meeting and I was immediately assigned to participate in a quasi-sexual food fight with two gay men.

I obligingly touched base via e-mail with Peter, who admitted that while he had little *personal* interest in degrading poor Jonathan further, he'd be glad to make it happen for the sake of helping me out. He'd read the first few installments of "I Did It for Science" on Em and Lo's request and insisted that he'd found the concept terribly amusing. Peter contacted Jonathan, who responded promptly, requesting that we provide him with a shopping list of items we'd like to fling in his general direction. The list included yogurt, eggs, soda, chocolate pudding, ketchup, chocolate syrup, crème fraîche, and whipped cream. As the day drew closer, a paranoid Jonathan promised to pay us $250 each to ensure that we didn't flake out, adding that he wanted to make it a weekly deal. My mind boggled at the thought of an easy extra $12,000 per year, or almost two years' rent.

The founding father of sploshing is a gentleman by the name of Bill Shipton. My first task was to get him on the phone to explain why on earth people would want to shower each other with pudding. Shipton is the editor and publisher of *Splosh!* magazine, which comes out of a notoriously dreary English coastal town called St. Leonards-on-Sea, a hamlet near where an entire branch of my family have quietly eked out their golden years with the minimum of fuss. I thumbed through a copy and wondered if poor old Aunt Mary and Uncle Tom would have had any inkling that a snaggletoothed woman by the name of Dirty Deidre was lying prostrate in a bathtub full of baked beans in one of the adjacent bungalows. Sploshing, as explained by its creator, seemed like a bit of slapstick, surrealist fun in the vein of Benny Hill or Monty Python. Similarly, sploshing seems to have been spawned by the British upper classes—presumably after realizing that throwing British food on your girlfriend is marginally preferable to putting it anywhere near your mouth.

Though we'd e-mailed several times I first met Peter in a Wild West–themed bar, an hour before we were due to go to Jonathan's place on the Upper West Side. It was a chilly March night that coincided with the six-month anniversary of the 9/11 attacks. I caught sight of the columns of light for the first time as I walked from the subway stop to the bar.

I saw Peter nursing a beer between two cowpokes. I quickly recognized him from Emma's thoughtful description: tall, but stocky like a rugby player, with a large, round, close-cropped and happy-looking head, mid-thirties, smiley. I sidled up next to Peter, who seemed pleased to see me if a little embarrassed by the circumstances. We spent the first two rounds talking about anything but the poor bastard we were about to abuse. Peter had a relaxed, lilting, and kind tone that reminded me of Bob Ross. He was as big a sweetheart as Emma had led me to believe. I was instantly relieved that I was embarking on this strange assignment with somebody so incredibly normal seeming.

It was only as we readied ourselves to go out onto the icy sidewalks of Amsterdam Avenue that we vocalized our own ideas at exactly what made Jonathan so keen to be used as a waste disposal.

"Listen, Grant," he said. He took a fantastically deep breath. "I probably should have told you this before, but there may be a stronger sexual element to what's going to happen tonight. And I just wanted to make sure that you are okay with that."

I cocked an eyebrow, inviting Peter to explain further.

"Well, I might be participating in the sexual side of things. If you are feeling it, you can jump in too, but it might get a bit weird. So you sure that's cool?"

"Weirder than a guy who likes having food thrown at him?" I said.

"Well, perhaps."

"I'm sure that it'll be fine," I said as we entered Jonathan's art deco building.

PETER TOLD the uniformed and mustachioed doorman that we were here to see Jonathan in 17H. He immediately stared us up and down with utter contempt.

He sneered and called up to our host's apartment. "You have-a visitors," he said coldly. Then he slammed the receiver down and pointed toward the mirrored elevators. Peter succumbed to a giggling fit that he finally got under control between the eighth and ninth floors.

"Also, you should probably know that I didn't *actually* go on a real date with Jonathan," he said. He continued to look straight ahead. Beads of sweat began to form in the meaty furrows of Peter's brow.

"Go on," I said. This was intriguing, but I started to get a little freaked out.

Peter thought about how the impact of what really happened could be lessened before quickly blurting out, "It was Christmas Day and I was cruising some Web sites. He asked me to come over to his place. I sort of knew he wanted some strange stuff before I left."

As open-minded as I told myself I had become, I found something about cruising for strange, anonymous, lonely gay sex on one of the holiest days in the Christian calendar mildly upsetting. The silence was thick and punctured by the soft ding that demarcated another floor.

"Okay," I said, unconvinced. "But why didn't you mention this to Em and Lo?"

"What?" he said. "I'd just met them, and we were in polite company. I didn't want them to think that I was some sort of sexual . . . *deviant*."

"You're not?"

Peter looked at me, disgusted that I seemed to be passing judgment on how he spent the Yule.

"No! I was bored and depressed. I always feel down around the holidays."

With that, the elevator doors slid open and dumped us into a long, narrow corridor painted a ghastly pastel pink.

"His apartment is that one at the end of the hall," said Peter in a theatrical whisper that was markedly louder than his talking voice.

The door at the end was ajar; a blue light seeped out of the crack. Following Peter's lead, I tiptoed up to the door behind him. Peter took a peek inside.

"Yeah, it's set up like before," he whispered. "We have to be quiet. The neighbors complained last time. Just follow my lead and hold tight."

Before I had a chance to think about what Peter had said, he rushed into the dimly lit apartment and I gamely followed after him. The first thing I noticed was the large flat-screen TV playing hard-core gay porn, which seemed to take up a whole wall of this neat and compact studio apartment. The TV was on mute. In the middle of the room was a massive tarp, and directly across from the TV was a bed upon which lay a stark-naked and furiously masturbating man who I assumed to be Jonathan. The man looked up at both of us from under his formidable unibrow, and although he seemed to quake with fear, he never compromised the lively rhythm of his onanism.

JONATHAN LOOKED Mediterranean and fairly athletic, though his troubled face was a mess of acne scars. Aside from the masturbation, his body movements were like a high-strung squirrel's. He pivoted his head to take in a view of myself, Peter, the porn, and his penis, each turn lasting a fraction of a second. After four go-rounds, Jonathan used his free hand to grab a Heineken and bottle opener that had been positioned on his nightstand ahead of our arrival. He scooted off the bed and landed on his knees, his head now inches in front of Peter's crotch. Peter took the beer, then reached down and grabbed Jonathan by his right ear and pulled him sharply upward.

The only sound in the room was the rapid wet slapping of our host's frenzied self-abuse, but I clearly saw Peter mouth "Suck my fucking cock" into the stretched lobe that he held mercilessly betwixt forefinger and thumb. Peter pulled down his sweatpants to mid-thigh, revealing his fully erect penis, which he maliciously poked in both of Jonathan's eyes before sinking it deep and hard into his gaping maw. Jonathan gagged, sputtered, and teared.

My coconspirator had gone from amiable teddy bear to Gestapo bully-boy sex fiend in mere seconds. I looked on from the doorjamb, still holding two plastic bags full of auxiliary yogurt and two dozen eggs we'd picked up at a bodega on Jonathan's block. Incidentally, Peter had insisted that the eggs be free-range and the yogurt organic, which cemented the image I was building of a caring, considerate person.

"Get fucking undressed," Peter said. I recoiled with fear and briefly reckoned how easy it would be to dump the groceries and make a run for freedom, leaving these two lovebirds in flagrante delicto. This was rapidly beginning to seem very distant from the definition of sploshing that I'd been given. This poor bastard Jonathan was being treated like a sexual ashtray by a guy who'd been a gentle giant minutes earlier. I began to think through how my failure to go through with this would go down with Michael Martin, Nerve's editor in chief. One of Michael's conditions for taking the head position at Nerve was that I should be

FREE FOOD ■ 129

paid full-time to write. Up until then, I wrote the column in between reordering ink for the printer, answering customer service e-mails, and bothering the female interns, and for no extra pay. When he joined the company, Michael made it clear that if ever I felt I was in physical danger during an assignment, I should leave immediately. I certainly didn't want to betray his confidence in me by using a lifeline—something I did only once in three years of sexual misadventures.

"We are about to fuck this faggot's shit up," said Peter as he intensified his thrusts into poor Jonathan's face.

I stepped backward into the bathroom and slowly peeled off my clothes, folded them into a neat pile, and set them on the tank of the toilet. I stopped short of stripping completely naked, thinking that my nudity would be mistaken as a green light for full involvement. More important, the ongoing fight-or-flight process had rendered my penis both tiny and useless. As if I wasn't already embarrassed enough. I didn't realize I was shaking until I caught a glimpse of myself in the mirror. I splashed my face with water. I'd seen this technique used in movies to provide a burst of clarity in harrowing situations, but it didn't do the trick. Most of the water ran down my elbows and onto the crotch of my light gray briefs. It looked as though I'd peed in my underwear and only served to heighten the tension. I splashed more water on more underpants to detract from the singular pee patch until the whole front section was wet through and charcoal in color.

"What are you doing in there?" said Peter at full volume. He placed emphasis on "doing," insinuating that I was wasting the opportunity to witness a homoerotic home invasion to clip my toenails or take a crap.

"Just a minute!" I said. I dabbed the excess water off my underpants with a towel then used it to wipe the accumulating beads of sweat from my brow. Jonathan made a guttural sound that was followed by a thud as he received what sounded like a powerful blow to the solar plexus.

I studied my face in the mirror. I was having a sense of a feeling that I get almost weekly. The feeling is a distant cousin to déjà vu. I feel like I have woken up in somebody else's life and am momentarily paralyzed as I try and retrace my life's steps and missteps to make some sense of how I arrived here, with them, in this moment, an opportunity, some bad luck begetting some good luck, a serendipitous meeting, a friend of a friend, dropping a name, being discovered, hitting my lowest ebb, my accent, a morsel of unrefined talent, the unflagging need to impress other people, once-in-a-lifetime opportunity, drunken grandstanding at a party, a good feeling, going with the flow, it's a small world after all, what the hell, I might die tomorrow.

"Grant!" said Peter.

"Don't use my name!" I called back, instantly incriminating myself.

"Shhhhhhh," hissed Jonathan, taking a moment's rest from servicing his master.

Whack went the butt of the beer bottle on Jonathan's skull. "Shut the fuck up!" said Peter.

As I mentally prepared myself to rejoin the fray, I reminded myself that I was being paid to be here, I was on the clock. None of the kids I grew up with would believe that a job like this even existed, let alone that "Grunt" Stoddard would be the person who ended up doing it. A social pariah back at home, I was now being paid to participate in bizarre sex acts, making up for lost time and enjoying an infinitely higher standard of living to boot.

I opened the bathroom door to see that Peter had stripped off his maroon sweatpants over his hi-top sneakers, but left his jacket and T-shirt on. He tipped his head back and dumped half of his beer into his own gullet and the other half into his fellator's eyes, which evoked a faint cry of pain.

"What did you fucking say to me?" said Peter. He rapped Jonathan hard on the cranium with the bottle whilst waiting for an answer. Jonathan momentarily took his pistonlike hand off his member to give the universal sign language for "please keep it down."

"Who do you think you are?" hissed Peter, reverting to his stage whisper. "I make the fucking rules here, you whoring come slut."

Thanks to Lisa Carver and her sex contest, this wasn't the first time I'd been in the same room with two naked and fully engorged men, but it was the first time I'd seen man-on-man action in the flesh. During sex, it seemed that there was nothing effete or sissified about the gay experience at all. It was something rougher, ruder, more brutish and manly than I had personally mustered before or since.

Peter briefly broke character and shot me a knowing wink.

"Are you getting all this?" he mouthed to me, pretending to be taking notes with an imaginary pad and pencil. I nodded that I was and Peter fought hard to stifle a chuckle. He pointed down at Jonathan's head, as if to say "get a load of this guy," and then held his palm to his beaming smile like an embarrassed Japanese schoolgirl. He looked down at my drenched underpants and shot me a quizzical look.

"Is everything okay?" he mouthed and grabbed two fistfuls of Jonathan's thick wiry black hair, pulling his head back and forth along the length of his cock.

"Fine," I mouthed back. "Water."

I took the bags of eggs and yogurt to the small kitchen nook and set them on the counter. I opened the fridge to find most of the items on our shopping list packed tightly onto the shelves. I picked up an egg and showed it to Peter, with my eyebrows arched. He shook his head no.

"Gimme five," he mouthed. He signed the numerical value with his fingers.

Without his penis ever escaping Jonathan's generous lips, Peter then pushed our continually masturbating host onto his back, got down on his haunches above Jonathan's face, and began drilling down into his face with gusto, his flapping hairy buttocks pulsing in the bluish light of the TV. Jonathan's eyes were fixated on the smooth studs enjoying an impromptu pool party. I watched in awe at the mechanics of Peter and Jonathan for a minute or two before I caught sight of a fiesta of family pictures atop Jonathan's Ikea shelving. There was our man Jonathan holding up a freshly caught fish with a young man in a frame with the word "Uncle" embossed upon it. Next to it was a picture of Jonathan at a wedding, kissing a lovely-looking girl on the cheek as a man I suspected to be his father looked on. The third picture was a younger Jonathan with several other guys wearing their Greek letters and giving effusive thumbs-up signs.

Jonathan tapped Peter on the shoulder like a submitting wrestler and motioned him closer.

"He wants you to start throwing stuff at him," amplified Peter. I walked over to the fridge and pulled out a large container of French Vanilla yogurt. Taking a large, icy-cold handful, I flung it at Jonathan's manically bouncing testicles.

"*Yymmppfff!*" he said, his airway stretched to accommodate Peter's bulky appendage. I was worried that I had somehow hurt him, a fear that quickly dissipated as his stroking increased in both speed and vigor.

"Give him more!" commanded Peter. I grabbed the bottle of Hershey's chocolate syrup and painted long sweeping brown lines the width of his hirsute torso and thighs and finishing with a flourish of concentric circles around his private parts. Another indecipherable yell emanated from deep within Jonathan's chest. He switched his masturbatory grip from the one-handed underhand grip to the unorthodox two-handed interlocking position, with thumbs pointed skyward, creating extra pressure between the heels of the hands. I ran back and forth from the kitchen nook with handfuls of eggs that I cracked one by one over his groin, great globs of crème fraîche that I catapulted between his hairy thighs with the aid of a serving spoon, bright arcs of ketchup squirted high into the air, while trying to get as little as possible on Peter, who continued to happily, obliviously bounce on top of Jonathan's face. Our victim briefly let go of himself for the first time and hooked his arms over Peter's thighs. The combined smell of the rapidly warming dairy products and my willing participation in a homosexual act was starting to make me feel dizzy, so I stepped off the Pollock-inspired tarp and took a breather.

"What is wrong with this fucking pervert?" asked Peter. He positioned his anus directly onto Jonathan's lips.

"I really don't know," I said. I was unaware that Peter was trying to initiate a call-and-response routine.

"It's because he's a disgusting little faggot, isn't it?"

"Yes."

"What is he?"

"Disgusting little faggot," I mumbled.

Jonathan's face emerged from between Peter's cheeks to shoot me a haunted glare that I found incredibly disturbing, before being quickly engulfed in flesh once again.

"Yes, but that's not all, is it?"

"Nope."

I hate when people make you grope around for an answer that they already know. It's terribly condescending.

"Well, tell him what he is!"

"Bad? A bad man . . . uh . . . boy! He is a very bad boy!"

Peter looked over his shoulder with a disappointed expression. "He is an ass-licking queer, the come-gargling lowest of the low that doesn't deserve to know happiness. *That's* what he is!"

Jonathan moaned in ecstasy, but I found that listening to these nasty things, let alone making up insults of my own, was incredibly challenging.

"Um . . . he is a worthless piece of shit?" I stammered, but my intonation was all wrong and the utterance sounded more like a question.

I knew that Jonathan really wanted to be humiliated and abused, but as the words left my lips I wanted to recall them all. I imagined Jonathan mincing around D'Agostino, spending his emergency savings on food that would ultimately be matted into his copious tufts of chest hair, and I pitied the poor man. I wondered if he had a huge cast of rotating characters that would come over to defile him and his apartment, or if his first time with Peter was the actualization of a fantasy years in the making.

Peter's frenzied thirty-second finale saw Jonathan's head loudly bouncing off the floor. Spent, Peter dismounted and stood up.

"I am really feeling the burn in my quads," he said before giving Jonathan a joyless punt in the ribs for seemingly no reason.

Jonathan had been furiously jerking himself off for over thirty-eight minutes, without resolution. He beckoned Peter closer and whispered something in his ear, inspiring his tormentor to spit in his eyes.

"He says that he can't pay us," whispered Peter. "He just lost his job."

The money would have been nice but I was far too shell-shocked to care.

"And he wants us to piss on him," he said. Peter sighed with gravitas. "He made me do this last time." This detail was also mysteriously absent from the story's first telling.

"Then we're out of here," said the big galoot. "I promise." He picked up on my reticence to honor his wishes.

I GRUDGINGLY STOOD on one side of Jonathan's prone body, Peter stood on the other. I exposed myself for the first time and took aim. Ordinarily, a knocked elbow at a urinal can prevent me from urinating no matter how badly I needed to go beforehand, so I wasn't entirely confident that I could complete the task at hand. To my total shock, I was instantly aiming a jet of aqua vitae at Jonathan's torso. He then raised his hips to signal that he wanted me to pee on his genitals and then opened his mouth, which I obligingly filled to the brim with hot urine, which produced a most satisfying sound. Jonathan writhed in ecstasy, his fist pumping ever faster. Peter stood with one hand on his hip and his eyes shut tight, attempting to clear his mind. I finished and stepped back, disgusted at the mess that was Jonathan.

"Would you mind looking away?" whispered Peter.

I spun around and again studied the smiling friends of the side of Jonathan I'd never get to know. Peter had hardly been human since his initial transformation when we first entered the apartment; it calmed me greatly to realize that the Jekyll and Hyde transformation wasn't permanent. I watched a few minutes of a rough but silent locker-room gang bang and felt glad that I was normal enough to get off without the need for abuse, pornography, urine, and groceries.

"Hey," said Peter. He sighed. He was visibly rattled. "Can you go into the bathroom?"

I obligingly walked in and wiped some of the culinary shrapnel off of my legs and scooped out the dollop of ketchup that sat in the depression behind my collarbone. I took another look in the mirror and wondered if tonight was yet another of those forks in the road that would send my life on a hitherto unimagined trajectory. It had become apparent that large swathes of my family were reading my column. My mother had recently called, after what sounded like a few glasses of wine, and said grandly, "What you're doing: Is it right?"

I said that I thought it was. I then averted a potentially damaging and definitely embarrassing confrontation by telling her how cool and open-minded everybody thought she was, which is partially true and totally did the trick. Up until tonight, it had all been racy yet forgivable stuff. Wrapping up a brutal, hard-core, gay home invasion by treating the victim to a golden shower seemed *not right*. Going to college, moving to New York City, and becoming a writer had set me apart from my peers back at home, but getting paid for chucking pudding at another man's erection while he suffers a merciless forty-minute throat-boning put me in another galaxy entirely.

I quickly got dressed and tried to make sense of the evening's events.

"It's no use," said Peter. He grimaced through the crack in the open door. "I really can't go. Can you go wait by the elevator?"

I took one last lingering look at Jonathan. He looked both sexually enraptured and terribly hurt, his body twitching in a glistening, Technicolor swill that I had helped create. His eyes traced me across his studio and out of his life forever.

"I'll be out in a minute," said Peter.

I quietly closed the front door behind me and took some deep breaths by the elevator.

Close to seven minutes later, I heard a splash and orgasmic moan before Peter came barreling out the door and down the hallway. He waved his hands above his head.

"Call the elevator!" he shouted.

Peter bundled me through the opening doors and hit the lobby button half a dozen times in rapid succession.

"Oh my God," he said. Peter gasped for breath, and finally satisfied that we were heading downward and away from Jonathan, said, "I drank half a gallon of water and I still couldn't go. In the end I went into the bathroom, pissed in a cup, and threw it in his face!"

The irony of his intermittent stage fright wasn't lost on Peter, who began giggling uncontrollably as we ran out of the building under the damning gaze of the doorman.

"Can't wait to read about this!" said Peter. We walked north on Amsterdam Avenue for a block. I felt awkward.

"Do you want to get a drink?" I asked as we passed the Western bar. The experience had left me weak and I wasn't ready to be alone just yet.

"I'd love to but I really have to run to a drinks thing, a work drink thing in TriBeCa," said Peter. "But this was kind of fun, wasn't it?"

"Totally!" I felt sad to the bone.

It was after 11:00 p.m. and the A train was now running on the local track, which meant I had forty minutes to ruminate upon the evening. Anna would be waiting. I needed to hold her to restore some semblance of normalcy in my life.

I said good-bye to Peter in a flurry of awkward pleasantries and promises of a burgeoning friendship between us.

"We should definitely hang out," he said a split second before I could.

"Oh, definitely."

"I mean I think we sort of *have* to now."

"Absolutely."

I haven't seen or heard from Peter since.

I waited on the freezing platform for almost fifteen minutes. I was cold and rattled.

I called Michael from a pay phone. I recounted the evening's events to him and he agreed that the evening was so far from the definition of the fetish that I should try sploshing with Anna in the comfort of my own home as soon as I felt up to it.

I needed a hug. I studied other people in the car and decided that they could tell what I'd been up to. I felt disgusted with myself. We stalled at 125th Street for another ten minutes and I got home just after midnight. Upon opening the door, Anna could tell something had happened to me.

"Just hold me!" I said and fell into the apartment and her arms.

"What happened?" she asked. I always teased Anna for being cold and ruthless, but on rare occasions such as this one, the caregiver, the nurturer, came through.

"I don't know if I can do this anymore. I think that it's going to affect me."

"Don't be ridiculous!" she said. "You'll be fine."

I'd been naked in a room with two fully engorged men having relations. When my sister was twelve, Pat Crouch, who lived across the street from our house growing up, told her that I was "going to be a gay." Prancing around with naked dudes for a living went a good way to realizing her prophecies. Explaining to Pat Crouch that I was purely doing it for money would have only exacerbated things.

In order to continue with a job that was becoming physically, mentally, and morally challenging, I found myself shifting my own definition of what was embarrassing or even potentially damaging. The envelope of what I would actually consider doing for the column seemed to grow exponentially with every passing day. Pushing the boundaries of what was and wasn't acceptable behavior had, in the previous few years, become a national pastime—the numerous celebrity sex videos, one president getting blow jobs in the Oval Office, the next having had a cocaine habit, Bob Dole hawking Viagra, the celeb-reality TV explosion—and behind it all was the Internet, ushering in a new culture of disclosure, irreversibly shifting the paradigms of modesty, privacy, and shame. When I felt that I was getting in too deep—as I almost always did—I consoled myself with the idea that in the subsequent few years the shift in what was viewed as being kosher would reach escape velocity, burst forth from New York and other coastal cities and flood into the towns and villages, winning the hearts and minds of those in the world's hinterlands, and that instead of a shameless sex pervert, I would come to be seen as some sort of brave pioneer, holding a mirror to mankind's basest physical needs in all their weird and wonderful manifestations.

Though as Anna fell into a deep sleep, I laid awake fretting about how wacky my résumé would look on paper.

NERVE ENDINGS

I HAD DECIDED that I would definitely need to break up with Anna some months before the actual event. I had become convinced that she didn't have my back. I felt that she should have done a better job of going to bat for me with her parents and that I would punish her with dismissal. I had recently found out that I could be finicky and incredibly ruthless with people if I felt slighted by them, and I could tell that Anna had no inkling of the kind of lather I worked myself into about the situation.

Anna's parents were upset that she had broken up with her yuppie boyfriend and immediately shacked up with another man. Furthermore, they were completely livid that her new beau was, in their estimation, a pornographer. Anna's father was a Vietnam vet of Prussian extraction, her mother an accented German woman of aristocratic lineage, which somehow made their distain for me that much more stark.

With the holidays approaching and me unable to return home because of a visa issue—I'd lost it in the back of a cab—I'd assumed that I'd be spending Christmas with the Braunschweigers. But shortly after Thanksgiving, Anna told me that I wasn't welcome at their Colonial Maryland home.

This came as a shock because, in general, parents loved me. Not as an ideal mate for their daughters, necessarily, but as a quirky, slightly fey but completely harmless placeholder while they sought out somebody, if not "better," then certainly taller. In the company of parents I am polite, charming, complimentary, self-deprecating, and can chat about current affairs at length without breaking a sweat. All of these attributes apparently count for little when you are extolling the virtues of their undergraduate only child's vagina to several thousand avid readers every month.

They just end up resenting you.

"They say that Christmas is just for family," said Anna on the A train journey home to Washington Heights.

"But I can't go home to mine," I said.

My losing my visa had meant that I couldn't even return home for my paternal grandmother's funeral some months earlier, which I felt terrible about.

"Did you tell them that I can't go home?"

"Yes. They didn't really care," said Anna.

We sat in silence as the train stalled at 103rd Street. Anna and I had been living together in Washington Heights for six months. We left the house each morning and commuted together, came home about the same time and made dinner together. It had been fun, this playing house with my beautiful, perky Aryan college senior. I began to think that spending the holidays together would be a logical continuation of our grown-upness.

"Well, I guess that's okay, we'll just have our own little Christmas," I said and put my arm around her, making her flinch. "I'll get us a nice tree and we'll cook dinner together. I'll buy a goose!"

"Are you out of your fucking mind? I can't *not* go home for Christmas, they'd cut me off!"

"Then what the fuck am I going to do?" I said.

"Well, my mom says that you ought to volunteer at a homeless shelter."

I'd always thought that one day I'd grow into the sort of good person who would volunteer a lot of his time to helping the disenfranchised, but I lost my shit at the suggestion that it's something that I really *ought* to do, as if it would serve as some sort of penance.

"And you're okay with that?" I said.

"I really don't have a choice."

"Stand up to them!"

Anna produced an emery board from her purse and absentmindedly filed away at her talons. I ended up spending Christmas with Becky and her family. Being spiteful wasn't my intention but I got some satisfaction when it made Anna bristle.

"They're wicked bleeders, the krauts," said my grandmother when I gave her my sob story at being shunned at Christmas. I'd long suspected Anna of being too cold and dispassionate to have a real relationship with. I'd spent the fall trying to push her buttons just to wrangle some sort of emotion out of her, but strategic and premeditated freakouts had become exhausting, predictable, and I was running out of plates to smash.

Ideally I would have wanted a clean break, but Anna was broke and had nowhere else to go. When she returned from Maryland I told her that for the sake of our relationship we should really think about getting our own places. I'd been forced into sharing a bed with an ex-girlfriend before and wasn't about to make the same mistake. Once we were in separate apartments, I would sever the ties, but not before.

A few weeks after we moved to our respective new homes on opposite banks of the East River it would be time to take action. I'd never dreamed that I'd be with a sexy fashionista like Anna, and now I was breaking up with her. Something had changed.

As breakups go, it was actually fairly pleasant. I was dog-sitting at a friend's beach house on the Jersey Shore one squally April weekend. I picked Anna up from the Asbury Park train station and we spent the time sitting around, cuddling, eating their food, drinking their wine, watching their movies. We eventually had a little cry together. But that was that. No mess, no fuss.

Michael Martin, Nerve's new editor in chief, was delighted with the news that I was now single, as it meant a whole slew of sexual scenarios with a rotating cast of unsavory characters was now possible, or perhaps even mandatory.

When Michael came to interview at Nerve I took an instant disliking to him. From across the room I could see that he was too good-looking, too stylish, and at twenty-five far too young to be an editor in chief. I didn't know then that in Michael I had a champion and that once he secured the position, one of the first things he'd do was make me part of the editorial team full-time. Up until Michael joined I sat in on editorial meetings, but my day-to-day work was focused on managing the interns, ordering office supplies, and monitoring the customer service situation. Before Michael took over, I felt that the previous regime had regarded me as a novelty. Michael, however, had believed in me enough to allow me to legitimately write for a living and persuaded Rufus not only to make that happen, but also to pay thousands of dollars to have my INS status put in order. In fact, after one visa application was rejected without reason, Michael ensured that Rufus paid for a whole new petition.

Michael's vision of "I Did It for Science" going forward would require a lot more commitment from me, however.

"I think that you are at the zenith of your powers when you are at your most uncomfortable," he said before mapping out his vision of me using glory holes, starring in porn movies, and offering myself up at gay clubs, and was willing to up my salary accordingly.

CHINATOWN

I HELPED ANNA MOVE to an apartment in the ass-end of Williamsburg, then moved to Chinatown in a taxicab. My new room couldn't accommodate a queen-sized bed or the chest of drawers I'd found on the street, so I bequeathed them to my estranged girlfriend.

I'd moved several times over the past few years. Every move began with me selling or gifting my things, packing a gym bag and a suitcase, hailing a cab, and calling 1-800-MATTRESS from an empty room. Up until very recently I'd viewed the furniture I bought or found as practically disposable. The cost of renting a moving truck would often be greater than the value of the items, and in the case of my Chinatown apartment, moving in had to be executed in utter secrecy.

New York's Chinatown is an ideal location for someone as thrifty and vain as me. One can instantly boost their "cool capital" by taking residence in an edgy neighborhood still resistant to gentrification. But unlike Harlem or Washington Heights, Chinatown is sandwiched between the neighborhoods a savvy twenty-something would be spending his or her time in. It's a short walk from the East Village, a stone's throw from the Lower East Side, SoHo, NoHo, Little Italy, Nolita, and the Financial District. If you were dropped there in the middle of the night, however, you would assume you were in Shanghai or Hong Kong. London's Chinatown is Disney-fied and Lilliputian in comparison. It's just a short, brightly colored, clean street full of non-offensive-smelling restaurants whose patrons are from every corner of the globe *except* China. Chinatown in New York is an adventuresome place, especially down near Henry Street, where nary a non-Chinese is spotted. The thickest odors hang in the air. What's most disconcerting about the smells, which reach their rank peak in the summer months, is that they completely elude categorization. You can never seem to pinpoint exactly what's making you wretch.

It's like rotten meat meets bad fish, hot vomit, trash, and dead mice. In fact, that's precisely what it is.

The whole place is like an obstacle course during trading hours. Live frogs and crabs escape their barrels and make a desperate dash for Division Street before being squashed by traffic or scooped up by the grocers and repositioned on display. Sometimes both. Kitchen staff dump out gallons of old acrid cooking oil onto the sidewalk, turning Market Street into a huge unsanitary slip 'n' slide. Metal doors to basement entrances are flung open and slammed shut without warning. I once glanced down into a subterranean kitchen containing three cooks standing knee-deep in brown water in which several objects I identified as duck carcasses were bobbing up and down. Men with filth-encrusted fingers and two full inches of ash hanging off their cigarettes scream at one another and their customers while hovering above containers of live eels, skate, and mackerel. Cantonese is a tonal language; the same word said slightly differently can mean two, three, or four entirely different things. Coming from Essex, that's something I can relate to completely; the word "cunt," for example, can be the most hurtful, spiteful thing to call someone, a precursor to violence. It can also, however, be a term of sincere affection, depending on the intonation and pronunciation.

The Chinese are effective squatters in every sense of the word. Instead of sitting on a stoop to smoke a cig or play dice, the Chinese manage to get down on their haunches, where they seem to balance perfectly for hours on end. Spitting is also very popular in Chinatown. The men and women, the old and the young, think nothing of theatrically hocking up inordinate amounts of phlegm and distributing it over the neighborhood's sidewalks with reckless abandon. It was a challenge just to walk to work each morning without getting bull's-eyed with a gelatinous green blob.

Chris had invited me to see the apartment before beginning renovations on it in the spring of 1999. He was turned on to the place by a woman named Peggy Chu. It looked like something from a horror movie, and to my mind completely unsuitable as a human dwelling.

Peggy Chu was Chris's martial arts instructor. Her mother had lived in apartment nine at 45 Henry Street through the '70s, '80s, and '90s and had recently died, leaving the one-and-a-half bedroom apartment vacant. Peggy's spiritual advisor, a Taoist monk, strongly recommended that she not take up residence there for fear of creating some sort of paranormal discord. Peggy then offered the apartment to Chris, for the bargain-basement price of $500 per month, conditional on him fixing up the place a little bit.

Thirty years of incense burning had covered every surface with a sticky film of red goo. Through holes in the floor and ceiling, upstairs and downstairs neighbors were clearly visible and seeping odors completely smellable.

The term "death trap" is too often flung around with little thought for its literal meaning. The tiny bathroom in Chris's fabulous find was the most dangerous enclosed space in the Western world. Two days after Chris had started his preparations to start work, a football-sized chunk of concrete had fallen through the bathroom ceiling, shattering the toilet tank's porcelain lid to smithereens and missing Chris's head by mere inches. A day later, Chris sat on the same toilet, only to experience a short freefall. The beams between apartment nine and the one below were rotted through, and Chris's weight—a lean, mean 125 pounds—had caused the stem of the toilet to jut through the ceiling of the Huang family underneath. The toilet bowl—being larger than the gap in the beams—prevented Chris from dropping in on them. After a fourteen-hour day at The Orchard, Chris would often spend five or six hours each night trying to get his place into some sort of habitable state.

As he renovated, there were always exciting new things to be discovered in the place. The flooring in the kitchen was lumpy and uneven. It was made up of layer upon layer of linoleum, each separated by a perfectly preserved layer of magazines and newspapers from each era of home improvement. There was one layer every ten years until the late '70s. The oldest was a fragile copy of *Life* magazine that detailed the National Socialist Party's rise to power in Germany in 1933. In addition, a small hole in the living room ceiling would inexplicably spew chicken bones, gnawed clean.

After a few months the place was unrecognizable. Chris had transformed apartment nine into a bright, clean, sunny, even homey living space. He managed to turn the small back room into a space to work on his various art projects. Chris finally left The Orchard despite being owed thousands of dollars in back pay. Unable to find work and pay Peggy rent money in cash, he bartered with his own labor, turning into a janitor, accountant, and moving live target at the martial arts school, where he could be found day and night, five to six days a week. I put the idea of crashing at Chris's place to him, and after a few days he agreed.

The back room, *my* room, was small—about six feet by eight feet. The position of the door meant that I could only squeeze in a twin bed. It didn't matter. It was clean, comfortable, and bright. My windows opened onto a wrought-iron fire escape painted bright red, which was festooned with a circular billboard ad for something in Chinese.

Even with the two of us sharing the one-and-a-half-bedroom place, we still had the lowest apartment occupancy in the tenement by two or three people. Chris didn't tell Peggy that he was taking rent money from somebody living in his "art studio." He put a lock on my door and advised that I keep it locked should Peggy unexpectedly drop by while we weren't there. Chris would only take $250 a month from me in rent. My friends all seethed with envy at my miniscule living costs, but the place came with a huge caveat: we could never be seen by the neighbors under any circumstances, which forced us to come and go in absolute secrecy. In the two and a half years that he'd lived there, Chris had successfully managed to avoid causing turbulence among the neighbors, no mean feat considering that two days after moving in he greeted the neighbors atop a porcelain throne.

To avoid detection, Chris established a few ground rules: We were not to arrive back at the apartment until after midnight if at all possible. Between midnight and six in the morning, hardly a soul would be seen out in the entire neighborhood. Before leaving the apartment we used the spy hole in the door and listened for footsteps before making a dash for the street. Should we run into somebody in the hall, we would not make eye contact, and in the most unlikely event of a neighbor striking up a conversation with either of us, we would say we were nocturnal plumbers, electricians, or simply delivering a package for Ms. Chu. This was an unlikely story because the community is so insular that no one would conceive of hiring a contractor from outside, and what could you possibly want delivered that you couldn't get in Chinatown? In any case, that was our alibi.

Chris also told me to be prepared to vacate the room and live elsewhere with little or no notice whatsoever.

Initially, Chris made attempts to make the place look as though Peggy was living there. The coat rack next to the door was full of Asian-looking coats and silk slippers were lined up under the huge oak-framed bed. One of the martial arts school's ceremonial dragon heads was hung over the bed in full few of anyone who might briefly glimpse inside when we darted in and out the door. We even had a parasol hanging off the gaudy chandelier. Our attempts at subterfuge were, in retrospect, slightly heavy-handed and had made the place look like a stage set from *The King and I*. I suspect that our attempts to blend in were only fueling the neighbors' suspicions.

After a few months our routine began to lapse. I soon found myself shepherding a rotating cast of slightly tipsy girls up the rank-smelling, ramshackle staircase. Chris was spending the wee hours of the morning playing flamenco guitar on the fire escape on the front of the building and the apartment was now free of the Oriental knickknacks we had been using for camouflage.

It was during this time that the infamy of my position caught up with me. PR reps for hundreds of pleasure-enhancing creams, pills, hardware, software, and products began calling my work phone at an astonishing rate. The folks at Aneros, the ergonomically designed prostate massager, reported an astonishing spike in sales after I took it (or it took me) for a test-drive. I read some of my adventures for Audible.com. I began to appear as a guest on a late-night chat show entitled *Naked New York with Bob Berkowitz*, which was shown on the Metro Channel. To my absolute horror, I was billed on the show as a sexpert and was respectfully treated as such. The idea of Grant Stoddard the sexpert seemed absolutely surreal to me, and positively ludicrous to anyone I'd slept with. Just a year ago I was the sexual nonstarter. Now I was being heralded as somebody with a better than good idea of how to give women sexual pleasure and spent a lot of my time perpetuating that myth in several media.

The strangest effect was that all stripes of women were suddenly paying attention to me. E-mails from Vassar freshmen arrived in my inbox professing their love of my "work" and would I be interested in having a drink with them sometime. Others didn't need to go through the artifice of a social drink and simply asked for directions to my apartment. I'd often just meet them at the F stop on East Broadway so that I could both check them out and fully explain the stealthy silence with which they were required to ascend to the apartment.

In regard to girls, even ones who had scheduled overt fuck dates with me, I was terribly backward in coming forward. Once they were in the apartment, unbuttoning clothes and getting touchy-feely, I'd always be pushing the idea of watching a DVD on them or asking them if they'd like to look at some pictures. In spite of my profession, or perhaps because of it, I was dreadfully squeamish about the idea of strangers getting together to do "it." Especially when the pressure was often on me to transport them to hitherto uncharted heights of sexual pleasure. With a reputation as a sexual Svengali preceding me, crushing disappointment was all but assured. When the movie had been watched, the beers imbibed, the snapshots shuffled with, and the conversation becoming strained and repetitive, the poor misguided girl and I would often just sit there looking at each other. They waited for me to pounce. Though I was thought to be a carnal black belt, I'd somehow never learned to initiate sex. I still haven't.

Since the days of playing kiss-chase in Corringham County Primary School as an eight-year-old, I've been much more at ease with being the prey than the hunter. Though when you are short, pimply, and have a chest that looks like two aspirin on an ironing board, it's not a smart tactic. Almost without exception, all the women I've slept with have inexplicably all crossed my path or jumped into my lap. Thanks in large part to my loveless, sexless teen years, I've never had the confidence to pick someone up in a bar, initiate a conversation with a pretty girl in an elevator. I've never had a one-night stand. Had I grown up in an era where it wasn't kosher for women to be sexually proactive, I may very well be a virgin today.

The type of girls who seemed to suddenly be offering sex ran the gamut in terms of sexual experience. I met Samantha, a tall, bookish twenty-five-year-old at a bar on the Lower East Side. After three drinks and repeatedly professing to be a fan of my writing, she asked to be taken home. To *my* home.

After sneaking up the stairs and remarking on my Anne Frank–type existence in the Chinese tenement, she peeled off her clothes, revealing a long, lithe body and largish perfect breasts that were almost mouth level on me. I thought she looked like a young Sigourney Weaver and I told her so. She undressed me and pushed me onto my single bed. An inordinate amount of reciprocal oral sex followed, and judging by her reaction, she wasn't about to call my sexual credentials into question.

She sat bolt upright.

"There's something you should know," she said as she rolled on a condom in a deliberate and textbook fashion. "I've never done this before."

"Had sex with a funny little Englishman in a squat?" I said in what proved to be a vain attempt at lightening the mood.

"No. I mean . . . had sex. Ever."

I was stunned. She was beautiful. She was slightly older than I was. Unlike me she had no excuse to be a virgin.

"Do you still want to?" she said.

At twenty-four, I'd imagined that my opportunity to take someone's cherry was consigned to the mid-1990s. At the moment of her admission, we were at the point of no return. The difference between doing it and not was a small thrust of the hips. I'd listened in on other men's experiences regarding the act of devirginizing women and the general consensus was that it was better to give the experience to some other poor sap, as the girl would almost assuredly become some sort of psychopath.

We both focused our glares on the space between my bits and hers.

"Aren't you a bit old to be a . . . ?" I said.

She rolled her eyes, as if she was dreading having to explain herself.

"I just wasn't interested in college. Then I dated some guys that were . . . just pricks. And now people are frightened to, because they think I'll be beholden to them forever. So I thought, who better to—" She looked down at her impeccably maintained vagina—"than you?"

I frankly couldn't think of anyone worse than me. The slow, sensual, gentle sex that I imagined the situation required was certainly not my forte. Besides, in heels this girl was a head taller than me. I imagined her throwing me around like a Muppet.

She had given me an out, but my ego suddenly kicked in and I subjected her to one of my top three lousiest sexual performances to date. It was awkward, clumsy, misinformed, intermittently flaccid, and over far too soon.

She put her proportionately large head on my chest. I wished that she would fall asleep and I could perhaps make up for things the next morning. But Samantha wanted to chat. To debrief, to pick over one of the most lackluster sexual unions ever performed.

"Is that how it's supposed to happen?"

"Well, kind of like that, yeah," I lied.

"Oh." She let out a huge sigh. "Don't people usually make eye contact or kiss?"

"Sometimes they do," I said. "But what you see in the movies isn't always accurate."

"Oh. I would have liked to have done it . . . facing each other. For a little while at least."

"Shhhhhhhh," I said, hoping to staunch the continual flow of dashed expectations.

I felt a giant tear roll into the faint line that bisected my underdeveloped pectoral muscles. From my ego's perspective, this was my lowest ebb. Not long ago I had been in her position. But somewhere along the line, I'd allowed myself to feel deserving of the hype and become a menace to women everywhere.

I made an attempt to make it up to her the next morning by taking her to a fancy champagne brunch in the Meatpacking District, and we didn't see each other again.

ALL THE WAY
AND BACK AGAIN

I PICKED OUT a pineapple-and-cheese skewer from the buffet table and looked across the plush hotel suite at Fiona. She shot me a smile that was simultaneously caring and seductive. It was only our third date but I had a good feeling about this girl from the moment I'd met her, a feeling that was at odds with my growing distain for the English, specifically the English abroad. Fiona was resoundingly English. I thought she looked like Kate Winslet, but blonder, and svelter. She'd grown up in a leafy part of Berkshire, in a village with a cricket green and a village hall and a pub with ivy growing wild up the walls. Fiona was very posh, and in a good-natured sort of way she made fun of my accent. She said I spoke like a chimney sweep.

We shared a bottle of wine on our first date and kissed some. The second date we had cocktails and dinner and she stayed over at my place in Chinatown. We did it five times and she fell asleep on my chest.

I imagined that she might put my parents on edge if I took her home to meet them. I'd warn my mother, who would likely say something like, "She'll have to take us as she finds us." Though I feared that Fiona's excellent diction and expensive Alpine education might snap the whole family into subservience.

I couldn't conceive of a person like me dating a girl like Fiona back at home. I suppose us both living in the alleged meritocracy of New York made that happen. This was my fourth year in America and her second month.

"Are you okay?" she mouthed. She'd noticed that my mood had changed over the course of the past three hours. She'd surmised that as I grazed the buffet I was working something through in my mind.

"I'm fine," I said.

I was at the party for work, and as such found it hard to let go.

She beckoned me closer to her. I squeezed my way through the gyrating crowd and stood by the ornate chaise longue she reclined upon.

"We can go if you'd like," she said. Fiona ruffled my hair with her free hand.

"No, really, it's cool. Enjoy yourself."

I wasn't being a martyr; I had a flight to London at 8:00 a.m. the next day. It was already 2:00 a.m. and I had planned to take a cab directly to JFK from the hotel. I stick rigidly to any plans that I make. I'd brought my suitcase to the party.

Still locking eyes with my date, I slumped down in an antique leather armchair.

Fiona smiled sweetly before turning to face the wrist-thick ten-inch penis she'd been absentmindedly pumping in her right fist and hungrily licked it from hilt to tip. Its owner, a quarterback-looking type, groaned with pleasure, prompting his girlfriend to sink her fingers ever deeper into his ass while fondling Fiona's large alabaster breasts. This reinvigorated the small Thai man with the blond bouffant who pounded away between her legs with a huge smile plastered across his face. Throughout the large suite, small clusters of pretty women and their slightly older, wealthy companions were in groups of three, four, or five, clusters of limbs, necks, and pelvises moving like pistons to a universal rhythm I couldn't lock on to.

I polished off another piece of bruschetta and thought about what was keeping me from enjoying being there. Perhaps it was partly the combination of odors: incense, tequila, lube, sweat, finger food, men's cologne, latex, the fifty sets of genitals being waved at each other. Another man had joined Fiona's clique and she fairly divvied up the oral sex to him and the quarterback. Earlier on I had fucked Fiona on the king-sized bed as another writer I knew looked on at close range.

"Hi," I said, embarrassed.

"You are doing a good job!" she said. I took it as mockery.

Together Fiona and I then went down on a tall Norwegian woman with an athletic body. My date went on to be the belle of the ball, but that was as much anonymous group sex as I could stomach.

In theory, attending an orgy should have been the zenith of my compact sexual career, but I managed to not enjoy myself to the degree I'd hoped. I'd imagined what it might be like thousands of times since I was shown a videotape of *Caligula* as a fourteen-year-old. Aside from the inordinate amount of time I'd spent browsing a case of CDs and skulking around the pâté plate, this was pretty close to the fantasy.

I was expensing the $150 cover fee to Nerve. All I had to do was find a female date. Bringing at least one girl was a prerequisite. I was shocked at how easy that part was. I was even more shocked that Fiona, a sexy, smart, knockout anthropologist of superior breeding, was so willing to accompany me.

Now the veteran of over a year of experiments, I never ceased to be amazed by just how easy it had become to find willing participants in my assignments. I had rather sheepishly asked one of our office interns to accompany me to the nude beach at Sandy Hook, New Jersey, only to find that she was thrilled to tag along and had no reservations about immediately stripping and doing a painstakingly meticulous job of applying sunblock. The intern, Joanna Angel, went on to be a stripper and later a star and director of hipster porn movies, and I like to think I played a small part in her career.

Likewise, I had a pick of attractive girls who were more than ready to go to the orgy with me. In a stunning misjudgment, I chose Fiona, chiefly because I could see myself dating her long-term. The orgy was my first assignment as a single man after dating Anna for the past year. I hadn't yet grasped the concept of casual sex fully. I didn't realize that, provided everyone is on the same page, it's perfectly fine to have intercourse with somebody you see no real future with. Some people actually find it preferable. I, however, have never been one of those people. I put this down to my loveless, sexless teen years and my wont to cling desperately to any female willing to have sex with me. Almost all of the time, girls had been ready to cling back.

I answered Fiona's online personal ad for my own purposes; I was, in some roundabout way, looking for a girlfriend. I wanted sex, sure, but also snuggles, spooning, movies, decadent weekend brunching, pet names, the whole bit. I was assigned the orgy article on the day I met Fiona in person and offhandedly told her about it over coffee. If nothing else, being paid a decent living to engage in bizarre sex acts with strangers was a surefire icebreaker. Many girls jumped to the erroneous conclusion that I was some sort of sexual wizard and were ready to see for themselves after a drink. Silly girls.

With hardly any cajoling from me, Fiona told me that she was in, and before I knew it she was making like a circus seal and I was jealous as hell. I was experiencing a kind of envy that can't even be dissipated by an unsolicited Russian Perfect 10 model popping up out of nowhere to furiously rub some life into my flaccid penis, like it was a newborn puppy.

"Hello," she said. For all the elbow grease she was putting into the task at hand, she looked terribly bored.

"Hi," I said. She was beautiful and her dirty blonde hair smelled of cigarettes.

"Is that your woman?" she said, nodding to the blonde head poking out from the middle of a pink huddle.

"Well, we're just getting to know each other."

"She from agency?"

I told her that she wasn't from an agency. I started to chafe.

The Russian was from an escort agency whose sole business was catering to men who couldn't find women to bring to sex parties.

"They have to sign contract. They no get to touch me if I not want. And I never want. Look at him. They all like him."

She nodded her head in the direction of a large hairy man wearing only his wig, a Rolex, and a gold Chai pendant around his chubby neck. He was rubbing a petite Asian girl's feet as she deep-throated her good-looking date.

"I fuck every man here but not him. He is animal."

Her grip tightened and I winced with pain and dug my fingers into the chair.

It was common knowledge that several celebrities had frequented this monthly soiree, but I hadn't successfully pinpointed any. It was hard to tell with the wigs on. The party's general theme was that attendees had to be dressed from head to toe in white and have some kind of fake hairpiece. The clothes had all come off hours ago, the wigs had stayed on.

Fiona momentarily stopped what she was doing and gave me the thumbs-up sign. I thought about how I would ask my Russian to stop.

"I think my girlfriend needs me."

She looked over at Fiona, who was now busy with almost three feet of penis, and cocked an eyebrow.

"I'm not so sure."

She let go and reached out for the nearest male member without missing a stroke.

By 3:45 a.m. I had watched Fiona have intercourse with four men, orally service another three and two women. She looked happy but exhausted. I was shell-shocked.

I'd sort of expected that the two of us might get to third base in a dark corner and spend the rest of the night gossiping about the other attendees and marveling at the alien world we'd somehow gained access to. Instead the party gave a collective groan when I finally found Fiona's thong and bra, pushed through her new fan club, and placed them on her shoulder. I already had my jacket on. It was time to go home.

Even as she dismounted the quarterback with the horse cock, she knew something in our burgeoning relationship was broken.

"Seriously, something's bothering you, isn't it?"

"Don't bring *him* next time!" offered the gentleman attached to an aggressive-looking erection.

"Can we talk about this outside?"

We found her clothes, she dressed, and we said good-bye to Apollonia, our host.

"Darling, you were breathtaking tonight," she said to Fiona.

"Yes!" agreed one of the men she'd had sex with, and squeezed his business card into her palm. "Please call me. . . ."

"Fiona," I said.

"Yes, Fiona. I would love to sample your unique effervescence once again."

Seriously. He *actually* said that.

With my suitcase dragging behind me we walked out into the warm August night. She tried to give me a hug but I recoiled.

"Okay," said Fiona. She took a deep breath. "You seem really quite upset with me."

"Well, yeah. You just fucked an entire party."

"It was your fucking idea!" she shrieked. "It was an orgy and you asked me to come!"

A cabbie pulled up beside us and rolled down his window.

"Fuck off!" Fiona screamed and the scared cabbie obliged.

"Well . . . you certainly ran with it. I didn't know how I would feel."

"Don't you do this, like, all the time? I thought this was your job, for fuck's sake."

"Well . . . I think that I really liked you."

"Liked? So you mean that's it, is it?" She began to cry. "I don't care about all this, y'know!" She theatrically ripped up the business card and threw the pieces in my face.

"*I* should be the one crying. You just fucked Uncle Miltie." I tried to stifle a smirk.

"Well, thanks a fucking lot." A cab arrived on cue and she jumped in. Instead of pulling away immediately, the cabbie paused to write down the location of the pickup in his log book. We looked at each other blankly for an inordinately long seven or eight seconds.

She wiped tears from her eyes as the cab pulled away.

"Who's Uncle Miltie?" said Fiona, breaking the icy silence and evoking guffaws from a pair of inebriated homosexuals mincing by. The question hung in the air, the last thing I heard her say.

I've never been able to sleep on planes, even after a long evening of booze, drugs, anonymous sex, and serial cuckolding. I fantasize that if something horrible happened to the crew, I would bravely volunteer to get the bird back on terra firma. I wouldn't let having no knowledge of how to pilot a commercial airliner get in the way. If I was asleep, I figured, I'd miss my chance at glory.

Consequently, I looked like the walking dead as I waited at the baggage carousel at Heathrow Airport. I hadn't showered since leaving the orgy, but had the presence of mind to wash my hands and face directly before greeting my father, mother, sister, and grandmother, who had come to pick me up.

"For a laugh" my mother had enlarged a particularly comical portrait picture from when I was six years old, duplicated it four times, mounted the picture on cardboard, cut around the shape of my head, punched eye holes and Scotch-taped pencils to the underside, making four masquerade masks with which to greet me at the airport. I was jet-lagged, cracked out, shagged out, and hungover, so what was supposed to be a sight gag almost birthed an anxiety attack.

I hadn't been home in two years and a lot had changed. I'd been writing my column for almost a year. I had started to get over feeling like a scumbag, but being at the orgy had sent me back there once again. I hoped that the stay in Corringham would take my mind off my sordid profession, that the humdrum of a working-class English village would help me to convalesce from my work. For the next two hours my family gave me tea, crumpets, and their undivided attention as we sat around the kitchen table. I gave them heavily censored accounts of my life in the Big Apple before sleep deprivation finally got the better of me. I should have stayed awake longer. After some glorious shut-eye, my two-year absence was seemingly forgotten about and the household chore rota had been affixed to the fridge with a magnet that professed that "*Anxiety comes from feeling unequal to the task.*" Beneath the text, a lion was pictured wearing a gold medal and giving a thumbs-up sign.

Unload the dishwasher, take out the rubbish, mow the lawn.

I would also have to find time to meet the deadline for my orgy story, as well as popping in to see all the relatives, keeping the fact that I was a sex worker on the down low. The main reason I came home was to apply for a new work visa. My first one had almost expired. I got three weeks' vacation per year. This is how I was spending it.

They say that people become their jobs; I was becoming mine and it wasn't a natural fit. Fiona had given me a lot to think about.

Fiona had also given me chlamydia.

That night at my place, I had just slipped it in without a condom for a second or a minute. Did I mention that we did it five times? That brief dip was long enough for me to catch a sexually transmitted disease of some description. I thought I was imagining the slight pain, but when I used the bathroom when we got back to my parent's house, it had become too acute to ignore. I hoped it was a urinary tract infection. When my previous girlfriends had UTIs they would disappear into the bathroom with a stack of magazines, a gallon of cranberry juice, and reemerge a few hours later, feeling a hundred percent better.

I limped down our street, past the smashed bus shelter and the graffiti-strewn pillar box to the corner shop on Lampits Hill. Or what I had referred to as a bodega for the past four years.

Raj, the shop's proprietor and only staff member, recognized me instantly.

"My goodness, I haven't seen you in a long time," he said. He looked me up and down. "A *bloody* long time."

I was a paper boy for Raj when I was thirteen and fourteen. Since then I was sent down the street to buy lottery tickets for my father every Saturday evening.

"Hi, Raj."

"Where have you been?"

"America. I live there now, in New York."

"New York, eh? Yes, very good. Well, what can I help you with, Mr. Trump?" He laughed heartily at his cleverness.

"Do you have any cranberry juice?"

Raj gave me a puzzled look, as if I'd asked for powdered rhinoceros horn.

"I am afraid not, sir, no." He folded him arms and looked at the floor.

I walked to another corner shop up the road, then about a mile to a medium-sized supermarket, where I found some cranberry "drink" in small juice boxes, which was the closest thing. I wasn't in New York anymore. I bought ten juice boxes and carried them home. I drew a hot bath and read my mother's copies of *OK!* and *Hello!* magazines from cover to cover, thinking that women's magazines were somehow vital to the relief of my symptoms.

Posh, Becks, Posh, Becks, Camilla, Posh, Becks, and so on.

The bath and the cranberry drink had been completely fruitless.

Two days into my stay it had become quite unbearable and I began dredging the Internet for information about what I should do.

Orsett Hospital is the place of my birth. Wings of the hospital had been shut down annually due to NHS spending cuts, and by 2002 the huge complex of buildings housed little more than an infirmary and the Sexual Health Centre, or "clap clinic," as it was known provincially. A brusque receptionist set up an appointment for me the following morning. The only appointment she had all week. Orsett is around six miles away from my parents' home in Corringham. Since the hospital had shrunk in size, one could no longer take the bus there from our town. A taxi would be over forty dollars round-trip and I wasn't insured to drive either of my parents' cars. I mulled my options over before asking the question no child wants to ask a parent.

"You want me to give you a lift to the flipping clap clinic?" said my mother.

She tugged theatrically on her thick black hair.

"My God, Grant, what are you doing with your life?"

"Don't make this any worse than it already is!" I pleaded. "There's no need to tell anyone else."

"Oh, do you think it's something I'd like to scream from the hill-tops? 'I'm taking my son to the clap clinic!'"

"You're *what*?" My kid sister had silently walked into the house and heard our conversation through the door.

"Nothing!" I snapped. "Mum's just being weird again."

As distraught as she seemed to be, my mother did a sort of Irish jig around the kitchen to demonstrate her supposed dementia. This satiated my sister's curiosity and she bounded back into her bedroom.

"I know the woman who used to work there, you know," she whispered. "I went to school with her. She might even still be there. God. How embarrassing."

We drove in silence to Orsett Hospital at eight thirty the next morning. I was dropped off outside the infirmary and walked around to the bleachy-smelling Sexual Health Centre. The building was divided into a men's and women's area. Sitting in the waiting room of the men's area was an embarrassed-looking sixty-year-old man under a jet-black toupee, a ginger bruiser in his late teens, and a thirty-year-old with too much jewelry and a terrible stutter. I wondered who was sleeping with these men, then remembered that I was one of them. I was embarrassed for having chlamydia and more embarrassed for the company chlamydia kept.

Over the past two years England had started to become very foreign seeming, antiquated and broken. But as I sat there in the husk of the hospital where it all began, I remember thinking that there's something very civilized about the government picking up the tab for that time you threw caution to the wind and just stuck your penis in a stranger. If one doesn't have decent health insurance in America by contrast, one should probably invest in a first aid kid and a crash helmet. My buddy Chris had some bad sushi and it cost him eight grand.

On the wall was a sign that read, IF YOU REQUIRE A HEALTH CARE TECHNICIAN OF YOUR OWN GENDER, PLEASE INFORM THE RECEPTIONIST 48 HOURS PRIOR TO YOUR ARRIVAL.

I filled out a questionnaire and some other paperwork. Like the decrepit red-brick shell around it, the Sexual Health Centre seemed very empty. Just one female nurse appeared to be on staff—was it my mother's school friend, Linda?

Like Fiona, she would soon have four penises in her grasp. The National Health Service would never acknowledge it, of course, but the nurse simply *must* compare the hundreds of penises she sees week in, week out: a big one, a small one, a ginger one, a pretty one, an ugly one, and—once in a blue moon—a circumcised one. The only common themes would be disease and irritation, infection and dysfunction. She was seeing unhappy penises attached to unhappy people. I've become hyperconscious of the working conditions of other sex workers. To that end I decided I would be concerned yet jovially pragmatic. I sort of *was* anyway. I had been rolling the dice for a while and finally got snake eyes.

"Arrrrghhhh!" came a disconcerting cry of pain from down the hall. I jumped in my chair. Nobody else reacted to it.

Wiggy and ginger nuts were awaiting test results. Mush-mouth was on his way out.

"*Fa fa fa fa fa fa fa fa fa fa fa* fanks very much, love," he said after scheduling a follow-up appointment with the receptionist for two weeks hence.

"See you in a *fa fa fa fa fa fa fa fa fa fa fa* fortnight," he added as he walked out to the parking lot.

"*Fa fa fa fa fa fa fa* fuckin' 'ell!" said Wiggy once the stutterer was safely out of earshot. "'E 'ad a lot to say for 'imself, didn't 'e?"

We all laughed, save ginger, who seemed to be praying and rocking in his chair, oblivious to the rest of us.

"Don't be so bleedin' 'orrible, you!" said the receptionist before succumbing to a wheezing cackle.

"Wot-choo talkin' baht, babes?" said Wiggy with a chuckle, "I'm only 'avin' a laugh, ain't I?"

"Oooh, you *are* a wicked little sod!"

"But you love me anyway though, don'tcha!"

Either Wiggy was a regular or oozed an easy charm. Perhaps that's what he was in for.

"Grahnt?" called a short, chubby blonde women with outsized spectacles.

I raised my hand.

"Come on, love, let's sort you out, then."

Her name tag said Linda. I appreciated her jolly demeanor and appreciated how she must have honed it over years in the discharge business.

"Now before we start, would you like to be tested for HIV?"

"Is it free?" I hadn't shaken the habit of taking anything if it was free.

"Of course."

"Then sure."

"Okay, well, now it's the law for anyone who takes the test to have a counseling session whether it comes up negative or not, all right, love?"

"No problem."

She readied the syringe. I rolled up my sleeve.

"Little bit of a pinch," she said. She filled the chamber. "All done." She sang.

"Now, what seems to be the problem?"

"It burns when I go to the bathroom."

"Going to the bathroom" is a turn of phrase than can sound both odd and vague to the Saxon ear.

"It 'urts when you do a wee, you mean?" said Linda, getting to the bottom of things.

"Precisely."

"Okay, well, what I'm going to do is take a little scraping from your urethra. I must warn you that it *is* quite painful, but it'll be over in a second. Okay, love, pants down." Linda snapped on some rubber gloves then referred to the paperwork I'd filled out.

"Stoddard?" She looked up at my face. She saw the likeness— everyone does. I made out the recognition in her eyes, but the circumstances probably prevented the follow-up questions.

She scrunched up her nose and took a long hard look at my business, rolling it around in her rubber-coated hands. My penis had overheard what was about to happen and was inching its way up into my body. If it happened to be larger looking, I might have pursued the personal connection we had, but in its current state my tiny penis would have brought dishonor upon my family name.

"You might want to grip the side of the bed, all right, dear?"

I braced myself. My sweaty palms gripped the aluminum bar along the side of the bed. The Q-tip–like implement went in and out. It wasn't particularly pleasant, but it was not the hellish pain I'd been led to believe.

"There's a brave soldier!" she said, in a very lovely and maternal way. "I've 'ad two men cryin' in 'ere, just this week. Ohhh and the profanities I 'ear when I pull it out. They turn the air blue!"

Linda introduced me to the woman who counseled me on not having HIV while she determined the results of the scrape. She came back with a choice. Chlamydia or Non-Specific Urethritus, N.S.U. for short.

"You can take your pick as they are both treated with the same antibiotics." She placed them in my hand.

Chlamydia sounded like a flower, N.S.U. like a state college. It was a toss-up.

"We need to check up so we'll have you back 'ere in a fortnight, all right, love?"

"Yes," I lied.

In a fortnight I'd be back where I suddenly realized that I felt at home, squatting in a tenement building in New York's Chinatown, being handsomely paid to have sex with strangers and write about it.

I bought a Coke from a vending machine and slurped down the first dose of antibiotics. It was already eighty degrees out, but unlike muggy New York the air was fresh and clean. I walked about a mile to the main road, where I was told I could catch a bus, but carried on walking.

I walked all the way home.

BRIDGE OVER
TROUBLED WATERS

AS MADCAP AS evading detection had been, Chris and I lived with a very real fear that the housing situation in the area was regulated in part or full by the Chinese mob, the Triads. News of two Caucasians, one of whom conspicuously sported more body hair than the rest of Chinatown's residents combined, taking up a space that would usually house one large and unspeakably poor immigrant family could put the both of us in harm's way.

Tensions were raised by all of the mysterious or sinister activity that was going on around us in Chinatown. Three prostitutes had been slain on New Year's Day, stabbed to death in an abandoned building opposite The Orchard's office on Orchard and Hester. Clues pointed toward mob involvement. A young girl from the neighborhood copy shop that we knew suddenly had a baby on her hip one day. Grace looked about thirteen and weighed eighty pounds soaking wet. The kid was at least six months old and already quite a porker. It couldn't have weighed much less than Grace, but she happily hauled him around the neighborhood.

"What do you mean *bought* him?" I asked her.

Grace's English was broken and I felt sure that the story behind the baby's sudden appearance had been corrupted in translation.

"Yes. I boughted him from man," she said, exasperated. It was the third time I'd asked. I was troubled and unsatisfied by her explanations.

"How much did you pay for him?" I asked.

Despite the language barrier, Grace suddenly realized that my line of questioning had gone from friendly to investigative.

"I don't want talk anymore!" she said, instantly upset.

We didn't talk about the baby or anything other than photocopying ever again.

Shenanigans were also afoot in our immediate surroundings. Every morning I would sneak down our steps to find a bag lady in her sixties hanging out in the hallway. She was white and had one of those early twentieth-century New York accents. *I saw a doughty boid on toity toid and toid.*

"Mawning, sweet-haught!" she said each morning. "You stay in school!"

I found her presence particularly odd as Chinatown is a less than desirable location for homeless people. No one in the neighborhood over the age of fifty was above Dumpster diving for the aluminum cans and recycling them for a nickel each. I just couldn't figure out why she always hung out in my building. One morning, I heard her having a conversation with somebody with a Chinese accent. I quietly snuck down the stairs and watched her wildly gesticulating with a clean-cut guy in his early twenties. The talking stopped before I could make out words, and I looked through a gap in the stairwell to see the woman counting out twenty-dollar bills that she was handing to him. I couldn't believe my eyes as she gave him over seven hundred dollars. A wad of cash large enough to choke a donkey. There could have been more but they quickly stopped as somebody came through the front door. I walked past them quickly but the woman gave me a knowing look, extended her stained index finger, and pointed at me in short jabbing motions. It seemed like everybody was trying to hide something, and as long as Chris and I didn't pry into other people's business they'd leave us well alone. The intrigue was killing me, but satisfying my curiosity was not worth risking the best deal. Almost all of my peers were spending a third to a half of their income on rent. I was spending less than an eighth, affording me a lifestyle otherwise unobtainable to someone earning thirty thousand dollars a year in New York City. The saving was great, but I really reveled in the bragging rights.

The temperature in July hardly dropped below ninety at night and the humidity meant that getting a good night's sleep was almost impossible. We had a puny air-conditioning unit but rarely used it, as it almost always blew the main fuse.

One particularly sticky night, I came home to find a note scrawled in red, dramatic Chinese characters pinned to our door. I called Chris, who joined me in thinking the worst: an eviction notice with an ultimatum, a promise of violence if we did not comply immediately. Chris rushed over and we took the note to a man he knew in a Chinese bar near his girlfriend's place in Brooklyn. We sweated profusely as the gentleman read it through and theatrically raised his eyebrows.

"Your neighbors," he said. He cleared his throat. "They want you to know . . ." He stopped to give direction to a busboy, leaving us on tenterhooks for five seconds, although it felt like an hour.

I wanted to grab him by the collar and give him a thorough shake. He faced us again and traced the characters with his finger.

". . . that they have something to give you."

"Oh, shit," said Chris.

"Is that bad?" I asked.

"That UPS delivered a parcel but you weren't home so they have it for you to pick up."

Relieved beyond measure, Chris and I collapsed in fits of laughter, much to the translator's astonishment, and enjoyed a cold beer before trekking back to Manhattan.

In July, Chris left New York for a month to visit his family, who lived in the remote, rough terrain of the northern Greek mainland, entrusting me with the apartment.

I awoke one morning about an hour earlier than usual and went to boil some water, which I drank with a few slices of fresh ginger, as per my newly New Age mother's latest recommendation. As I walked into the kitchen, a section of the ceiling directly above my bed collapsed. This wasn't light plasterboard of the twentieth century but a thick heavy plaster attached to a kind of cement several inches thick. Chunks of wood, animal bones, and decaying rags came down with it too, filling the apartment with a thick dust. The weight of it all crashing down broke my nightstand and shattered my lamp and alarm clock. If I'd have still been in bed I'd have been robbed of my trademark Bee Gee teeth and aquiline nose. I considered it a spooky warning shot. I turned on a few fans, took a few changes of clothes, and camped out at Brian's house on the Bowery for the weekend.

I returned on Sunday night to an apartment that was hot, dark, rank-smelling, and full of choking dust. Having the two fans on apparently blew the fuse shortly after I left and there was no electricity. The fuse box was in the basement that the super of the building had under lock and key, meaning that I couldn't change it myself. Whatever was in the fridge was stinking to high heaven, and from what I could make out from the flickering, buzzing fluorescent lights in the hallway, the whole place was an utter disaster area. I stayed the night regardless, sleeping in Chris's bedroom, which was relatively dust-free. I was awakened at six in the morning by a persistent pounding on my door, which I tried to ignore in vain. The woman who immediately started screaming at me was demanding that I turn off my shower. I told her that it's the middle of the night and that I wasn't using my shower and even invited her in to look, but she just repeated *"Turn off shower!"* as she stormed back down the stairs. I went straight back to sleep and was awaken three hours later by more screaming and shouting coming from the hallway. I went to pee and saw that my kitchen and bathroom were now under an inch and a half of water. The leak was coming from the apartment above ours and it was now *that* resident who was getting an earful from the woman who'd given me my wake-up call.

I e-mailed Chris in Athens. He suggested that I mop up the mess as best I could, buy a fuse, and put it in a bag with a note written in Chinese that said the fuse in apartment nine needed replacing. He told me to hang the bag on the super's door handle, bang on the door, and run away as fast as I could. I asked Brian's roommate Victoria to write the note in Cantonese. I returned that evening to find that power had been restored. I could now concentrate on another pressing problem—namely, the gaping hole in the ceiling that seemed to be growing by the hour. I cleared the rubble and dust from my room, but whenever the kids upstairs ran around, more debris would fall through. I began to have horrible nightmares about the mysterious bones constantly falling through the ceiling being those of a human baby. I was beginning to think the Taoist monk was right when he suggested that the apartment was haunted.

Chris returned from Greece with a renewed energy and within a day of his return he expertly installed a new ceiling, gave the plumbing an overhaul, repainted, plastered, and had the place looking better than ever in no time. Paying so little in rent actually left me with extra money each month for the first time in my life. I decided I would use this extra cash to first visit my parents, sort out my visa, and then really make inroads on making 45 Henry our own. After so long on the move, I was extremely excited to have a stable home. I'd been here six months, survived detection *and* the apartment's attempts to kill us both. Things looked like they would be running smoothly from then on.

Toward the end of my ten-day trip to my parents' home, I got a cryptic e-mail from Chris saying that he'd packed my stuff up and put it somewhere until I got back. I couldn't imagine what had happened. Had Peggy found out? Had another supernatural disaster rendered my room permanently uninhabitable? Had the Triads taken a baseball bat to Chris's knees? I called Chris, who apologized for the terse e-mail but explained that there had been a sudden and unfortunate turn of events regarding the apartment. Alex had moved in.

Alex was a sixty-year-old Siberian man who taught sambo at Peggy's school. Despite sounding like a dance, sambo is a lethal type of no-frills hand-to-hand combat employed by Spetsnaz—the Soviet equivalent of the British SAS or American Green Berets—perfected against the mujahideen in Afghanistan. Peggy had suddenly needed to find a living space for the illegal immigrant killing machine.

I jumped in a cab at JFK and went straight to the apartment. Chris wasn't picking up. His last instruction to me was simply to get out as soon as I could. Chris had always said that I may need to leave at a moment's notice. It just seemed so cruel that it would have to happen now. The place was a real shag pad and afforded me a disposable income. I was living high off the hog and having lots of sex: my American wet dream come true.

I opened the apartment door. All the lights were off. I threw my bag down and started feeling my way toward my bedroom when I bumped into a large object in the middle of the living room. I tripped and tumbled into the kitchen. After a few seconds of fumbling for the light switch I opened the fridge door, which cast an eerie light over the obstruction. A short bald man with a barrel chest and hands like bunches of kielbasa was standing perfectly still in the middle of the room. He had been standing there like that in the pitch dark.

"What the fuck?"

"My name is Alex."

He still hadn't turned his face to look at me and his gaze remained on the back wall of the living room.

"I come to live in here." He turned his head to look at me for the first time.

"Sorry."

His Brezhnevian face softened and he even cracked a brief but apologetic smile, revealing a tangle of silvery bridgework. Alex was earning money in the United States through teaching sambo and was sending the proceeds back to his wife and kids in Siberia. He hadn't seen them for almost four years.

Alex gave me a hand with moving out. Not a huge task, as there was just a suitcase, a guitar, and two garbage bags full of clothes. Once again, I left everything that wouldn't fit in the trunk of a taxicab. I put the suitcase and the guitar in the trunk of the waiting taxi and went to shake Alex's mighty paw. He shook my hand firmly, placing his left hand on my elbow, and in doing so relinquished his grip on the bags, dropping all of my clothes into a deep, muddy Chinatown puddle.

It didn't occur to me that I really had nowhere else to go until I was in the taxi. I had keys for the Nerve office, so I told the driver to take me to the corner of Broadway and Spring. I stashed all of my worldly belongings under my desk and fell asleep on the couch. I figured that until I found a new living situation, I could live in the office and join the New York Sports Club across the street so that I could still shower regularly. I could also have a schvitz anytime I wanted and, if the mood ever took me, pump a little iron.

Michael woke me up the next morning.

"Do you know how to play bridge?" he asked.

I hadn't thought about bridge since living with Mrs. Montague. For her the game was both her reason for living and the bane of her existence. One night I'd made the mistake of asking her how to play and subjected myself to a two-hour primer that left me confused and confounded.

"I have no idea," I said and made for the coffeepot.

"Well, you're going to learn tonight."

Michael was referring to a biweekly bridge class that was taking place that evening. According to the ad that had been posted on Craigslist, Doug, the bridge expert, has a "thick, ten-inch cock." This claim is the most striking feature of the ad he placed online to conscript novices to his "clothing-optional" bridge class, which took place twice a month on Wednesday evenings at his apartment in uptown Manhattan. Aside from his purported dimensions, the main body of the ad is about guys in their mid-twenties to mid-forties learning and playing bridge in a relaxed atmosphere. "There is to be no touching before, during, or after the class. The class is clothing-optional with pupils invited to wear as much or as little as you feel comfortable in."

Still ruing the previous night's eviction, I e-mailed Doug and expressed a desire to learn and insinuated an undercurrent of voyeuristic intent. Within what seemed like nanoseconds I received a reply that again stressed the relaxed vibe he sought to create during the class, the strict no-touching rule, the phallus that encroached upon a foot in length, and my responsibility to be height/weight proportionate. "Because no one wants to look at a bunch of fat guys playing cards." I was asked to report my stats or ideally to send along a recent picture. Attached to his e-mail was a menagerie of playful pictures of Doug smiling coquettishly while brandishing what looked like a length of radiator hose, dressed in wingtips, black socks, and a yellow and black letterman jacket.

With some frightfully fruity underwear purchased just for the occasion, I stood on a chair in the Nerve bathroom and tried to take a self-portrait looking both sexually alluring and eager to learn a card game whilst precariously balanced. I sent the picture along to Doug and received a reply some hours later that made no judgments on my twinkish shot but did suggest that I arrive at his apartment early so that I could be shown the basics. "I will be naked," he advised.

I'd surmised from our e-mail exchange that Doug was much more of an exhibitionist than a voyeur. As I strolled the alien world of the Upper West Side, I meditated on whether bridge or any activity that was predicated on sitting around a table was ideally suited for exhibiting one's genitalia as, for the most part, his phallus's majesty would be obscured by the playing surface. As I walked along I made a mental short list of other activities that might be more effective to that end. They included yoga and jump rope.

Doug wanted me to arrive at seven with the other pupils arriving at seven thirty, but I decided that ten minutes alone with Doug and his special something would be more than sufficient. I was jet-lagged, suddenly homeless, and about to kick back with a naked man in his sixties. With my heart thumping, I walked into a very grandiose but dimly lit marble lobby that smelled strongly of hearty, simple, Central European foods. I told the doorman the apartment number.

"You're here to play cards?" he asked. "Go on up."

Apartment 8H; the home of the whopper. I knocked on the door and waited nine long seconds before Doug appeared around the door, seemingly dressed.

"Grant?" he asked with a broad and kind grin. "Come on in!"

I was in Doug's place for several more seconds before becoming aware of a swaying movement around my host's mid to lower thigh. I'd assumed naked meant bereft of clothing, but Doug was wearing a rather jolly animal-print T-shirt, slippers, socks, and a pair of bookish spectacles with a velvet cord that linked the parts that hook over one's ears. His loins and legs were especially pink, naked, and open to the elements. Doug seemed puzzled by the six-pack of beer that I'd brought along, more as common courtesy than from a need or desire to get tipsy.

"You did grocery shopping on the way here?" he asked.

"I just picked up some beers."

"Oh," he said, seeming slightly miffed. "We actually don't do *that* here, but you are welcome to indulge if you'd like."

This exchange was the evening's only conversation that didn't directly relate to the folly of bridge. A shame, as I had prepared nuggets of small talk and benign chatter on a variety of subjects.

"Well, we have ten minutes before the others arrive so let me just run you through the basics."

The dual decorative themes for Doug's place are "fruits of the forest" and gold lamé, which seemed too disparate a pairing until I spied a wreath of gilded plums that neatly tied the two motifs together. Doug sat down at the circular glass table in the middle of the room and urged me to sit opposite him. *The table is glass! Of course*, I thought. Doug placed an ace, a king, a queen, and a jack on the table as I took my seat. The placement of the cards seemed deliberate as they perfectly eclipsed his much-hyped appendage. Doug explained the numeric value of the picture cards and the pecking order of the four suits and immediately quizzed me. As I began to deliver the answers to his questions, Doug slid the cards around, allowing partial glimpses of the monster member, a sort of dance of the seven veils. I found that I had to use every ounce of concentration as the relatively simple questions came with a peek-a-boo glimpse that I found very distracting. I couldn't help notice Doug's grin widen as he deliberately sabotaged my ability to count to four. With a Herculean effort I answered most of his questions correctly, prompting my host to sweep the cards off the table and reveal the element that made this card game something special. There it was. Based on its size, I was convinced that Doug owned the world's only bifocal tabletop. I tried not to look directly at it by focusing on a coffee ring on the glassy foreground. I was struggling with whether I ought to vocally acknowledge its presence when I was saved by the doorbell. The star of the show went to greet the other pupils, with Doug following several moments later.

Sam and Dimitri had arrived. I was glad that the other bridge wannabes were here to give me an idea of how to behave in this unique scenario. Sam set himself down on the sofa, waking a noticeably annoyed white Persian cat.

"Be careful with those black pants," said Doug, grinning. "You'll leave here with pussy hair all over you and we wouldn't want that, now would we."

"It'd certainly be a first," parried Sam. We all laughed mischievously.

I hadn't been invited to disrobe and wondered what the others would be "feeling comfortable in." One- and two-lesson veterans respectively, Sam and Dimitri looked like stereotypical denizens of the neighborhoods in which they resided. Dimitri, heavily muscled, tanned, and wearing a baseball cap, khaki shorts, and tight white tank top was from Chelsea. Sam was a nebbish, bookish, buttoned-up gent from midtown. They each clutched Xeroxed handouts that had been their bridge homework from last time. Sam held a copy of *Bridge for Dummies*.

"Throw that away," said Doug disdainfully. "You can't learn what I'm about to teach you from a book." I took this as alluding to some hanky-panky, but he went on to talk about the card game as if it was delivered to mankind from a higher being and should be handed down, person to person. The conversation was so immediately and wholly bridgecentric that I wasn't even introduced to the other guys; we threw around a cursory nod as cards were being dealt.

Bridge seems to have a language all its own, as foreign to English as Urdu. Terms like "singleton," "doubleton," "trump," and something called "the Gerber method" were all mentioned with nary a regular English word to give any clues as to what it all meant. "If you are feeling confused, that's okay," said Doug with a chuckle. "You should be."

Sam and Dimitri remained fully dressed. I watched my fellow players' gazes intensely. Sure, they had been to Doug's class before, but I was surprised that no one was doing or saying anything to reference the fact that one of the four of us wasn't wearing any pants. The others seemed as if they actually wanted to buy in to what Mrs. Montague called a recipe for madness. They wanted to learn how to play bridge, regardless of the distraction. We silently looked down at our hands, tallying points. We looked as if we were studying some prehistoric species of sea cucumber through a glass-bottomed boat. I had counted my cards incorrectly during the past two hands, so this time Doug got up and walked around the table to look at my hand over my shoulder. Despite my fear that his schlong would swing into my ribs, no contact took place. Doug returned to his place satisfied that I'd leaned something. I had. But he thought it had to do with cards.

At 8:00 a din filled the room as five clocks chimed out the hour simultaneously. The racket was an indistinguishable cacophany but the clock nearest to us was definitely playing *"Deutschland Über Alles."*

"Is this tune what I think it is?" I asked Doug as he shuffled the deck.

He neither confirmed nor denied it but instead closed his eyes, tilted his head back, and pursed his lips as he conducted an imaginary orchestra by moving his forefingers in a wide U-shaped motion.

I decided I could probably use a drink. I offered everyone a beer, but they politely declined while looking at me as if I had a drinking problem. I hardly drink at all, but I felt obligated to get rid of at least some of the beer. Returning from the fridge, I noticed that in my thirty-second absence Sam had stripped down to a pair of black boxer briefs. I'd decided that if Dimitri took his clothes off, I would follow suit. No one was taking a blind bit of notice of either of the two partially naked players, which I imagined was a little disheartening for Sam, as he'd really put himself out there. He looked nervous—perhaps about his gynomastia, more commonly known as having man-titties. I made sure that he caught me looking at his adolescent-looking physique so he would feel that stripping hadn't been an entire waste. Unencumbered by clothing, Sam soon became a different type of player, bidding high, taking risks. Dimitri was very kind and gave me guidance when he could see that Doug's instruction left me more bewildered.

Ultimately, Doug's mighty penis seemed incidental. No one was overtly looking at it or talking about it. I wondered what he got out of our indifference toward it. Was he getting off by having his equine penis ignored? His ad said that he loved showing off his "cock and nuts," but he really made little effort to draw our attention to it. Doug always steered the conversation away from anything that had nothing to do with cards and really got quite passionate when any of us had played a good hand or conversely made a "silly, silly mistake." In the few hours I'd had to speculate on how the evening would go, I never once entertained the idea that there would be an entirely scholarly atmosphere with little or no mention or deference given to the pink elephant under the glass tabletop in the living room. Doug spent too much time tsking our silly mistakes to revel in his exhibitionism.

I'm not sure what made Doug bashful, but as the evening progressed he became prone to crossing his legs. Earlier on he exhibited his unit as if he were showing a selection of prizewinning fruit at a garden show. With the third rousing rendition of the German national anthem ringing out, bridge class was over for the evening. We left in a staggered fashion, Dimitri first, me a minute later, while Sam stayed behind to ask more questions.

I got back to the office a little before eleven and crashed on the sofa. Rufus wouldn't mind me spending a few nights here but would no doubt nix my plans for making it my primary residence. Still on Greenwich Mean Time, I found myself wide awake at four thirty. I made a cup of coffee and climbed the fire escape six flights to the building's roof and watched the summer sun begin to rise. The vistas were perhaps more impressive when the towers still stood, but looking downtown as the sun turned the city's buildings orange, it was hard to imagine that they were ever really there. Anxieties about finding a new place to hang my hat were pushed out by the feeling that made my body buzz. Goddamn, I love this town.

HATE MAIL

THE 3,549 E-MAILS in my inbox said more or less the same thing: that I was a despicable person. I refreshed the screen every few seconds—3,551, 3,558—the number was growing ever faster. A few of the e-mailers were disappointed but pragmatic about what had happened in the woods of rural Maryland. Some wanted to take me to court. Others promised me physical harm. They said I betrayed them, deceived them. The word choices, the frantic grammatical errors, and the heavy use of uppercase type were frightening indicators of how acutely I had enraged an entire subculture, a group of people who were actually defined by their collective urge to inflict pain on others. Within a few hours they had mobilized against me and I was running scared. E-mails came in waves that corresponded to time zones.

Eastern, Central, Mountain, Pacific, from sea to shining sea. Then a second wave of venomous prose from Europe.

For a few weeks in July, I was the scourge of everyone who'd ever donned a gimp suit, brandished a bullwhip, or attached electrodes to a pair of testicles. The BDSM community wanted me dead.

I'd first heard of Leather Camp during a Nerve editorial meeting. Leather Camp is a five-day retreat in which extremely kinky people from the United States and abroad get together and enact their wildest fantasies. The idea was that I would attend and report back on the scene. Michael Martin was initially lukewarm about the idea, but I shot the organizer an e-mail expressing an interest in joining in anyway. He replied saying that Leather Camp doesn't need publicity; that it sold out every year; that its location and schedule is a closely guarded secret; that he is trying to foster an environment free of judgment; that journalists are absolutely forbidden to attend.

"Now you're *definitely* fucking going!" said Michael, suddenly adrenalized with intrigue. "What don't they want people to know about? You are going undercover."

None of the installments of my column had ever hinged on my using an assumed persona. Usually I was courted by companies to promote their products and services and, among a specific subset of people, my name had clout. I could help companies sell hundreds of chin-mounted dildos or bottles of supplements "specially formulated" to make one's semen taste like applesauce, just by giving them a quick mention.

The brief was to go live among these folk at their summer retreat and report back on what I found. Should anyone ask, I was to tell them that I was attracted to BDSM and thought that Leather Camp would be a good way to find out what worked for me.

I had already delved into some BDSM-type activity in my column before now: I'd been shrink-wrapped in latex, infantilized by a dominatrix, and had seven shades of shit beaten out of me by a female wrestler. These articles were blogged—and usually ridiculed—on BDSM Web sites, so there was a fairly good chance that people might recognize my name. My pseudonym was Simon, which I thought went well with my accent. I have found that when forced to lie, keeping the lies parallel with the truth can help thwart revealing inconsistencies. To that end, I said that I was a customer service administrator, which I was up until twelve months earlier.

A portion of the Leather Camp Web site dealt with travel arrangements and carpooling. I ended up getting a ride with a guy called Manflesh. I traveled to Brighton Beach, Brooklyn, to meet up with him at his parents' home.

Manflesh was red-haired, soft-spoken, and in his mid-twenties. He had borrowed his parents' vehicle for Leather Camp: a large silver minivan with a large disabled sticker on the back and a mechanism for getting wheelchairs in and out of it.

"Hey, for a minivan, this thing can really move," he assured me, then faithfully observed the speed limit the whole way down past the Mason-Dixon Line.

The location of Leather Camp was shrouded in secrecy right up until the event, though it was always based within a two hour's drive of Washington, D.C. Previous years had seen local communities getting wind of the goings-on at a Leather Camp event and arriving at the premises in heated protest, presumably with pitchforks and torches.

Manflesh astounded me with tales of Leather Camps past—this year was his sixth—until we were well into Delaware. Like the time he and all seven of his cabinmates kidnapped a bi-curious male (consensually, of course) and wouldn't release him until he'd fellated them all. I imagine that his curiosity was quenched after that. Manflesh took a satisfied drag on a Parliament and looked longingly out the window.

"It was intense," he said. "You know, for a beginner, you are taking on a lot by coming here. It'll be a baptism by fire."

"How do you mean?" I asked. I began to panic.

"Leather Camp is fucking hard core. It's no joke. That's why we love it and you probably will too. It's great because, for four or five days, it's life as it should be: no rules, no judgments, no limits. But after four or five days, the weekend is over and—*Bam!*—it's back to reality."

At a typical BDSM event (bondage, domination, sadism, and masochism), Manflesh probably got more tail than I'd had in my entire life. He told me that he'd been whipped, flogged, pissed on, shat on, and generally bothered countless times since he discovered the scene at the tender age of nineteen. In fact, he was scheduled to give a two-hour tutorial on pissing that weekend. Last year, ten and one-third women showered him with golden degradation.

"One of the girls was three months pregnant," he explained the fraction cheerfully.

This time around, Manflesh had rallied fifteen through a BDSM Web site; he assured me it was not to be missed. I took my Blimpie sub from my lips and gazed out the window, ruminating upon what the weekend would have in store.

I was in the death throes of a four-month relationship with Sophie. Sophie had some understandable misgivings about my attending a country retreat for sexual miscreants. Sophie was not really the jealous type, but her hormones were currently out of whack due to her being on fertility medication. She was "donating" her eggs.

I assured her that I was just going to be there in an observational capacity, though I really couldn't gauge how I'd feel once I was there. I'd never been into the theatrical nature of the BDSM scene, though some of what Manflesh had said saying piqued my interest. Apparently, the previous year's big hit was the "merry-go-suck-and-fuck," in which eight "bottoms" assumed prone positions on a merry-go-round while a corresponding number of "tops" stood around the circle's perimeter. Condoms were changed with every spin of the wheel.

As we headed closer to camp, the clouds cleared. In the final mile of our journey, we passed through a quaint little village that listed the times of church services on its welcome sign. There I was, driving in with a man who made the Marquis de Sade look like Pat Boone. Did Littlebrooke's residents know that four hundred more of us were on the way?

We slowly pulled up the gravel driveway to the checkpoint, where two fifty-year-old women in Stars-and-Stripes T-shirts checked our credentials.

"Let's see yer dicks!" one of them yelled.

"We gotta check that you ain't vanilla!" said the other, laughing.

After three hours with Manflesh, I was feeling more vanilla than at any point in my life. He was poised to unbuckle his belt when a car came up behind us and we were waved into a parking area. About twenty-five yards from our car was a fifty-year-old man dressed as a little girl, with a bright red wig, pink dress, white knee-high socks, and Mary Jane shoes. He looked like a dry-cured Strawberry Shortcake. He skipped along the dirt road before hopping into a buggy and taking the reins.

"Hyah!" he squealed, jerking his steed into motion.

The steed was a sixty-year-old man. He wore a harness, black boots, blinders, a bit for his mouth, a butt plug replete with faux horsetail, and a cock ring. He pulled Strawberry Shortcake a few yards before the old man–little girl called out, "Whoa."

The centaur obligingly came to a halt. While the passenger buckled his shoe, his horse whinnied loudly, thrashed his head back and forth, and dragged a foot along the ground.

Manflesh put my mind at ease when I confessed that I hadn't brought any fetish wear whatsoever.

"That's fine," he said, "about half the people don't. Leather isn't a literal term. Leather is a state of mind, an umbrella term that covers all sorts of people who are into all sorts of things."

As we loaded our luggage into a golf cart, I heard what I thought was a rifle range in the distance. As we trundled over the brow of a hill, I saw a large meadow dotted with several crucifixes. Attached to each was an individual being whipped, flogged, and/or beaten. It was just like that scene in *Life of Brian*. But instead of looking on the bright side of life, the whippees were emitting the most bloodcurdling screams I'd ever heard. The air was full of agony.

The camp was flanked by three hills and a small lake. Manflesh and I registered, got our cabin assignments, and went our separate ways. He had already secured a private cabin with several of the scene's luminaries. Their cabin was called "Oink" because, as my new friend explained, "We're all fucking pigs."

I was assigned a cabin on the opposite end of the camp. It was about twenty feet by thirty, with ten stripped twin beds around the perimeter and some cubbyholes in the center of the room for personal effects. I thought I was the first to arrive, but in the far corner of the room lain a rotund blonde-haired woman in a pair of terry-cloth shorts and one white ankle sock. She was lying topless and facedown in a noisy slumber. My shuffling caused her to open her eyes slightly.

"Hi," I whispered. "Sorry to wake you."

She grunted and cut a spectacular fart that sent me scurrying outside for air.

From the porch of the cabin I saw a petite blonde woman leading around a huge, white, naked, entirely hairless man wearing a zippered gimp mask and "SLAVE" tattooed over his pubic bone. What was really unusual is that the gentleman seemed to lack any identifiable genitalia. In the area where one would normally find a penis, there was something that looked like the tied-up end of a balloon. His testicles were not in evidence. I wondered if he had tucked everything inside, like Samurai warriors did before going into battle. He was completely at the mercy of his owner: I saw her walk up to a swing and place a dog bowl full of a brown substance ten feet in front of it. Her slave got onto all fours and hungrily ate from it. At the end of her swing's arc, his tormentor would spit, and her saliva would land on her slave or in his food. Every thirty seconds or so she would get off the swing, walk over to him, and flick her cigarette ash into his bowl for him to consume.

My cell phone didn't work. I couldn't unburden myself of any of the nightmarish vignettes being played out before me. I suddenly realized that, for perhaps the first time, I was truly alone. I ran across the camp to find Manflesh. He said that his crew was all around our age.

With the large, plushy pig toy on the veranda, cabin Oink wasn't too hard to spot. Twenty paces from my destination, I was almost stampeded by a team of six "ponies" that were pulling a chariot at speed, provoking laughter from Manflesh and his cabinmates.

"You gotta watch out for that if you are going to last the weekend!" he called out.

Manflesh introduced me to a dozen of his friends, who were all very nice and had tons of questions about my kink, my sexual orientation, and my funny accent. There was Malcolm, a stout Uncle Fester type; Candy, a shy blonde woman in her late twenties; Julia and Dominique, two girls also in their twenties who could have been the two nerdy, spookily inseparable girls from any high school.

"How are you doing, Jeff?" called Manflesh to a man dressed up as a pony and being flogged nearby.

"Another day in paradise, man!" he answered as large welts began to appear on his back.

At that point, I'd been asked "Are you a top or a bottom?" at least ten times. I just said that I wasn't entirely sure but hadn't ruled anything out and that I expected the weekend to shed some light on things. That usually stopped people from digging much deeper and exposing me as an outsider. Having a shared history in the scene, everyone else had plenty to talk about. There were inside jokes, slang, and a lot of jargon I found hard to decipher.

"Have you seen Bolt-Thrower lately?"

"No, last I heard, he married Desire and disappeared off the scene. Moved to Tallahassee."

I held up my end of a conversation by constantly asking for explanations. Everybody was talking about "doing a scene" with one person or another: "I've got a bondage scene with Cumbucket on Sunday at two, a humiliation scene with Donkey-boy on Friday morning." They kind of scheduled them all in like power meetings.

With as much fanfare as he could muster, Manflesh produced his "new toy": a 10,000-volt cattle prod designed for cattlemen involved in carrying out something called "close work." I swallowed hard. The device emitted a soft buzzing sound, like that of a honeybee, which belied its ability to render a human being helpless and in unspeakable pain. Manflesh said he wouldn't use the prod until somebody had used it on him first—he wanted to know what the pain would be like.

"I'll do it," said everyone in near perfect unison.

With about an hour to go before the opening dinner, I headed off to the pool. A huge majority of attendees at Leather Camp were older than my parents. Some were grandparents. Many were obese and leathery. There were about ten older walrus-people sitting on lounge chairs around the pool's edge. A man who looked like Santa Claus stood next to my chair. In addition to his pillowy beard and trademark belly, he wore black sandals, orange-tinted aviators, and, most interestingly, a pair of assless hot pants showcasing an ornate barbed-wire cock ring.

By the time of my trip to Leather Camp, I had two years of immersive sexual research under my belt and had noticed several common themes among the attendees at these sorts of things, whether it be a trip to the nude beach, porn shoot, a sex party, or any other sociosexual event: people looked either like NASCAR fans or the sort of people who spent their weekends reenacting historical battles. They were almost always overweight, overtanned, and bereft of almost any body hair. Most interestingly, they would use any excuse to whip themselves and each other up into a nationalistic fervor. These people may have their genitalia unencumbered by clothing but would always be wearing hats or T-shirts with slogans like "Welcome to America, Now Speak English!" "These Colors Don't Run" replete with weeping eagle/World Trade Center backdrop, or, most worryingly, "Nuke 'em All! (let Allah sort 'em out)." Manhattanites like myself could easily forget that, with every mile west beyond the Hudson River, this variety of American became more numerous and commonplace. To that end, these events don't attract society's misfits but rather the hoi polloi. In fact, the only demographic that's notably lacking are urbanites.

I was walking to the cabin to change for dinner when Manflesh, Candy, and Malcolm appeared by the pool and started doing a scene about ten yards from where I was sitting. Malcolm was standing behind Candy, pulling her hair and biting her neck as Manflesh slapped her tits from the front. To my horror, Manflesh pulled out an ornate pocket-knife that looked like a miniature scimitar. He crouched down, pulled up Candy's skirt, and ran the blade over her exposed vagina. Candy was moaning and thrashing around; I couldn't tell if she was actually being cut or not and I was about to pass out.

Manflesh looked over at me and smiled. I fumbled for my cell phone and had a pretend conversation while looking hard into the woods in the other direction. There was no way I was going to get involved in this. When I pretended to hang up, Manflesh was striding toward me. "You can get a decent signal here?"

"Er, yeah," I said unconvincingly.

"Who is your service provider?"

It seemed like an extremely normal conversation to be having while a knife-point rape was being played out five yards from us. "T-Mobile."

"That's amazing. You must be the only one who can get service out here. May I borrow your phone for just a second?" I gave him my phone, thinking I had been truly caught out. My phone service was spotty in parts of Brooklyn. Miraculously, it worked, and after a brief conversation, Manflesh handed it back to me with a smile. "It's time for dinner," he said. Shell-shocked, I followed him, Malcolm, and Candy to the dining hall. The dining hall was the only place on the campground where a dress code was enforced. Genitalia and breasts must be covered.

On the ride down, Manflesh had told me to keep my expectations low about the camp cuisine, but dinner was actually quite enjoyable: two different types of salad, gammon steak baked with pineapple, sautéed potatoes, mixed winter vegetables, and orange sherbet for dessert. I sat with Manflesh and the others I'd met outside his cabin. During dinner, camp announcements were made by one of the event's organizers, the charismatic Vincent.

Vincent had the best voice I'd ever heard. He sounded like a slightly deeper Lee Marvin. But announcements about general conduct depress the hell out of me, even when they're delivered with a sub-bass cowboy drawl. "Do not have any open flame within ten feet of your cabin. Please clean up after yourself. We are not your mother," and so on. Then Vincent started talking about his giant dick. You see, cabin decoration was one of the events at Leather Camp. A grand prize was offered at the end of the weekend. Vincent's cabin had been festooned with a four-foot inflatable penis that had disappeared, and the theme of its return had worked its way into Vincent's nightly dinner shtick. He reached into his pocket and counted some change. "A seventeen-cent reward for the return of my big dick," he drawled. The diners erupted in laughter and applause.

I got up to leave and somehow got introduced to a couple in their forties. We shook hands, and in a Southern drawl the woman said, "I just love your accent! Bill, don't you just love his li'l accent? Say, where are Ginny and Todd now? Bris-bane?"

"Cranbara," the man said.

"Mel-borne?" she continued.

"It's Cranbara."

"Cairns?"

The couple went on to explain the finer points of the vacation on which they visited the Great Barrier Reef, Ayres Rock, Alice Springs, Sydney, Melbourne, and Canberra, saw crocodiles in the wild and visited an aboriginal village. Before I could get a word in, the husband was trying his best to pull his wife away. "I'm sorry, mate, will you excuse us?" said the woman apologetically.

Not having the heart to tell them I wasn't, in fact, Australian, I offered them a hearty, "No worries, mate!" and made a break.

More and more people were arriving at camp, and the fervor was growing. I really got the feeling that people were grateful for the opportunity to come to Leather Camp. Old friends were being reunited all around me, catching up on subjects ranging from home improvement to the differences in the campsite from last year to this.

I snuck over to the pay phone and put in a call to my girlfriend. I missed her terribly. Some of the "I Did It for Science" assignments were contingent on having a significant other, some required an insignificant other, and a third grouping required me to be footloose and fancy-free. During Leather Camp I was in the death throes of dating Erica. During our tumultuous first five months, I had tried to induce a female ejaculation from Erica, had sex with her under the influence of five different narcotics in the space of one wacky weekend, and even had her accompany me to a gay bar, where I made out with twelve strange men, all in the name of experiential journalism. Erica was a good sport. Now, she was my only lifeline to the normal world.

I went back to the cabin to find a sunburned baby boomer having himself a stiff drink on the soft bunk next to mine. "Name's Dan," he said, extending his hand. "Havin' fun yet?"

"Oh, sure," I said.

"Ready for some vodka and ice?" he asked.

"Yep!" I said. Dan filled up half a sixteen-ounce cup with Absolut and threw in a little ice.

"See, I come from a long line of skydivers who say, 'If you've survived the day, drink your ass off.'" Dan told me that he was a 743-jump veteran, and that skydiving was "the biggest fucking rush imaginable." His speech was slurred and he could hardly walk.

I submerged my lips in the vodka.

Later, it was *Fantasy Island* night down at the swimming pool. The area was decked out Hawaiian-style: tiki torches, leis, fake palm trees, attendees in hula skirts and coconut bras. To rapturous applause, Vincent and another staff member arrived on a golf cart dressed as Mr. Roarke and Tattoo. Vincent took a stick from his bag.

"What's this, Tattoo?"

"De cane, Boss! De cane!"

The crowd lost it.

When you're in the countryside, the setting sun is the harbinger of lonesomeness. By nine o'clock, dinner had come and gone. Manflesh and his friends were nowhere to be seen; I had no one to talk to. I looked out at the crowd and saw people laughing, hanging out, embracing. It was then that a cute blonde girl, early twenties, ran across the pool area to join in the limbo competition. Out of six hundred people, she was singular in her attractiveness. I decided that would be my chance to make a connection. The limbo music started, and in front of hundreds of onlookers, I and fifteen others got ready to compete.

The cute girl was destined to win; that was clear from the start. She had captured the hearts and minds of the audience the moment she decided to remove an item of clothing every time she went under the bar. After the rest of us had been eliminated, she battled it out with a six-foot-four woman for supremacy. At that point, the blonde girl was totally naked, and the crowd shifted position to get a better view of her vagina as she made the winning pass. I stood near her pile of discarded clothes, which facilitated our meeting. She came up and shook my hand.

"You were great out there!" I said. She was in no hurry to put her clothes back on, even in the chilly night air.

"Thanks so much!" she said. "I'm a performer, a huge exhibition-ist, and I'm also very supple. Wanna beer?" She produced two Coronas from her book bag. Her name was Aimee; she was twenty. Still naked, she chatted with me for a while.

Aimee beckoned some friends over and introduced me to them. They were a coed group in their twenties and thirties who weren't scary at all.

"Oh oh oh!" said Aimee, flapping her arms around. "It's time for s'mores by the campfire!" We rushed down the hill to a small lake, where a roaring fire was under way.

I NOTICED THAT "VIRGIN" was a word everyone liked to misuse and throw around there. The standard questions about what I was into identified me as a virgin. In fact, I was the virgin. Around the campfire, Aimee and her friends were conspiring.

"Are you into pain?" they asked me.

"Absolutely not," I replied.

"How about some light bondage?"

Like lite cream and lite salad dressing, lite bondage sounded a lot less hazardous to my health. "Um, okay."

"Goodie!" said Aimee, clapping.

"Why don't we take him to the dungeon now?" asked Claudia.

Resistance was futile. Arm in arm, they led me to their cabin, where they picked up some toys, then we jumped in a golf cart and went to the dungeon. It was really chilly out, but I think my uncontrollable shivering was due more to nerves than anything else. Devirginizing people like me seemed to be a real treat for Aimee and Claudia. They could barely contain their excitement.

The dungeon was actually a gymnasium fitted with swings, suspension bars, stocks, and a contraption in the shape of an X that people could be tied to. As we entered, a woman screamed as her "play partner" used a lighter and aerosol can to send massive plumes of fire toward her body. Elsewhere, a man pressed a woman's feet back to her shoulders while another gent slapped her vagina. Aimee and Claudia brought me to a padded table at the back of the dungeon. They told me to strip down to my boxers, then put a blindfold on me and cuffed me securely to the table.

Screams were coming from all corners of the room. Being blindfolded, I could only vaguely guess what was causing them. For the next twenty minutes, the girls gently flogged me, ran their nails over my skin, and tickled me with an oversized feather. It was about this time that I heard a third female voice hovering somewhere above me. Then I felt a heat source near my face, and a vaguely familiar smell. A vagina! From the razor-thin strip of vision my skewed blindfold gave me, I could see that the vagina did not belong to Aimee or Claudia, who were slipping my underwear off inch by inch. I sealed my mouth and turned my head like a toddler, refusing to eat. The mystery vagina got the hint and disappeared. I could hear more and more people around me. Aimee uncuffed my right arm and told me to jerk off for her. Despite what I could sense was a growing audience, I found this particularly easy to do. Three minutes in, Claudia removed my blindfold. I was masturbating for a crowd of fifteen men and women. Aimee was on all fours above me, her head down by my ankles, and her ass inches from my face. Claudia was torturing Aimee's nipples with metal clamps. "You'd better come, Simon, or I'm going to pull blondie's nips off," said Claudia. Aimee shrieked in pain and sounded like she was beginning to sob.

"Come, come, come, come." One of the audience members began the low chant, which the others picked up.

I pumped my fist mercilessly, knowing full well that it would take a while and that I could be an accomplice in Aimee's disfigurement.

"Hurry up, Simon!" Aimee yelled.

The chanting got louder and faster. "Come, come, come, come!"

"I think that he wants to hurt you, bitch," Claudia said to Aimee. "Do you like this?" she said, looking at me and slapping Aimee's pert ass.

"Yes," I said.

"Would it speed things up if it was in your face?" she asked.

I nodded and Claudia backed Aimee up then gently rubbed my testicles. I'd never cheated on a girlfriend before now. Not so much as kissed another girl, and here I was with my tongue in the ass of a blonde debutante while masturbating in front of a growing crowd as another woman held my balls with an iron grip.

"Come, come, come, come!" yelled the crowd, sounding angry now.

Finally I was done. Rapturous applause echoed around the gymnasium.

Claudia slid a finger through the pool of semen I'd deposited on my chest and put it into my mouth before she allowed me to get off-stage.

"Well, what did you think?" Claudia asked.

"I thought it was very interesting," I said. I wasn't lying. After all that activity, I was bushed and ready for bed, but someone came up with the idea of going to the dungeon's group grope room, where there were two adjoining inflatable beds, with some disposable paper play sheets in a box beside them.

Two guys and a woman were finishing up their scene, dutifully getting dressed and throwing away the paper sheets. Aimee laid out some new ones, and everyone else started making out and stripping. It was cold, so Aimee left her socks on. Within a few seconds, limbs were entwined in an eight-person clusterfuck. The people involved were arguably the youngest, leanest, and most attractive at Leather Camp, and within a few minutes a number of people put down their toys and piled into the room.

"Join in!" said Claudia, giving me a saucy wink and tugging at my penis. Mindful of my girlfriend, I inched to the back of the room to check out the scene with the other onlookers. I wasn't aroused, exactly; more grateful to be included in the scene. There was no slapping, flogging, hot wax, or anything of that nature, just a good old-fashioned orgy: eight people looking to put the right parts in the correct places. Fifteen minutes later, it downsized into something that looked more like a group grope. "Aftercare," as it's known: following a scene, people reassure each other with cuddles and kisses. It kind of says, "Although I spent the past hour breaking your skin and calling you a filthy little whore, it was just pretend. We were just playing!"

I hardly slept a wink that night. Apparently I was assigned to the snorey cabin, where everybody else was at least twenty years my senior. I had finally gotten comfortable on the spiky, funny-smelling bedding when a bunch of people straggled in and flopped onto their beds, one by one. That, coupled with the numbing cold, meant that I was still awake by the time my cabinmates were getting up to greet the day. I was so cold and tired that I couldn't be bothered to get up and put on more clothing. Although they were more pierced and tattooed than conventional baby boomers, the campers still had a propensity for getting up at 6:30 on the dot. Noisily, they arose and went out onto the veranda for cigs and coffee, finally allowing me a couple of hours of shut-eye. I woke at midday feeling like hammered shit.

"You didn't miss much," said Dan, who had come to the cabin to change into his birthday suit.

"Aside from three cute submissives jerking off some guy at the pool. He took ages to come, but he didn't mind about that."

"Um, is it warm out?" I asked.

"Well, it's just warm enough to walk around naked, which I find is the best way to advertise," he deadpanned, giving his considerable Johnson a wave, as if to prove his point.

Lunch was three different types of what was labeled as pizza. I sat down with Trevor and Claire, a couple from the monumental cluster-fuck the night before. When not "in the moment," they seemed shy. It was only Claire's second event, and she was only marginally more in tune with the scene than I was. Trevor was worried he was about to be kidnapped.

Kidnapping is big at Leather Camp. You either had to consent to being kidnapped, or perhaps a partner or friend volunteered you for it. At some point, you'd be pounced upon by four or five assailants and receive an abduction made to order. It could be sexual in nature or just a good old-fashioned beating. Either way, Trevor was concerned that his kidnapping would come at an inconvenient time, like on the way to dinner or when he needed to go to the bathroom. He started getting animated and waving his arms around, spilling a cup of hot coffee that barely missed my lap. I didn't know what had happened to my appetite, but I could barely eat anything.

The weather was overcast. Glancing at the schedule of events, I decided I would catch the two-hour "Takin' It Up the Ass" tutorial, which was due to take place at 2:00. On the way out of the dining hall I bumped into Aimee, who was chatting to her boyfriend on the phone. He was turning up at camp tonight and she was terribly excited. Aimee was competing in the stripping contest that night, and she asked for my help in selecting a song and figuring out her choreography. Against my wishes, she picked Alannah Myles's "Black Velvet" from the songbook. We went to the pool and I watched her dance/gymnastic routine take shape.

Satisfied with her moves, we headed up to "the Barn," which was, as the name suggests, a barn. Inside, twenty people were sitting around looking bored and perplexed.

"This is a lot less stressful than a lot of other SM events," explained Aimee. "Tutorials happen, or they don't. Other events are more regimented, but this is like, 'Fuck you, I'm on my vacation!'"

With the night's theme being Mardi Gras, Claudia was running a mask-making competition. We ran over to the dining hall and got busy with the glitter glue, sequins, and feathers. While we tinkered with design concepts, the conversation turned to what other attendees had told friends and family about where they'd be that weekend. It was rare to hear people talk about the outside world, and I was happy they were. The premise of camp was that people could be "who they really wanted to be," meaning that, for the most part, the trappings of the real world were checked at the front gate. I, for one, love the trappings of the real world. Without them to embrace or react against, I was getting really, really lonely. With my mask complete and Aimee running off to do a photographed "suspension scene," I looked around camp for familiar faces, but again found no one.

I walked over to the lake's edge, where a fire had been lit and deserted. I don't like being alone. I'm not sure what's scarier: asking a sixty-year-old guy dressed as Pippi Longstocking to pass the Elmer's Glue, or sitting there by the lake with nothing but my thoughts. I hadn't felt so isolated since I was a bus driver at the oil refinery about five years before. At least then I had a book, the radio, and the occasional grease monkey to chat with. But having to essentially fib to these people all day about who I was and why I was there was making me feel like I was without an identity. It seemed that the more people were into it, the more I was feeling left out. I'm sure that I could have gotten into more situations, but I found it hard to have common ground with people. If you want to know the truth, I almost had a little cry.

I wasn't alone. A rustling in the bushes alerted me to the presence of three medievalists—one male and two female—caressing and canoodling together. The man was wearing Cossack boots, black jodhpurs, and a baggy shirt that looked like liquid chrome with a belt resting midway up his belly. The man gave me what I could only describe as a Shakespearean wave or hand flurry before turning back to his ladies and sipping some Bud Light, which he no doubt wished was ale or mead. Across the edge of the lake, a couple of guys—clothed and looking like civilians—were fishing for the elusive handful of bigmouthed bass rumored to be skulking around in the weeds. I took heart in the fishermen and a Cessna that flew overhead. All this sex, sex, sex was driving me absolutely crazy.

I found Claudia and Josh in the dining hall. In keeping with the Mardi Gras theme, shrimp gumbo, jambalaya, and corn bread were on the menu. In the buffet line, I stood next to a guy who was so manly he made the Brawny towel dude look positively fey. On his back was a woman of similar age—his partner or wife, I presumed. She was pretending to be his daughter, exhibiting the characteristics of a hyperactive seven-year-old girl and addressing the man as "Papa."

As was becoming the trend, I put more on my plate than I was able to eat. Josh and Claudia introduced me to Martha, a smiley fifty-year-old with Farrah Fawcett hair.

"Oh, don't tell me, you are a bottom, aren't you?" she cooed. "Look at those wonderful baby browns! You wouldn't hurt a fly, would you?"

I *guess* not. I tend to dislike pain, being restrained, or getting generally bothered; I would only give someone a sound beating if they stole my stuff. So I suppose I'm a bottom by default.

During dinner, Josh developed a pronounced facial tic, like his eye was trying to jump off his face. I hadn't noticed it the night before. It seemed to happen every ten seconds and was accompanied by maniacal laughter from Claudia. It transpired that Josh was wearing a mini version of an invisible-fence dog collar around his cock and balls. Claudia held the remote control.

Vincent made his nightly announcements. The abductors of the inflatable dick had cobbled together a ransom note out of letters clipped from a newspaper. Vincent upped the reward for the dick's return to forty-five cents. The dining room erupted with laughter and applause. Vincent then revealed why the "Takin' It Up the Ass" seminar was a nonstarter.

Apparently some poor bugger had fainted and was carted off to the hospital in an ambulance. He had taken too much or not enough of his blood-pressure medication, and as an impossibly large object was inserted into a willing ass, he hit the deck faster than Anna Nicole Smith on a fistful of Vicodin.

There was another special announcement to be made: that day was the one-year anniversary of Peter and Madeleine, who had wed at

Leather Camp last year. Applause all around. Peter then grabbed the mic and presented the camp organizers with a plaque conveying heartfelt thanks. It was really touching. The four of them got a two-minute standing ovation. I got a little choked up myself.

After dinner, everybody filed outside for the stripping competition. Aimee was the first contestant. She did a perfect dance, ending with a headstand, split, and precisely executed bridge. The crowd went apeshit. Peter was up next. Despite his formidable bulk, he did some tantalizing leaps and landed in a split, soliciting oohs and aahs from the audience. Perhaps the biggest crowd-pleaser was a man named "Pluto's Revenge," a six-foot-four member of the Oink cabin who wore a Mohawk, handlebar mustache, and wraparound shades. He threw his lanky frame around for two minutes while wearing a leather thong pouch. During the routine, he launched his sunglasses into the pool. For the finale, he recklessly somersaulted into the shallow end. When he didn't come up for five seconds, everybody thought the worst. There was uncomfortable silence, then murmuring. But Pluto reemerged victorious. He was wearing the sunglasses and holding his marble sack high above his head.

Another routine of note was Samantha and Craig's. As well as being boyfriend and girlfriend, they were both blonde, skinny, and tall. Dressed identically in pigtails and Catholic-schoolgirl uniforms, they did a naughty take on a mirror dance, backed by Nine Inch Nails' "Closer (I Wanna Fuck You Like an Animal)." At the end, they writhed on a section of indoor-outdoor carpeting wearing nothing but knee-high boots.

It's worth mentioning here that out of ten entrants in the stripping contest, six of them chose "I Wanna Fuck You Like an Animal" as accompaniment. After it was played three times in a row, the DJ declared the song banned. The other strippers were chagrined. "That's fucked up!" one of them cried behind me. Attention was momentarily deflected from the stripping when a woman in a Mardi Gras mask and front-mounted dildo went down on a fellow audience member. The contest ultimately ended in a tie between Aimee, Pluto's Revenge, and an Audrey Hepburn–type performer known simply as Dancer. Each prize was a bundle of Leather Camp dollars, which could be used at Casino Night or the next day's slave auction.

Aimee's boyfriend finally came to camp, and she couldn't have been happier about it. They'd only been dating for a month, but she was already wearing a collar that indicated she was, in some way, his property.

After the stripping contest, I bumped into Claudia, and we strolled past the torch-lit pony races and down to the pavilion, where Casino Night was being held. Blackjack, poker, and roulette were being played at tables all around. Attendees wore differing degrees of fetish wear. I learned how to play blackjack and even came away with hundreds of (fake) dollars.

Being away from the city's energy made me lethargic, and I was fading fast. In addition to breakfast, lunch, and dinner, a midnight snack was provided. That night it was cold cuts and rolls. I start talking to Claudia about how she got into the scene. She was really attractive and in her mid-twenties.

"I was a sorority girl," she said and smiled. "That's how I learned to top and bottom. It set me up for being a switch. I didn't know it at the time, but a few years later something was definitely pulling me toward the scene."

My curiosity was piqued, to say the least.

"But you know, I was a great pledge too," she said. "I was all, 'Yes, ma'am, yes, ma'am.' I loved it, even the really evil shit." Apparently, in one hazing ritual the pledges had to strip naked so the seniors could use a permanent marker to circle each girl's less taut body parts.

I said good night and went back to the cabin. The remaining two unoccupied beds had been pushed together and an inflatable bed had been put over the top. Cliff and Liz were our cabin's only couple. They were in their fifties, and they brought everything but the kitchen sink to camp: a night-light, two drink coolers, an electric blanket, a collapsible coat rack, a set of those plastic drawers on wheels with all sorts of medical and cosmetic supplies in them. The woman looked like Olive Oyl, and her husband was the spitting image of Mr. Kotter. I lay in bed wondering about their relationship. I wondered if there were vanilla couples where one partner had discovered the scene and the other just kind of went along with it. That's how Olive Oyl seemed. She looked like she wanted to be anywhere else but in this cabin.

Unlike the night before, I fell asleep immediately. I kept my clothes on and used two towels as auxiliary blankets. It was still bone-chillingly cold, but at least Dan wasn't making such a racket. I woke up at 6:00 on the dot, freezing. I went into the shower room and found that Cliff and Liz had even brought their own massaging showerhead. Unbelievable! I took advantage of their creature comfort and hung out under the shower for the better part of an hour. The majority of my cabinmates were still asleep. It was 7:30, and the rain outside was nothing short of torrential. Breakfast wasn't served until 9:00, but the kitchen staff already had some coffee brewing while they prepared eggs, bacon, and oatmeal. I sat down at one end of the huge dining hall, the only person there. I started talking to a kitchen staffer who was wearing a David Beckham jersey. I guessed he was English, but he was actually from Poland, on one of those Camp America programs.

"I'm from Gdansk," he told me in perfect English. Not only did Stacek nail my country of origin, but he could identify what region I was from by my accent.

"What do you think of America?" I asked him.

"I much prefer England," he said. "This place is weird." I hoped he had seen other things than camp. "Next week, there will be more people here that will be naked and having sex everywhere. It's a strange place, America."

"This isn't normal," I said.

I was about to argue the case for my adopted homeland, but as I opened my mouth, I caught sight of a sexagenarian male dressed as a female toddler and applying rouge at the other end of the dining hall. I shook hands with Stacek, the only person I had met outside of the scene in days, and I stared out at the gloom.

Before I'd left for camp, my editor had told me there were three categories of kids who went to summer camp. Some kids assimilate immediately, disappearing into the throng before their parents have left the parking lot. Others might feel lonely and uncool for the first few days before falling in with a like-minded crowd; they ultimately had to be dragged away. Then there are the kids who piss the bed and want to go home.

I had pissed the proverbial bed. As I sat in the dining hall, watching the rain drive against the window, I was overwhelmed by the need to leave. The continuing monsoon threatened to compromise the rest of the weekend's events; it had driven people inside, into more intimate, insular activities. Everyone at camp seemed to be having the time of their lives, and I was not included. Not being straight up about what I was doing there was starting to become a massive burden; I would make a useless double agent. I just wanted everybody to get on with having fun.

As soon as I had made the decision to go, I felt a massive sense of relief. In fact, the end of every sexual situation related to the column was marked by a feeling of dread, anguish, and insecurity being suddenly lifted. Making a break from Leather Camp was that feeling multiplied by a hundred.

I ran through the downpour to camp HQ and checked in my bed linen. There were only two trains to New York that day, and I was determined to catch the earlier one. There was no precedent of people leaving camp before the diabolical activities had reached their heady zenith at the Renaissance Fair, and consequently the camp's organizers were reluctant to let me go.

Jorge, one of Claudia's crew, who I'd meet in the group grope, very kindly offered to drive me the twenty miles to the nearest train station, through torrential rain, after I'd explained that there'd been a family emergency that I had to get back for.

"Well, family is very important," he said with his thick Venezuelan accent. "We'll make sure you get back to New York okay."

I got on the train, thankful that I'd made it back undetected and in one piece, though I doubted that I'd ever really be "okay" again.

FISH AND CHIPS
ON MY SHOULDER

BASED ON THE CONVERSATION I know will follow, I often dread to open my mouth. My diphthongs, my glottal stops, my singsongy inflection conspire against me and commit me to having the same conversation, every day, two, five, ten times a day since the late nineties. I'll have to write off the next ten minutes.

I love New York City. I belong to it and it belongs to me. Like most adopted New Yorkers, my love informs my politics and worldview, my lifestyle and relationships, my dress sense and street smarts, my hopes and aspirations. I walk the walk just fine, but whenever I talk the talk, I am stopped dead in my tracks.

"Hey, where are you from?"

I'll say "here" or "New York," depending on where I am. I'll try to neutralize my accent, but it's too late. I know where this is going and there's no way out.

"No, I mean *really* from?"

If I have the energy to make them guess, just less than half of people will say England. The remainder will guess either Australia or New Zealand. Every twentieth person will guess South Africa or Ireland. I'm not sure if this corresponds with the commonly held view that in general Americans aren't all that worldly, or that by accident or design my accent has morphed over time.

"I was *raised* in England."

My choice of words is conceited. If I can't be identified as a New Yorker, I'll accept "citizen of the world." Anything but being backed into this one again.

Now, I'm aware that my accent has done me infinitely more good than harm at this point. It's opened doors, created opportunities, allowed me to jump the line, endeared me to otherwise indifferent people; it's kick-started thousands of conversations, it's gotten me laid well and often.

In major U.S. cities, being English is almost always relatable. People always want to tell me that they spent a semester abroad in England, that they have family who live there, that they love soccer, Monty Python, Benny Hill, and Mr. Bean. An effective conversationalist uses first impressions to find common ground. It's cruel to derail a person's line of questioning but I attempt in vain to do just that, every time. It's not malicious; I'm trying to avoid being defined by a place that's never really felt like home and instead be allied with a place that does. No one lets me.

"What town?"

"A small village outside of London. I've lived here for years though. How do you know Brian?"

"West, north?"

"East of London. Hey, are you wearing Issey Miyake?"

"What's it called?"

"You would have never heard of it. I can barely remember it myself."

"Seriously, what's the name of your town? I lived in England for a semester."

Oftentimes my inflection, the cadence of my voice starts to feature in their sentences. My accent is almost always contagious.

"What did you study?"

"Economics. What town?"

"Corringham."

"Never heard of it. Are you a cockney?"

He or she is almost always trying to be friendly, personable, yet it's got my blood boiling.

Bad teeth, gray skies, warm beer, pale skin, blood pudding. I am always overcome with the urge to create distance between me and all that; to prove that that's just not me. I wouldn't identify myself as a self-loathing Brit. In fact, I'm slowly beginning to like myself. Oblivious to my attempts to sever the national umbilical cord, people often introduce me to other Englanders.

I don't dislike British people per se. I just don't like them *here*.

"This is James," says the ruthless man introducing his friend. "James is another bloody Brit!"

Other "Brits" are my kryptonite. Well-meaning Americans always manage to conjure up an estranged countryman and set me up on a sort of expat playdate, unaware that their very presence strikes at the heart of my special powers—my presumed wit and charming accent. The intermediary will watch us shake hands and leave. Probably thinks we must have a lot to talk about, but I am instantly transported to my unhappy place.

I'd always railed against the archetypal Brit as portrayed in the American media, but I confront it whenever I meet an estranged countryman.

"Where are you from then?"

James's accent is always clipped, if a little slurred; nonregional. His hair is foppish and curly.

"Just east of London."

I always give a vague response and hope that his or her concept of geography is thrown off by the alcohol that's causing him or her to sway. Nope, it's clicked. It usually does. Oh shit. He's pointing, smiling.

"*Essex boy!*"

In England and throughout the package vacation zones of southern Europe, the county of Essex has the unenviable reputation as a capital of utter barbarism, the nexus of tackiness and uncouth. I've referred to it as the New Jersey of England in the past, though in reality it's not nearly as quaint.

It's frosted hair, souped-up cars, bumper-to-bumper traffic, gangsters, random violence, ecstasy dealers, binge drinking, tanorexic girls, vandalism, designer-brand clothing, shopping malls, funky-house and theme-pub franchises. The urban areas smell of sulfur, the countryside smells of pig shit. Depending on the prevailing wind conditions, the odor in Corringham changes hour by hour. Essex is a cultural blind spot, a geopolitical punch line.

"Au-right, geeezaah!" James apes an Essex accent and slaps me on the back. The performance is too theatrical but technically accurate.

"What are *you* doing 'ere then?" James continues the impersonation.

I was blissfully unaware of the British class system until I moved to New York and met the Jameses and the Tobys, the Nicholases, the Emmas, the Sebastians, the Brunos. They are all in media, PR, or finance; overpaid, oversexed, and over here. The men have the Hugh Grant thing going on and use it night after night, whittling their bedposts to toothpicks.

"I'm a writer," I'll say.

"Oh, you're a wri-ah!"

I make a fist and think about throwing it into their crooked teeth. All that money spent on boarding school, summer vacations in the Dordogne, winters skiing in Val D'Isere, and to have a mouth that looks stuffed full of smashed crockery. Twisted bicuspids, discolored canines, and unruly incisors aren't the only things they bring with them from Oxfordshire, Cambridgeshire, Berkshire, Hampshire, and Surrey. They bring their colonizing instinct and stick together, a clan, a posse, a clique. Every year there's more of them. Tarquins and Olivers and Annas and Bridgetts. They meet to drink and watch cricket and rugby, only they call it "Ruggah." I have more in common with a house cat than these people and no one can see it but me and them.

THE LONG FRENCH KISS
GOOD-BYE

IN HEELS, the supermodel seemed a good foot taller than me.

"*What* did you just say to me?" she said.

It was the third time she'd asked me to repeat myself.

She sounded German, perhaps Dutch. The pickup line would have sounded garbled even if there *wasn't* a height difference, a language barrier, a pulsing bass beat, or the effects of drugs and alcohol to contend with. I balanced precariously on tiptoes and yelled in the general direction of her eardrum.

"*I said, Your daddy doesn't have a penis, he has a paintbrush!*"

Even as concepts for my "I Did It for Science" column went, this one was patently preposterous. In an editorial meeting the previous week, I'd inadvertently leaked that despite being a kamikaze sex writer,

I'd never used a pickup line on anyone. In fact, though I was checking off bizarre once-in-a-lifetime sexual experiences at a dizzying rate, I'd never done the normal stuff like ask for a girl's number, French kissed a complete stranger, or had a one-night stand. I still haven't. Within an hour, a short list of twenty of the most egregious lines had been made for me to unleash at a Ford model party that Wednesday night.

The model jumped back and held my shoulders at arm's length.

"*You . . .*"

I braced myself for a stinging slap or knee to the groin.

Brian laughed and took a picture.

"*. . . are so funny!*"

She wrapped her arms around me, shoved my face to her clammy breasts, and swiveled at the hips several times.

"A paintbrush! Ha ha ha!"

She snapped her fingers at the bartender and pointed to me. Another free drink.

This was the fourth. I'd been making models laugh all night and they'd been rewarding me by buying me drinks on their boyfriends' tabs and promptly disappearing. I tried not to take it personally, reminding myself that models are required to flit in and out of clubs all night. I'm not a big drinker and was only now realizing that my humiliation and my drunkenness were inversely proportional.

The night had started with Anna and me sharing several flasks of sake at Decibel. It was one of the semiannual occasions when we have a drink and talk about the tumultuous year that we dated each other. I walked her to her friend's place on 3rd Street and Avenue A and was asked to stay for a glass of Riesling and a few chunky lines of coke. I left to join Brian and Vin at Cherry Tavern for a Tecate and tequila shot. Outside, I wretched twice. Nothing came up and the three of us headed over to the model party at Plaid.

I surveyed the dance floor for my next glamazon. If my liver could take it, I still had eight or nine pickup lines to bust out. In the distance I saw Brian threading himself through the crowd toward me.

"Hey!" he said.

I could barely focus my eyes on him.

"How do you like your eggs in the morning?" I slurred. "Fertilized?"

"Never mind all that," he said. He pulled me across the dance floor by my shirt collar. "There's this totally cute French girl who really wants to meet you."

Even in my inebriated state I knew that this was Brian code for "I want to close in on a cute girl, so please make time with her clubfooted friend."

Laure and Louise were both nineteen years old and both adorable, swinging their arms and legs around with a seemingly laissez-faire attitude toward the beat, as French girls in discotheques are wont to do. They were spending the summer in New York, interning for an importer of Bordeaux. It was easy to tell to whom we'd each been allotted. Laure was taller, blonde, and sun-kissed. Louise was shorter with paler skin and a stylish jet-black bob. She wore a black tank top, a short black-and-white polka-dot skirt, and black heels.

"Louise, this is Grant," yelled Brian. He came close to my ear and yelled, "Your one."

As they were both slim, pretty, and jerked their bodies in the same arrhythmic manner, I would have been happy with either, though I was acutely aware that they were seeing me at my drunkest and sweatiest. By the sixth week of a New York summer, people sort of surrender to the swampy air that has you schvitzing before you've walked a block from your apartment. In pairs we danced and talked.

"Your name?" said Louise, hooking her shiny black hair over her ear and putting it near my mouth.

"My name is Grant," I said.

Louise raised her eyebrows and tugged Laure's arm.

"*Laure! Laure! Il s'appelle Grand!*" she said as they succumbed to fits of girlish laughter.

A bouncer pushed past me and I spilt free gin and tonic over my shirt to more giggles from Louise. Laure and Brian were already making out and slapping each other's asses in time to the music. With seemingly nothing left to lose, I proceeded to treat Louise to some of my comedy dance moves, which are, in truth, modified only slightly from my *actual* dance moves.

"You are cool!" she said with a wink.

She must have been as wrecked as I was.

"What are you doing later?" I asked just before an urgent need to throw up hit me like a kick in the gut.

"Well, per'aps we should 'ang out because I fink that your friend and Laure are going to . . ."

I left Louise mid-sentence and hurtled toward the exit and ran across the street from the club and started spitting out that awful-tasting liquid that tends to precede a Technicolor yawn.

I'm going to be sick, I'm not going to be sick, I'm going to be sick.

My body kept me guessing until I was a block from my house. I threw up outside the window of the Dynasty diner at the corner of 14th and B to the disgust of its nighttime patrons. As I got home, my phone rang several times. It was Brian; I didn't pick up.

Hungover, I stumbled into the Nerve offices at around noon the next day. I sat at my desk and kept one eye on the bathroom door.

"Oh, man!" Brian said and laughed from across the room. "You were wasted last night!"

"I don't want to talk about it." Even thinking about what I drank last night could restart the heaving.

"You actually left that girl while she was still *talking* to you."

The pain of the hangover had nudged out any memory of the two teenage Parisians we had met. Brian filled in the gaps in my memory with snaps of the previous night on his digital camera.

"Wow, they're pretty cute!" I said.

"Well, the one you *could* have taken home totally thinks that you are totally not into her. She got kind of upset. After you left she said . . . ha ha ha . . . oh, man, she said, 'What eez wrong wiv your friend? Is 'e . . . 'ow you say . . . a faggot?' Ha ha ha ha!"

"Did you set her straight?"

"No, I told her that she was probably right!"

"Thanks."

At around four, I kept down half a sandwich. At five I was called at my desk and summoned to Starbucks. I threw up the sandwich. The Starbucks on the corner of Crosby and Spring was where Rufus fired people. An enormous culling took place in the spring and summer of 2001. After each outgoing staffer left Nerve's employ to the sounds of world Muzak and the smell of mocha lattes, the venue became known internally as Charbucks. Rufus was pissed at me.

BY THE FALL of 2002 Rufus Griscom had already had some success in transitioning Nerve-branded content into a wide array of other media: the Nerve HBO show; cobranded movie projects; Nerve online personals were spun into a separate company that powered personals for a plethora of Web sites; Emma Taylor and Lorelei Sharkey coauthored a hardcover sex guide, *The Big Bang: Nerve's Guide to the New Sexual Universe*, and followed it with *Nerve's Guide to Sexual Etiquette*. Rufus now had designs on spinning some Nerve content into a TV series and decided that a small-screen version of "I Did It for Science" could be a feasible project. Rufus had off-handedly brought up the possibility during an awkward moment in the elevator. Through spatial association, the elevator became the only venue where this formless project was touched upon.

"Why, Mr. Stoddard, sir!" he'd routinely say as we entered the elevator in the lobby.

Rufus often referred to and addressed me as Nerve's unofficial mascot, a distinction I secretly enjoyed and tried to aspire to. I liked Rufus and thought him charming, quite Gatsby-ish. He is tall, slim, and bespectacled, with a triangular nose and prominent, noble-looking chin. He has a crest of thick, straight floppy hair and flings his arms around in wild gesticulation.

Third floor.

"Well, what a wonderful bouquet of bed-head you are presenting us all with this fine morning."

The timbre of Rufus's voice is somewhat odd and comical. His uvula, the circular muscle at the back of the throat, seems perpetually tensed, as when yawning. This can make him sound Kermit-like. The sound becomes more noticeable when he is excited or enraged, which is patently hilarious.

Fifth floor.

"So how about 'I Did It for Science' TV? That'd be quite something, wouldn't it?"

"Totally."

Sixth floor. Our floor.

We had this brief conversation about four times in as many months, always in the elevator, until seemingly out of the blue Rufus and Alisa invited me to accompany them to a VH1 meeting at 1515 Broadway.

Rufus's girlfriend, the tall, blonde, perky, and Texan Alisa Volkmann, had been recently brought in to share Ross Martin's position as the head of Film and TV projects. Shortly thereafter, Ross and his pregnant wife, Jordana, moved to LA, where he set up his own production company, Plant Film.

"We want you to see what a TV meeting is like, so you have an idea for when we pitch the 'I Did It for Science' show," he said as we scooched into the backseat of a town car.

"Totally!" said Alisa. "A TV version of your show would just be rilly, rilly hilarious. And VH1 would be a totally koo-uhl home for it."

The idea that the adventures of my genitalia could be the basis for a weekly half hour of nationally broadcast television certainly appealed to my ego, though I was unsure that I would be willing to bare all to a mainstream TV audience and skeptical that a network existed that would deign to show something quite so tragic and foul. VH1 had recently made the leap from showing Genesis videos to clip shows about the glitterati. Surely a show about a pasty, nervous, pigeon-chested weakling with an erection would be a colossal step backward.

We shoved away through the line of banner-waving kids who were there for MTV's *TRL*. We filed into a conference room, where we all shook hands with frosted-hair TV execs whose teeth were bleached too white.

"And who might this be, Rufus?" said the one with the whitest teeth. He made little effort to finesse his distaste for the random scruffy person sitting in.

"This, guys, is Grant 'I Did It for Science' Stoddard."

Blank faces all around. I began to feel like a complete asshole.

"Nerve's most intrepid and most widely read columnist?"

No recognition whatsoever. Rufus was always overstating the cultural reach of his media empire and often making us all look like tools in the process.

"O-kay, so we have no time to talk about anything other than the matter at hand. Another meeting is using the room in, like, ten minutes."

"Absolutely," said Rufus. "Grant is just here to—"

"Great, let's begin."

The matter at hand was VH1 wanting to peripherally use Nerve personals for some reality dating show pilot. Over the next eight minutes, Rufus and Alisa began shooting out increasingly half-baked show ideas that would insinuate Nerve into the project to a more significant extent. Rufus's voice got funnier. They hit a wall. I sank into my chair.

"Rufus, we already *have* our show." White Teeth used his hands in the international gesture for calm the fuck down.

He and the other execs were exasperated. "We just wanted to know if you wanted to help us."

"I just don't see the value for Nerve," Rufus said and folded his arms.

"Then I think we're done here."

The five execs got up and coldly shook hands with Rufus. People for the next meeting filed into the conference room and began sitting down.

"You *guys*!" said Alisa. She always spoke like a cheerleader. "Grant here is a fucking superstar!"

At that moment, I felt like less of a superstar than at any point in my life. I jerked into my overcoat without looking up. White Teeth gave Alisa the hand.

"Alisa, that's our time here."

"'Kay, but you *guys*, he is totally funny and he dressed up as a girl for his column and it was like, rilly, rilly hilarious."

"Alisa, I need for you to *hear* me right now."

"Yeah, but . . ."

"You have to leave."

We were shooed out and down to the street, where we took a silent subway ride back downtown. In the ten months since, the TV show had been scarcely mentioned again.

MR. STODDARD, SIR! Take a seat!"

Rufus had taken his usual spot in the busy Charbucks. For all the firings and "serious chats" he had hosted there, Rufus never actually made a purchase, preferring instead to pop next door to the more chi-chi Balthazar for coffee.

"Well, the fall season is nearly upon us, the smell of pencil shavings hangs thick in the air."

Rufus took great pains to appear his chipper self, though it was easy to tell from the look in his eye that he felt spurned.

"What's on your mind?" I finally said after he let loose with yet another amusing anecdote from his heady days at Brown. The nausea was back with a vengeance.

"Well, Grant. It's come to my attention that you are in talks to make a TV show with Ross Martin."

It was true. Sometime after the VH1 debacle, Ross had pitched the idea of a travelogue-style show that I would host—coincidentally—to VH1. The network had bitten and wanted to set up a meeting with me immediately. Ross—who flew in from California—his production partner, Corin, and two VH1 execs met at a hotel bar, got drunk, and talked about what the show would be.

The show was built around the following premise: Charming if slightly clueless British guy goes from coast to coast taking part in Americana that the rest of the world might find strange. A drunken, cursory brainstorming of possible segments included participating at the Lumberjack Games, becoming a rodeo clown, attending the Montana Testicle Festival, alligator wrestling, having dinner with members of the Flat Earth Society. It would be equal parts *Jackass*, Hugh Grant, and Alistair Cooke and a vastly preferable concept to dressing up in a gimp suit or inserting things into my rectum for yuks. Everyone professed to being "very excited," though I soon learned that in TV talk, one must vocalize their extreme excitement at all times. The show would be called *Granted*, the tag: "'Bloody bloke' Grant Stoddard looks at the America we take for granted." It seemed too good to be true, an eponymous TV vehicle in which I got to have adventures, be myself, and make a good chunk of change in the process.

Ross, Corin, and I then flew to a TV conference in New Orleans the next day, prompting VH1 to play their hand, and within a very short-seeming period of time, they had green-lit a pilot shooting over four days in LA in October.

I summarized the concept to my now red-faced boss.

"Let me get this straight," said Rufus. "So you try new things as an outsider and reflect upon the experience?"

"Well, in the very broadest sense, yes, that's right."

"It sounds suspiciously like the concept of your column, which, as you're no doubt aware, Nerve has the rights to."

Ross had mentioned that Rufus would be seeking "value" for Nerve as soon as he got word that we were working on something. A cornerstone of his business plan was to acquire a taste for anything vaguely related to the company he'd begun in a bedroom and then skillfully steered through the dot-com bust and into profitability. A current and slighted ex-employee working on a project that could be misconstrued to be a spin-off of Nerve's intellectual property was understandably hard for him to swallow.

"Rufus, I can assure you that it has nothing to do with the column or Nerve or anything."

I meant it. He shook his head dismissively.

"Well, to be honest, Grant, I'm disappointed," he said with a melancholy smile.

We shook hands; I returned upstairs to my desk and accidentally locked eyes with Alisa. Her eyes were red from crying. She narrowed them and shook her head at me.

I ran to the bathroom and threw up again.

That evening Nerve editor in chief Michael Martin summoned me to have dinner with him at a bar on East 5th Street. He had two large Jack and Cokes and told me that my presence was no longer required in the office but that he persuaded Rufus to allow me to continue contributing my column, which had become a fan favorite under Michael's watch.

"Rufus is hardly gnashing his teeth with glee at the arrangement, but I convinced him that it made sense," he said. "You need to come by and clear your desk tomorrow."

Though I'd always envied people who wrote from home on their own schedule, I was sorry that my transition to a freelancer was less than smooth or deliberate.

I came by the office around lunchtime, when I was fairly certain that Rufus and Alisa would be finding value for Nerve over some oysters at Balthazar. This was the first time in my life I'd been told to clear my desk. I found two cardboard boxes and filled them with most of the following items:

1. Penis-extender weight kit with instructional video
2. Liberator Shapes, foam sex platforms
3. Peppermint-flavor "ass-tringent"
4. Enzyte male enhancement pills
5. Condomania assortment pack
6. Passport
7. Viagra sample pack
8. Immigration paperwork
9. TongueJoy, tongue-mounted vibrator and attachments
10. New Sex, guide to female ejaculation DVD
11. Aneros prostate massager
12. No More Mr. Nice Guy: A Proven Plan for Getting What You Want in Love, Sex and Life, hardcover

13. CB2000 male chastity harness
14. 2001 and 2002 tax documents
15. Thirty-nine condoms from online herpes dating community (HDate.com)
16. *American Bukkake 12*, DVD
17. Credit card application forms
18. *Knee Pad Nymphos #2*, DVD
19. One gram of low-grade cocaine
20. Self-hypnosis cassette and instructional booklet
21. Assorted jelly cock rings
22. First Impressions dating consultants' questionnaire
23. Payment-past-due notices from immigration attorney James O'Malley and Associates
24. *How to Succeed with Women*, paperback
25. Seven issues of *Adult Video News*
26. The Accommodator, chin-mounted latex dong
27. Sweet Release semen-flavoring supplement (crisp apple)
28. Tend Skin, ingrown hair/razor bump formula
29. International money-wire transfer application forms
30. Kama Sutra–brand assorted flavor massage oils
31. Kama Sutra–brand "honey dust"
32. Edible underwear (women's)
33. *Satisfaction: The Art of the Female Orgasm*, hardcover
34. Vigel topical female sex-enhancing cream
35. Make Your Own Dildo molding kit

Brian helped me down to the street and put me and my sleazy paraphernalia in a cab.

"Hey, I'm going to Laure and Louise's apartment tonight," he said over the din of a passing fire truck's siren. "You should come, it'll cheer you up." It sounded like Brian needed me to play wingman again and I wasn't in the mood.

"No, it's okay," I said, "I still haven't recovered from the other night."

The next day, Brian called to tell me that I had remotely cock-blocked him. Apparently, he had arrived at their loft to find both girls dressed to the nines and a miffed Louise asking why *he* had turned up and *I* hadn't. The three of them drank wine on the fire escape until Laure took Brian by the hand and led him into her bedroom. Things were beginning to escalate when Louise, in hysterical tears, began thumping on the door, exclaiming, "*Laure, tu est une put!*" before collapsing into a sobbing heap on the floor, putting an understandable dampener on the evening. Brian was shown the door. Being more confident and easygoing, Laure's attentions had been courted more ferociously over the summer and Louise was seemingly at a breaking point. A similar dynamic existed between Brian and myself.

"So next time, if she hasn't already written you off as a complete faggot, you *have* to come with me, okay?"

And so began a short series of double dates during which I did little to prove that I wasn't a *pede*.

Even though she was merely a teen, Louise intimidated me greatly, what with her Galois and ennui. To her annoyance I had not yet tried to kiss her, though I very much wanted to.

"Why do you not smoke, little Grant?" she said over sake at Decibel. "Are you afraid, afraid you will get sick, that you will catch the . . . cancer?"

"Well, that's one reason, yeah," I said.

"Well, I 'ave news for you, little Grant." She blew a huge plume of smoke into my face. "We are all going to die."

For all of her world-weary Parisian posturing, Louise would privately tell me that she loved my English accent when I spoke my smattering of remedial French. She said it drove her "mad completely."

Louise complained to Laure, who complained to Brian, who complained to me that no one was getting what they wanted and it was all my fault.

"Just fucking lay one on her, you pussy," said Brian.

Louise was so French and young and stylish and cute that I had a hard time believing that she'd be into playing tonsil hockey with the likes of me. Brian was putting a lot more effort into trying to pair us up than I was.

"He has got a TV show, y'know," he said to Louise as we picnicked on top of their roof. She looked at me in disbelief, shrugged, and looked back up at the stars and enjoyed a huge drag off her cigarette. The three of them had all but lost their patience with me.

The levee finally broke when we asked the girls to a Cake party that we'd been invited to through Nerve. Cake parties were occasions where a predominately hot and female crowd all got into their skivvies or less and fooled around on the bar. Brian and I had been friends with its founders since we lap-danced for three hundred handsy women at a Cake party for an "I Did It for Science" installment.

Among the gyrating naked bodies, the hard-core porn playing on a big-screen TV, and with me dressed only in my underoos, I finally plucked up the courage to make out with Louise and wrapped her tight young body up in my arms. I didn't even mind the cigarette taste on her tongue, something I'm usually extremely squeamish of. In fact, I quite enjoyed it.

"Thank fucking Christ!" I could hear Brian scream over the music.

After one more drink, we found our clothes and made our way outside. Brian optimistically hailed two cabs and gave me a wink.

"I think I am going to hang out with Grant," said Louise.

"Ah! *Qui est la put, Louise?*" said Laure. She cocked an eyebrow and folded her arms in callous satisfaction.

Without a word, Louise kissed me on the cheek and dutifully got into the cab with Laure, who was still smug with her perfectly timed retort, and drove away.

"What the fuck happened there?" asked Brian.

It soon became clear that the girls were waging a war of attrition against each other and that thanks in part to my prolonged hesitation, we were in the cross fire. We went on two more double dates before Brian lost interest and stopped calling Laure. When she wasn't not putting out, Laure had gotten existential with Brian about their stilted dating.

"Really, Brian, you live 'ere in New York, my 'ome is in Paris. We are some friendly . . . 'ow you say . . . strangers? You want to make love wiv me but really"—Laure took a long drag on her cigarette and exhaled—"what eez the point?"

This coincided with Brian lining up a sure thing elsewhere who wasn't such a total pain in the ass. Conversely, I redoubled my efforts to fool around with Louise. I felt that after the drinks, the dinners, the repeatedly being called a faggot, I needed to close the deal: I wanted to get some value.

The girls were leaving for Paris in a week. Over our next three dates, I took Louise to bars in concentric circles around my apartment, but before the end of the night Laure would suddenly materialize, despite neither of the girls having a cell phone and me keeping our various destinations shrouded in secrecy. On their penultimate night in town, Laure actually arrived as Louise stood on my stoop deliberating on whether to risk spending the night.

"Tomorrow is our last night, little Grant," she said as Laure herded her into a waiting cab. "Maybe I will stay at your 'ome."

The Bordeaux company was throwing the summer interns a good-bye party in the basement of Puck Fair, an Irish pub on Lafayette and Houston. For someone who was now effectively jobless, I had already spent hundreds of dollars on entertaining Louise and her contrary chaperone, so I arrived three hours after the party started, at around eleven thirty.

"Little Grant!" yelled Louise from across the room. Even though her teeth were stained gray from the wine, she looked cuter than ever. "I am so glad that you came 'ere!"

Previously, we had only kissed at the end of our dates, but Louise grabbed my face with both hands and darted her boozy, ashy tongue into my mouth. Laure was furiously making out with an orange-haired though not terribly unattractive Dubliner in the corner, which bode well for me finally wrapping up this stop-start summer fling.

"What do you want to drink?" I asked as she eagerly stroked my leg.

"I will 'ave a apple martini," said Laure, who had briefly pulled her tongue out of ginger nut's mouth.

"Ahh, me also!" said the intended recipient of the offer.

The design of the martini glass is the stuff of nightmares for me. Delivering two filled-to-the-brim martini glasses across a rowdy Irish bar filled me with trepidation. One needs the steady hand of a gun-slinger to get them safely to the table without incident. An attribute I apparently do not possess.

"'N' just what da feck d'ya tink ure doon, noi?" said a fat woman with an underbite and an almost indecipherable Belfast accent. While hoisting the drinks over the Ulster bruiser's frame, I'd received a knock and spilt a little from each glass onto her ill-fitting tank top and my ice-blue dress shirt.

"I'm really sorry," I said.

"Well, sorry in't gonna dry off me feckin' tits noi, is it, ya wee bender."

Louise was waving me over from across the bar. It had taken ten minutes to get the drinks, and it looked like I was about to be beaten by this flabby and angry creature.

"Well, okay, the next one's on me," I said and told the barkeep to put the next one on my tab.

"Dat's a bit more feckin' like it, short-arse."

A round of shots arrived at the table followed by another and another. Though she'd had a three-hour head start on me, I seemed to be a lot worse for wear than Louise, who was slurring in neither French nor English.

After several drinks and hours watching Laure molest the poor plumber's apprentice, Louise looked at me and squeezed my hand.

"Grant, tonight I fink it is time that I will sleep at your 'ouse."

It was three a.m.

I quickly collected my credit card to find that the chubby bruiser and her mates had two rounds at my expense, bringing my tab to over $140.

"Oi! I said *one* drink!" I yelled at the barkeep.

"Sarry, pal, but dats not what you tol' me, so pay up and piss ahf."

Louise was excitedly tugging at my hand, so I reluctantly signed the receipt, gave him a lousy tip, and wrote *Wanker!* at the bottom.

Hand in hand, we walked back to my place on 14th and C. I was out of cash until I got my final Nerve paycheck on the first of the month and couldn't afford a taxi.

"My feet 'urt," complained Louise, who was now wildly wobbling in her heels.

"Nearly there," I lied. We were still a mile away. It was one of those nights when the temperature had seemed to actually increase with the setting sun. The metal shutters, the pavement, the sidewalk were all radiating the day's heat back at us. The smell of hot garbage seemed to stick to one's hair, clothes, and skin. I was conscious of the patches under my arms. Louise just looked dewy and fresh.

As we walked up the stairs in the flickering fluorescent light of my building, I realized just how drunk I'd become. Since meeting Louise to now, I'd drunk more than I had in the previous six months, and I suddenly seemed to be feeling the cumulative effect of all that booze. As I struggled to put the key in my front door, I realized that I was definitely too drunk to perform.

We entered my place and were hit in the face by the smell of cooking bacon. The apartment is above Jack's Deli, which exists to cater to the hard-hatted workers from the power plant. They begin frying up at around a quarter to four. I usually relish the strong aroma, but it generally isn't conducive to seduction. I turned on both of the huge air conditioners I'd been gifted.

"It'll be cool in here in a minute," I promised. As Louise looked through my book collection and the posters that hung on my walls, I caught sight of the boxes of Nerve flotsam that I'd taken from my desk. Since meeting Louise, I had played down the fact that I was a sex columnist, an illusion that would be instantly shattered if she caught sight of two giant boxes full of dildos and condoms with the word "herpes" written on them.

"May I 'ave a drink of water?" she said as I casually kicked them under the bed.

"Yeah, in the fridge," I called from my bedroom.

"Ah, Grant, you 'ave a bottle of pinot grigio 'ere. May we open it?"

"Mais oui, we may!" I said. No reaction. As a reflection of how drunk I'd become I considered that fucking brilliant.

Though I did have a chilled bottle of white wine in my fridge, I didn't have one of those easy openers with the arms that you push down.

"'Ere eez a corkscrew," said Louise, finding a rusty and ancient-looking little pig's tail in the silverware drawer and handing me the bottle.

"I must go to the bafroom to . . . freshen up."

My toilet is in a separate little room that is located out of my apartment and down the hall. Though it is for my use only, it is *technically* an outhouse. I have to explain this to guests and hand them a key to the padlock that keeps my WC shut. As it only houses a crapper, there is no pretense of one going in there to freshen up. If anything, the opposite is true. I found it sort of funny that Louise would use the very American euphemism of "freshening up" with me. As fellow Europeans, Louise and I ought to have been above that puritan nonsense. Also, because there is no sink in there, I am well aware if a person does not wash his or her hands after visiting the toilet room. My bathtub and bathroom sink are located in my kitchen.

"Okay," I said. I explained the drill and gave her the key.

I started to fathom how an old-school corkscrew worked when I remembered that one of my boxes contained one 100-milligram dose of Viagra.

Two columns ago, I had reported the experiences of having sex under the influence of five different drugs: cocaine, ecstasy, mushrooms, weed, and Viagra. I still had some coke and Viagra left over!

I ran into the bedroom and started rifling to find the smallest item in the box, eventually found it, and put the whole 100-milligram pill in my mouth. In my experiment I had only taken a 25-milligram dose, which resulted in a prizewinning erection that I terrorized my then-girlfriend with, an afternoon she rues to this day. I was totally sober then and figured that I probably needed an increased dose to combat the effects of the alcohol now. I also found the coke in a bullet-sized dispenser. I ran back to the kitchen and swallowed the large pill with some water, took two large bumps, and got to work on opening the wine and promptly broke the cork in half just as Louise walked through the door.

"What 'ave you done?"

Not being able to open a bottle of wine is embarrassing under any circumstances, but in front of a French girl it was completely emasculating. I jabbed at the remaining half of the cork with a stainless steel chopstick but it didn't budge.

"Ah, poor little Grant, 'oo cannot even open a bottle of wine."

Louise sat down on the corner of my bed, choosing not to wash her hands.

"How about a line?" I said, poking my head around the door after finally giving up with the wine.

"What?"

"Would you like a little coke?"

I rarely indulged, but offering it made me feel and sound like Scarface. I didn't even really want any more but I somehow had to run down the clock while I waited for the sildenafil citrate to inhibit cGMP specific phosphodiesterase type 5 (PDE5), which is responsible for degradation of cGMP in the corpus cavernosum. The molecular structure of sildenafil is similar to that of cGMP and acts as a competitive binding agent of cGMP in the corpus cavernosum. Now given that I'd taken four times the amount that had given me a thumper for the better part of a weekend, I was fairly confident that I could overcome my case of brewer's droop. All I needed was just a little more time.

I figured I'd put the blow on a CD case and make a really big deal about meticulously chopping it up, which I could drag out for five or ten minutes.

"Pffff! I absolutely fink no."

She looked horrified. Louise's body language shifted from languid and suggestive to closed and distant. I was trying to push narcotics on a teen and it had inexplicably backfired.

"No, me neither," I said. "My friend had some and I'm . . . holding it for him. I just didn't know if you . . ."

"Grant, please, I would like it for us to go to bed."

Though I already had the thumping headache, I felt sure I needed to give the Viagra more time to work its magic.

"Let's watch some television!" I said and pulled her through my railroad apartment to the living room. It was four a.m., and there only seemed to be infomercials on.

"'Oo eez dis man wiv 'is chickens?" she said after watching a studio audience get jazzed by a rotisserie oven.

"That's Ron Popeil," I said. "He is a famous American inventor."

She looked at me, apparently unsatisfied with my reasons for making her watch late-night infomercials after a three-and-a-half-week campaign to get her back to my place.

"Set it and forget it!" I said at an inappropriate volume that made Louise recoil.

"Well, zis eez very strange to me, and I am very ty-aired. I must get up and pack tomorrow and . . . your face! It eez very red. Are you okay?"

The headache, the red face. I had documented the chain of events in my experiment. I knew that I only needed to kill around ten more minutes before I'd have a chemically enhanced erection that would be the talk of the Champs-Elysées.

I got the drip, and couldn't help fidgeting with my nostrils.

"The roof!" I said. "I need some fresh air. It's beautiful up there."

I grabbed Louise and pulled her up four flights of rickety stairs to the roof. The Chinese families who lived on the top floor of the building often slept on the roof in the summer months, in lieu of having a way to keep cool at night, though thankfully there was no one up there. The heat had melted the tar on the roof, making the surface like a giant piece of flypaper. Great gobs of it were stuck to Louise's shoes as I led her across the roof to admire the view.

"That's Stuyvesant Town," I said, suddenly realizing how underwhelming the view must have been to her. "If you strain your neck and look between the two buildings in front of us, you can see the glow of the Empire State Building . . . but they turn off the lights at midnight."

"I see."

"And that's the famous East River; the historical borough of Queens is on the other side. That's where the airport is. Next to us is the ConEd power plant, can you hear it buzzing? And those buildings are Alphabet City projects. A hundred years ago this neighborhood was called *Kleine Deutschland* and was full of Germans. *Allgemeine!* I expect you could have seen the World Trade Center from here, but I didn't live here then so don't quote me on that. Below us is Fourteenth Street, which is mostly just dollar stores and fried chicken joints. So . . ."

Silence.

"And maybe a Rite Aid."

"It would 'ave been nice to 'ave that wine up 'ere."

Silence.

Louise suddenly looked sort of bluish, which indicated that the Viagra was working. I excitedly made out with my Gallic smurf and painfully knocked teeth with her twice. With my hands exploring her tight rear, I sprang an instantaneous erection and pushed it into her taut midsection.

"Let's go to bed," I said triumphantly and led her down the stairs, leaving two sets of tarry footprints that led into my now chilly apartment.

In what is a break from tradition, I undressed the girl first before shedding my own clothes. Her breasts were small and perfect, her skin white and even, the musculature of her abdomen discernable by accident rather than design, her bulbous little bottom caressed in surprisingly sensible white cotton underwear. We kissed and she tinkered with my fly for what seemed like ages before I yanked my pants off myself. My erection threatened to poke a hole through my underpants as I lowered her onto my bed and slid my hand into hers. She stopped me.

"Grant," she said hesitantly, "tonight, I fink I just want you to 'ug me."

"Huh," I said and cupped her left breast.

"I just want you to, to 'old me, before I leave for Paris."

"Yeah," I said and spooned her, sliding my inhumanly turgid penis between the gap in her thighs. She jerked away from it, as if it had burned her. She made me set my alarm for 8:00. Her flight was at 12:45, but she needed to get down to Canal Street and pack.

"Here, lie on my chest," I said.

We shifted positions.

Everything was blue now, and with my hand I could feel the raised veins on my forehead popping out. My penis tented the comforter. I stroked Louise's hair and lovingly kissed her dainty little fingers before curling them around my penis. She'd have to be impressed, I thought.

"Grant, no, I must sleep."

It was getting light outside.

"Sleep on the plane, baby."

Louise turned her back to me.

"Good night, Grant," she said. "Cute English boy."

The strange mix of chemicals racing around my body made sleep impossible. I spent the next three hours looking at the back of Louise's head and the erection that would not back down. I reset the alarm for 7:30 in the hopes that Louise would want to fool around upon waking. I listened to the thunder in the distance come closer, until it seemed that the clouds had settled on my roof. It was the loudest thunder I'd ever heard but Louise didn't stir. I must have finally gotten to sleep minutes before she woke up.

"Shit!" she said, maniacally buzzing around my room foraging for clothing. The clock said 9:41.

"Laure is going to kill me! What 'appened to the alarm?"

"I don't know," I croaked.

My head was spinning and my erection showed no signs of remittance.

I put on some pajama pants and walked her downstairs.

"Taxi!" She was already out in the road, arm extended.

The rain was still torrential and it was chilly outside. A cab pulled up and she held the door open as she kissed me on the cheek. I gave her a business card with my now-defunct e-mail address and phone number.

"I will write to you!" she promised and playfully batted my hitherto ignored member with her hand.

"I will write to you too!"

She sped off without waving.

I walked back upstairs, toweled off, and awoke at about the same time as her plane was due to leave. A monster hangover, the unsatisfying conclusion to a summer fling, no longer receiving a regular paycheck, and the Viagra Web site's insistence that I seek urgent medical attention all ganged up on me at once and I suddenly felt lousier than I had in my whole life. The rain pelted against my cracked windowpanes and rattled on the tops of the air conditioners as I considered making the walk to the ER at Beth Israel, under an umbrella and half a pace behind an angry erection.

Summer had ended.

THE TALENT

THE LIMO THAT PICKED ME UP from Long Beach Airport was chock-full of candies, snacks, and bottles of mineral water. I'd been in a limo once before, during a bachelor-party-style weekend in Montreal in November 2002. That one was stretched, white, full of liquor, and the transport that delivered us to more restaurants, bars, "full-contact" strip clubs, peep shows, diners, and roadhouse brothels than I care to remember. It glowed purple underneath and I'm sure we were deservedly referred to as assholes dozens of times.

This limo was black, modestly unstretched, and had a courteous uniformed driver by the name of Terry.

"You movin' out here, bro?" he said.

"Well, maybe. I'm shooting a pilot, and if all goes well, then . . . y'know?"

I'd been to Southern California once before and hated it. But then my trip was just thirty hours long, and the lion's share of it was spent on the set of a porno movie. That trip was Ross's doing too. This stay would be for several weeks, most of it spent in preproduction for the pilot of *Granted* and then a four-day shoot. And if we went to series . . . who knows?

"Shit, if you like warm weather and beautiful babes, you ain't gonna leave in a hurry," said Terry.

While I certainly *was* a fan of beautiful babes, I also rather liked the seasons, but I chose not to get into that with Terry, as he might reckon me a fairy, and he seemed to be on a roll.

"And if you are gonna be on TV, man, I tell ya, you'll be gettin' so much freakin' pussy you'll have to beat it off with a stick. But hey, that's Hollywood for ya. Where you comin' from?"

"New York."

"New York Ci-tay," he said under his breath. "I always wanted to go there."

I arrived at Ross and Jordana's home near North Hollywood around nine to find Ross waiting in the driveway. It was great to see him again. When he left Nerve, he promised that he and I would work together again soon, and true to his word, here we were. The house was a charming one-level, three-bedroom with a good-sized swimming pool and a two-car garage that Jordana used as her painting studio. I walked in and set my bags down.

"Welcome to Valley Village, California!" Jordana said and gave me a big, good-feeling hug. Their son, Dashiell, had just turned one and was already asleep, but we crept into his room to take a peek. He was beautiful and I told them so.

"Wait 'til you see his penis," whispered Ross. "It's massive."

We ordered Chinese food, caught up, and I was overcome with the realization that, TV show or not, I was completely starting over, in a new place, with new people, with a new job, and within a very short period of time had a whole new ready-to-wear life in the sunshine. A few days before I got on the plane, I sublet my apartment to a Texan debutante via Craigslist for almost double what I paid. I saw some friends, tied up some loose ends, and didn't even stop to think about how efficiently I seemed to have packed up and moved on.

This was all brought sharply into focus the next morning when I got a phone call from my ex-girlfriend Sophie. I had begun breaking up with her on Memorial Day, and by late August she had sort of gotten the message, though not before she broke into my apartment and stood over me as I slept.

"Hello?"

"I've been doing some thinking and I think that we should go out again."

"Now? Christ, it's six thirty a.m.," I said.

"No, it's not, it's nine thirty," she replied.

She hadn't heard that I'd moved, but then I didn't have much time to tell anyone.

"I'm in California."

"What are you doing *there*?"

"I'm making a TV show. I sort of . . . *live* here now."

She began to cry then hung up. We had spoken less than three weeks ago, when the TV show was merely a pipe dream.

Now that I was up, I decided to figure out how to use a cafetière and make some coffee.

"This is Dashiell!" Ross was already up and brought Dash into the kitchen so we could meet properly. He was still wiping the sleep from his eyes but already starting to giggle as I shook his little hand.

"Want to go hiking in the canyon with us?" asked Ross.

To my untrained ear "hiking in the canyon" sounded like a formidable physical challenge.

"Um, I don't have any . . . equipment," I said. I was thinking boots, pickax, guide ropes.

"You'll be fine in a sweater, jeans, and sneakers," he said.

It seems that in Los Angeles, hiking in a canyon actually means taking a relatively brisk walk up a hill and down again, and the use of the term sort of made me chuckle. Had Ross assimilated to being a West Coaster in just a year? In any case, as I'd landed in darkness, it was useful to look at my new surroundings from some high ground. In Los Angeles you can't fool yourself into thinking that you live in an entirely man-made place, like you can in Manhattan. You can use natural topography to get your bearings, as opposed to bridges and sky-scrapers.

"Hollywood is on the other side of these hills," said Ross as we reached a point with a view of the San Fernando Valley. At eight a.m. the air was clean, cool, and fresh, though I could feel the temperature rising by the minute.

It's strange to think about how I'd first surveyed Manhattan from the observation deck of the World Trade Center, thinking about whether I could ever call the city home, whether I would soon be navigating its arteries instinctually. And it's funny to think about how I first perceived the city at street level. Becky had parked in Hoboken and we took the Path train in, eventually emerging on leafy 9th Street and Sixth Avenue before walking east through Washington Square, past NYU and onto Broadway as an armada of yellow cabs flew by the Tower Records store at East 4th Street. I got a hot dog from a street vendor and was overcome yet fully satisfied with the New Yorkness of it all. This view, even from the "wrong side" of the Hollywood Hills, was impressive in a sort of serene way, but I wondered if it was a place I'd ever think of as home.

We deposited Dash back at home and crawled to Santa Monica for the first day of preproduction. A portion of a floor at VH1's Santa Monica offices had been devoted to *Granted*. The name of the show was affixed to each of the brightly colored pens, and the wallpaper and screensavers for each of the dozen computers in the *Granted* zone were ridiculous life-sized snapshots of my mug. The ten-person production team had been assembled and I moved along a line of them like the queen at an important movie premiere.

"Everyone, this is the notorious Grant Stoddard," announced Ross to my embarrassment. "He's our talent."

"Please don't call me that again," I said to Ross when I got him alone for a second. The total cost of the pilot was heading for the better part of a hundred grand, and from my interactions with the production team, it was becoming clear that no one knew that my experience "on camera" was limited to a few home videos. Being constantly referred to as "the talent," given that I was completely unproven, seemed sarcastic and served only to heighten my anxiety.

Just getting to this point had been an adventure in and of itself. Despite my assurances that *Granted* the TV show had nothing whatsoever to do with the "I Did It for Science" column or its hypothetical TV spin-off, Rufus threatened litigation on intellectual property grounds and through his old boy network could make sure his saber rattling could be well heard. In the pre-pilot stage even the mere whiff of legal hurdles could quash our TV show with Viacom, and with that in mind the VH1 people put pressure on Ross to capitulate with Rufus's demands just to keep the project alive. Rufus's first preposterous set of conditions included naming the show *I Did It for Science* or having some Nerve cobranding in the title of the show. Caught between a rock and a hard place, Ross eventually agreed to give a percentage of the show's prospective profits and to add wording in the end credits reflecting Nerve's involvement in the development of the "Grant Stoddard character."

This led me to wonder if my character had in actuality been developed by Nerve. It was certainly true that my suddenly being obligated to participate in bizarre sexual activity had certainly broadened my outlook on sex, people, and life in general. It was also fair to say that the company had given me an amazing opportunity to start and build upon a career in writing that would never have presented itself otherwise. It was assured that Nerve had gotten me laid, a *lot*. Surely, if it wasn't for Nerve, I wouldn't have had the opportunity to make an eponymous TV show. But the assertion that Rufus Griscom and Nerve somehow fashioned my persona from scratch was completely inaccurate. Rufus's percentages weren't even coming out of my share, but out of Ross's.

Rufus was ruthless in the pursuit of value, and we felt as though we were being shaken down in spectacular fashion.

Everyone at VH1 had been urged to bone up on my writing and the regular appearances I'd made on friends' photo blogs and had become intimately familiar with some of my more intimate moments. I had a dozen insta-friends, who already knew a good deal about me. This felt extremely odd but appealed to my ego.

Most days were brainstorming sessions in which we hashed out the segments we would try to include in the pilot. Logistical and financial constraints meant that all the segments would be shot in LA, though I'd envisioned the real contrast of the show to be the relationship between myself and subject matter more readily found in the interior of the country.

With that being the case, we quickly tailored the pilot episode to our surroundings. One of my ideas was for me to emcee a karaoke night for washed-up celebrities. The execs in New York said they were "psyched" about the idea and we started creating a list of who these possible D-listers could be. The following day, the execs called to say that they continued to be psyched about the idea but especially loved the thought of me singing karaoke dressed as a woman and that this segment should be "tweaked slightly" to that end. They'd read the "I Did It for Science" column in which I'd dressed up as a woman and incidentally found it "rilly, rilly funny," funny enough to try to shoehorn into a show about wacky Americana.

And so began a pattern in which the execs seemed to latch on to a tiny and inconsequential part of each idea and run it off on some tangent that somehow made perfect sense to them. In 2005 VH1 launched a show called *So You Think You Can Sing?* in which minor celebrities sang karaoke songs.

Back in New York, Michael Martin was throwing all sorts of freelance gigs my way so that I wouldn't see that much of a drop-off in my income. In among putting the pilot together, I also had to interview Ricky Gervais, then a complete unknown in America, and orchestrate and participate in a threesome with a girl and another guy for my "I Did It for Science" column, despite knowing nary a soul west of Weehawken. Some magazine work for *Glamour* and *BlackBook* was also sent my way, and I would regularly sit Dashiell for an hour or two. Despite having so much to do, I felt that time moved slower out here and I could get to work in earnest.

Ross, Jordana, Dashiell, and I lived together as a nuclear family, though I could never really figure out if I was the funny uncle, roguish bachelor, guest of honor, eldest son, or babysitter. But, I was certainly made to feel integral to their home, despite my klutziness increasing exponentially. In my first week I blocked the toilet in the guest bathroom, damaged the upholstery in Ross's car, shattered the porcelain faucet handle in their shower, put dish detergent in the dishwasher that filled the kitchen knee-high in suds, and woke everyone in the house by having the two other participants of my threesome jump in the pool to pee at three in the morning due to the aforementioned blocked toilet in the guest bathroom. Jordana classified these extremely embarrassing episodes as (Gr)antics.

In addition to the preproduction of *Granted*, Ross was also taking meetings for a handful of other projects. I was only needed at the VH1 offices for a few hours each day, though Ross left the house before nine and often didn't return until the wee hours of the morning. This left Jordana, Dash, and me together most nights.

As we drew closer to the shooting date, the show began to shift tone and form to the point that it was quite a different project from the action-packed anthropological travelogue I'd initially envisioned. The concept had shifted much more toward the slapstick, pratfall end of the spectrum in which I would be a roving Mr. Bean–type character. I felt that we'd lost control of the project entirely, but Ross assured me that the execs were doing exactly what they needed to do in order for the show to go to series and, once green-lit, we would get to steer it back.

The five segments we eventually settled on were:

1. Me and a group of friends going to restaurants and seeing what we could get for free by telling them that it was our birthday.

2. Me hanging out at a truck stop and offering truckers tea and scones as part of something called "Trucker Appreciation Day."
3. Me participating in a staged audition for a fake reality TV show.
4. Me dressing in drag and singing at a karaoke bar.
5. Me training with high school cheerleaders then taking them around Los Angeles to spread cheer among its citizens.

According to the call sheet, at all times I would be surrounded by a minimum of fifteen people. Ross and Corin Nelson, associate producer Jen Ehrman, assistant producers Brian Wahlund and Cherry Jimenez, my seventeen-year-old PA, Andrew Karlsruher, production manager Jennifer Dugan, makeup artist Lucy Fleetwood, VH1 execs Rob Weiss and eight-months-pregnant Lauren Gellert, who had flown out from New York for the shoot. Then there was the four-man camera crew, headed up by a guy named Christian, along with his men Brett, War-Dog, and a terribly nice chap who was referred to only as the Donger. This entourage was then expanded with the introduction of fifteen teenage cheerleaders, a handful of gnarled truckers, a slew of singles at a karaoke bar, a group of instant best friends, and over a hundred reality TV star wannabes, waving their eight-by-tens around and trying to appear zany and unpredictable.

In the few days prior to their departure, Lauren and Rob were constantly having conference calls with Ross and Jen Ehrman tweaking, finessing, massaging, and frequently leaving us all wondering if they were high on drugs.

"What I'm about to say comes from a place of love. . . ."

Rob would always preface another step away from our original concept and toward unrestrained physical comedy.

Despite being Ross's production partner on this project, Corin Nelson had been absent throughout the weeks of preproduction due to her recent appointment as the executive producer of the ill-fated *Sharon*

Osbourne Show. Ad hoc ideas flew out of her mouth as quickly as she'd conceived them. If an idea was well received she'd continue to flesh it out on the fly; if it sunk it was immediately discarded, never to be thought about again.

Corin was constantly fluffing my ego and stoking my imagination.

"America is going to want to fuck you," she'd tell me on a daily basis. "You're going to have your pick. I hope you're ready for what's about to fucking happen for you."

The first day of shooting was at the Viacom offices in Santa Monica. The premise of the segment was that with reality-based programming being so pervasive, auditioning for reality TV shows had become an American way of life. Concept-wise, it was sort of a stretch, but the idea was a firm favorite of the execs in New York.

In just a few hours, six hundred people had answered an ad Brian Wahlund had posted on Craigslist. The post was an open casting call for a new reality series that MTV was producing and it instructed applicants to send a picture and brief bio.

The idea was that from the moment the hopefuls arrived, they would be pumped up to believe that this particular project would be the biggest thing MTV had ever produced and would make the single successful applicant a household name the world over. A series of cuts would be made and the final six applicants would each be given ten seconds to prove why they should be the successful applicant.

Around a hundred people were shoved into a large greenroom. For many, this was just one stop on a day full of open auditions. I recognized a few faces from back home in the East Village, but my concocted back story was that I'd just moved to LA from merry old England, so I couldn't say anything. Jen Ehrman, Cherry, and Andrew ran around the greenroom taking down particulars of the candidates, and we pretended not to know each other. One hundred was cut to forty, which was cut to twelve, then left only six applicants, the sixth being me.

There was Dave, a clean-cut-looking porn impresario from Orange County; Ebony, a pretty young actress; Dan, a peroxide-blond pretty boy who managed to be both fratty and fey; Tiffany, a rail-thin Tara Reid–esque party girl; and Beth, a nondescript shy girl.

As the girls all hugged and kissed each other good luck, we were led from the greenroom to a windowless audition room, where Ross asked each of us to behave in strange ways: act like a chicken, be a tree, pretend to be a mugger, and so on, then all interact with each other. With international fame seemingly within reach, everyone took to their assigned roles with conviction. And after two minutes Ross calmed everyone down.

"Okay," he said. "The head of the network is watching this on a live feed elsewhere in this building. You each have fifteen seconds to look into the camera and explain why you should be the sole subject of MTV's most revolutionary programming to date."

In truth, Rob and Lauren *were* watching on a live feed.

Ross pointed at Dave.

"Go!"

Dave leapt forward.

"Hey! My name's Dave, I got no tattoos, I don't smoke, drink, or do drugs; I'm the boy next door. Your friggin' next-door neighbor is doing porn, bro. Whad'ya think about that?"

"*Cut!*" said Ross. "Beth."

"Let's see. I'm Beth. Um . . . people like me. I'm fun and personable. Good to be around . . . and . . . um."

"*Cut!* Ebony."

"Hey, my name is Ebony. I'm a strong, sentient being who is both pishon . . . wait. . . . I am passionate and iticolade . . . sorry, articulate um . . . and . . ."

"*Cut!* Dan!"

"'Sup, MTV?" Dan suddenly picked up a hitherto undetectable blaccent. "My tag's Dan and da question you gots ta acks yo'self is can you people handle *this*?"

Dan shucked himself out of his tight white T-shirt and flexed his gym-rat body. Ross sadistically let Dan silently flex for about twenty long seconds, leaving him to rack his tiny brain to fill the dead air.

But instead there was the most sphincter-clenching awkward silence as Dan's eyes shot around the room, begging for Ross to yell cut.

"Yeah, baby!" he finally said after half a minute had elapsed.

He kissed his bicep.

"It's a gun show!"

"Okay, that was real nice, Dan, thanks and . . . cut."

Embarrassed, Dan shuffled back to his place on the line.

"Okay." Ross cleared his throat, looked up at me, and skillfully stifled a grin. "Is it Grant or Graham?"

"It's Grant."

"Australian?"

Ross knew that being erroneously pegged as an Aussie was intensely annoying to me. We both stifled a smirk.

"English."

"Okay, Grant, show us what you got."

Jen Ehrman, Ross, Brian Wahlund, Christian, Brett, War-Dog, and the Donger all knew what was about to happen, but did remarkably well to conceal their anticipation.

I could just imagine Rob and Lauren in the adjacent room leaning in closer to the monitor that was showing the live feed.

Ross had told me that this would all be about the reaction of the five other finalists, something we wouldn't be able to easily reproduce, so I'd have to get it right the first time. I wasn't thrilled with the segment, but in theory the reveal was really funny, if a little base.

I began marching on the spot with my elbows and knees locked straight.

"My name is Grant Stoddard,

"I walk about the town,

"Sometimes with my trousers up and sometimes with them *down*!"

On the word "down" I bent over, grabbed the fronts of my tear-away pants, and yanked them off in one deft motion, revealing my naked lower half, save the knotted tube sock I'd tucked my penis and testicles into.

My unwitting costars' jaws dropped as I heard four loud gasps behind me. Their eyes were flitting between Ross and my bare behind.

"Oh yeah, oh yeah!" I said, transforming the march into a cancan, then a rough approximation of Riverdance, while yelling, "Pick me, pick me, pick me!" the stuffed sock flying hither and dither.

"Cut!" yelled Ross, holding back laughter. "Okay, well, Grant seems to have upped the ante, but I'm feeling nice, so does anyone want to take another shot at this?"

They didn't.

"I think he just shut down the audition," said Ebony.

I had.

The next morning we awoke at five thirty to be at a Burbank Catholic school at sunup.

I had been outfitted in a tight tracksuit top, running shoes, over-the-knee tube socks, Bjorn Borg–style sweatbands, and a pair of skin-tight, lime green, terry-cloth booty shorts that left absolutely nothing to the imagination. Minutes before the shoot began, a meeting was called in the school parking lot to discuss whether parading my clearly visible package around in front of fifteen eighth-grade girls was grounds for a lawsuit. Though Rob spent an inordinate amount of time assessing my situation, he decided that I should probably wear underpants, but even when not "commando" I looked as though I was smuggling five servings of fruit about my loins. It seemed that the comedy premise of the show was entirely genital in nature.

The segment started with me running out of a wooded area, vaulting over a creek and into the throng of the ponytailed adolescents.

"Hello, ladies!" I yelled as I sprinted toward them.

"Hi, Grant!" they yelled back in well-rehearsed unison.

"Girls," said one of the two impossibly glammed-up coaches, "let's show Grant what we've been working on for him."

The girls snapped into formation. A crowd of bemused early-morning onlookers began to assemble on one side of the field.

"Ready? Okay!" they all shouted.

The girls then proceeded to spell out my name with their pom-poms, yelling each letter in time.

"G, G, G, G, R, R, R, R, A, A, A, A, N, N, N, N, T, T, T, T, what does it spell? GRANT! Whooooo!"

The girls put me through my paces, eventually hoisting me up on their dainty shoulders to be the zenith of a pyramid and helped me dismount without injury.

"I'd like to get me some a that!" said one sassy and buxom Lolita to her friend while pointing at my crotch.

Ross and Corin were being fed lines by Rob and Lauren for me to say, finally decimating my concept of a documentary-style travelogue. The situations were now quite skitlike.

"Honey," said Corin, running over to me while still receiving instruction on her earpiece from Lauren and Rob. "You're a fucking superstar, but we need you to say, 'Girls, would you like to help me spread cheer around Los Angeles?' but say it more British. Call them 'Love' or 'Birds' or some shit like that. Okay, so *way* more British. Go!"

The idea of "turning up the British" was sort of abhorrent to me, but I'd do my best to humor everyone if it meant the show would stand a better chance of being green-lit for a series.

"So, girls, would you like to help me spread cheer around Los Angeles?"

From the corner of my eye I caught Lauren immediately address Ross and Corin on their earpieces.

"More British!" they both mouthed to me, pointing skyward.

I turned up the British and ended up sounding like Dick Van Dyke in *Mary Poppins*.

"Blimey, loves, what do you say to spreading some cheer around LA?"

"*Yes!*" mouthed Ross and Corin, giving enthusiastic thumbs-up signs.

On the ride over to the next location with the cheerleaders, Ross made me write down all of the most ridiculous British slang and turns of phrase, which he wanted to pepper all of my subsequent dialogue with.

There was "knackered," meaning tired; "bollocks," meaning bullshit; "blimey" and "crikey" as interchangeable exclamations; "throw a wobbly," meaning to have a tantrum, and so on and so forth.

"So every time you say one of those words a subtitle will appear on the screen, giving a translation," said Ross.

"But I would never say *any* of these words."

"Trust me," he said. "It'll be hilarious."

By ten a.m. it was already over ninety degrees in North Hollywood, where we were due to "spread cheer" to a picket line of employees from Von's supermarket. My waxy makeup was beginning to melt and I was becoming increasingly strangulated by my tiny terry-cloth booty shorts. By 2003 the reality TV craze was so pervasive that a crew's prime concern is to not get another reality TV crew in frame. In that one North Hollywood parking lot three other crews, albeit more modest than our thirty-person entourage, were roaming around in hot pursuit of reality.

After terrorizing several dozen Los Angelinos, Andrew, Ross, and I cooled off in Ross and Jordana's swimming pool before shooting the third of the five segments that afternoon. The concept of the "birthday" segment was so formless and inane that even as the cameras started rolling none of us had any idea what on earth we were supposed to do. The brief was that the fifteen-person crew plus five "friends" would appear at several different restaurants and see what we could get for free by telling them that it was my birthday, and then exponentially request more and more menu items on the house. The problem of course is that when a party of six is accompanied by a television crew, waiters are waving their eight-by-tens around and are ready, willing, and able to do anything for a measly bit of camera time. Having no real friends on the West Coast, my group of pals was made up of Jordana's cousin Steve, Ross's friend Amin, Corin, Susan, a friend of Jordana's, and Gabrielle, the girl I'd enlisted to help me in the threesome the week before. With no direction, canned lines, and overly accommodating waitstaff hamming it up for the camera, the segment ended up like a low-wattage version of a *Punk'd* skit and was completely unsalvageable as far as I could tell.

The last day of shooting began at daybreak at a shady-looking truck stop in downtown LA. Toothless crack whores scuttled between the tractor trailers like roaches from the beam of a flashlight as our crew arrived just after dawn. As I chatted with the truckers, I felt that the segment was much more in line with my idea of the show and hoped it would be apparent to the powers that be at VH1. I didn't even mind Corin's constant coaching to be more British, which in addition to saying "blimey" and "crikey" also involved serving tea and scones to the truckers, who regaled me with tales from the road. It was our interaction that was driving the comedy of this segment, not me in tight shorts. I tried chewing tobacco, played with their CB radios, and even got to drive a big rig the length of the parking lot.

The last segment to shoot was the one Rob and Lauren were most "totally jazzed" about, me dressing up as a woman and trying to pick up guys at a karaoke bar. I spent the afternoon having my legs waxed and being made up at a beauty spa before heading out on the town. How this all figured into the theme of the pilot remained unclear.

After the three-day shoot I flew to JFK and caught a flight to London, where I met up with Brian, Chris, and Fatty. We'd had a European vacation booked for several months. The shooting schedule meant I'd regrettably missed the first leg in Reykjavík, Iceland. From London we flew to Athens then Crete, where Brian's parents had a time-share. We flew back to London, and the four of us spent a couple of days in Corringham, staying at my parents' house. I got to spend a week in New York before heading back to LA to do voice-over work on the pilot. There was no money left in the show's budget to accommodate this, and so I flew out on my own dime and took up residence in Ross and Jordana's spare room and rented a compact car.

After the insanity of the preproduction and three-day shoot, life back in the Martin household seemed serene. I was only required for voice-over sessions in Santa Monica for a few hours per week, and with little else to do I began to get the distinct impression that I'd outlived my use, worn out my welcome, and was increasingly getting under everyone's feet. Los Angeles, it seemed, was a fine place if you happened to be working, but a lull in productivity felt like creeping death. I became so homesick for New York that I began to manifest physical symptoms. I'd never felt like this when I left Corringham for New York.

Ross suggested that I spend my time working on a proposal for my book. It had already been eighteen months since I'd met with several literary agents, who seemed eager to help me sell an account of my time at Nerve. Furthermore, he insisted that I disappear off into the wilderness to write it.

THE RANCH

THE CIRCLED W RANCH occupies over four thousand acres of land just outside the town of North Fork, which is located in the exact center of California. Jordana's grandfather had bought the land in the late 1950s from a Native American tribe. The land straddles a hill range and seeps down into the valleys on either side. Over the past half century the head of cattle had been greatly reduced and the land had been parceled and sold to family and friends. When they married, in 2000, Ross and Jordana had been given a beautiful home on one of the ranch's highest elevations. It overlooks a deep valley, and above the opposing slope one can easily see El Capitan and the white-capped mountaintops of Yosemite National Park in the distance.

I'd visited the ranch during a break in the preproduction of the show. Ross, Jordana, Dash, and I had arrived there in darkness, leaving me unaware of the stunning beauty of the place until I was awakened to see the sun creeping over the mountains and illuminating the interior of the valley below us. I sort of fell in love with it immediately.

"Stay at the ranch," Ross had generously suggested after the show wrapped.

He didn't want me to leave California before we knew the fate of the *Granted* project.

"You can write without distractions, without having to pay silly New York rent, you can borrow one of the pickups to drive, you'll get inspired and still be able to drive down to LA to take meetings when you need to."

As much as I missed New York, it did seem like an amazing opportunity. I couldn't remember spending more than a few hours in my own company. Perhaps it was not having enough alone time that prevented me from being a prolific writer, I thought.

I bought a laptop and Ross and Jord took me up there to show me where everything was, how everything worked. The pickup was available for me to use, but I was only allowed to take it as far as Oakhurst, meaning I'd have to keep my rental for trips to and from LA at a cost of a thousand dollars a month. Other unexpected costs included having a high-speed Internet connection installed. Due to its relatively remote location, one company had the monopoly on almost every utility service available and charged high premiums. A local phone call was charged at over seventy cents per minute. I swear that when I called about the propane tank, the plumbing, the DSL connection, and the telephone bill I was chatting with the same person.

Being in such a remote place meant that writing about strange sexual experiences—my bread-and-butter gig—was going to be somewhat of a challenge. Since moving to California I'd successfully had a threesome and somehow convinced three strangers to let me take pictures of them naked. In LA those kinds of things were comparatively easy to pull off, but forty-five minutes from Fresno, in the foothills of the

Sierra Nevadas, my options were limited. Nerve was paying me fifteen hundred dollars a column, my only steady income, and it was proving barely enough to live on, despite paying no rent.

I decided that because I had at least three months ahead of me, there was no need to rush headlong into writing. To that end, I demarcated my day along themes of rest and relaxation: awaking at my leisure, coffee on the porch, picking rosemary from the garden to make elaborate omelets, followed by an hour-long run around the grazing area of some truly bewildered cattle. After lunch, some light reading before going out to collect kindling for the fireplace. After catching up with e-mails and events from the outside world, I'd make a nice fire, make dinner, and get through a bottle of Charles Taylor cabernet sauvignon. "Two Buck Chuck" was selling at Trader Joe's at $1.99 a bottle, and I'd bought two cases on my way through Fresno.

After a few days without seeing another soul I began to wonder how quickly I would get used to my own company. I encouraged friends in New York to call me as often as they could, though day to day I really had very little to report. Every day was clear, crisp, and sunny, up to eighty degrees in the day, down to forty at night. Each night coyotes serenaded me as squadrons of bats flew in to pick off the moths fluttering around the porch light.

Several parcels of land on the ranch had been sold to close family friends, who'd built vacation homes there. The Kesselmans were at their home quite a lot of the time, and after a week of my leisurely routine they extended an invitation for dinner to me, being new and all. The Kesselmans were my de facto next-door neighbors on the ranch, though they lived almost a mile away. Sandy and Hank were in their fifties, tall, good-looking, and incredibly charismatic. Hank had a wide range of interests, from mastering classical guitar to delivering spot-on impersonations of Ali G. I found this so incredibly surreal, because before Ali G that affect wasn't heard outside of Pakistani and Indian areas of west London, where I went to school. Sandy was a trained clinical psychologist and an ordained Zen priest in the Suzuki-roshi lineage. When performing her priestly duties her name was not Sandy, but Grace.

"We have our meetings every Sunday morning at eight forty-five," said Hank. "If you'd like to join us you're very welcome."

Having dinner with other people reminded me just how starved I was for human interaction, so I jumped at the chance to spend Sunday with a group of people. After coffee, Hank showed me the zendo, which was the converted second story of a barn, and ran me through what a meeting is like. Hank then loaded me up with an armful of Kurosawa DVDs and gave me a light scolding for walking over and not using my car.

"We lost a horse to mountain lions one night last year," he said gravely. "They'd make short work of you. I'm giving you a lift back."

I was enthralled at the idea of danger lurking all around me. Until then it hadn't occurred to me just how particularly mild a place England is: seldom too hot or too cold, free of poisonous reptiles and long since cleared of large carnivorous mammals, rarely subject to earthquakes, volcanoes, tornados, or tsunamis. It made me think about how a region's environment informs its inhabitants' dispositions and how my life would improve as a result of my becoming more rugged, independent, even manly. As a young child, I would listen to my grandparents' old 78 of "The Ballad of Davy Crockett" repeatedly. I somehow felt that in moving to the ranch I was taking a small step to becoming a bit of a frontiersman myself. This made things particularly awkward as I realized I had no clue how to build an effective fire, use the stars to navigate, or stay sane without being surrounded by several million other human beings.

As well as the cougars, the ranch was full of coyotes, large deer, and the odd bear or wolf. Some years ago, someone had given the ranch a few wild boars that had multiplied exponentially and roamed around in gangs terrorizing all in their path. Aside from the Kesselmans, the only other semipermanent residents on the Circled W were the outgoing and incumbent ranch managers, Tom and Jesse respectively. I would see them from afar on my mid-morning jogs, AC/DC accompanying me on my iPod. I often wondered what these guys thought of the city-slicking Semites and their friends who came in from Los Angeles and San Francisco to play at being cowboy at the weekend.

I'D ONLY STAYED in touch with a small handful of people from Corringham, and Charlotte was one of them. I had invited her out to visit me at the ranch and, to my amazement, she jumped on a plane about a week later. I excitedly drove down to LAX to pick her up and met up with Ross, Jordana, rising comedian Freddy Soto, and his wife, Cory, for dinner in Beverly Hills. From there, I took Charlotte to an incredibly sketchy part of downtown LA in the name of science. Most of my experiments had been pretty tight in terms of a clear objective. Attending a porn star's Christmas party was a bit of a stretch as decent fodder for an "I Did It for Science" installment, but it appeared that after almost three years, I'd just about exhausted every conceivable sexual kink and proclivity known to man. Living in the middle of nowhere had only served to exacerbate the problem. Being my friend, Michael Martin knew too much about my financial situation to say no and green-lit an article about being a guest at Kylie Ireland's annual Yuletide soiree. Before she left for LA, I asked Charlotte if she'd mind popping into a sex party with me. Though she was stunningly beautiful, bubbly, and charming, I always found Charlotte to be prudish and resolutely asexual, at least with regard to me. I'd had a silent crush on her since we were sixteen, both sales assistants in a men's clothing store in the local shopping mall, though much to my chagrin, we quickly became more like brother and sister.

"I really like her shoes," said Charlotte.

Her eyes had been nervously flitting around the large loft space in the ten minutes since we'd arrived and had finally seen something that she could bring herself to say out loud.

"Yeah, they're really nice," I replied. "Prada?"

"Hmmmm, I'm not quite sure," said Charlotte, squinting her eyes and leaning ever so slightly forward.

We talked about the shoes as if they weren't the items being worn by the women preparing to be fisted on the bench next to us. Despite being around five feet nine, the woman in the nice shoes had corset-trained her waist to a circumference of under nineteen inches, giving her the appearance of some sort of human-wasp hybrid.

"I think your hands are too big," she said to the frustrated gentleman between her legs.

She propped herself up on her elbows so that she could get a better view of the action and direct accordingly.

"Put your thumb flat to your palm," she said as the man's forehead vein bulged with concentration.

"Maybe I'll get a pair like that while I'm out here," said Charlotte.

"Yeah," I said. "Although you certainly won't be needing them at the ranch."

Given the size of the man's mitts it seemed that the wasp-waisted woman should be in physical pain, yet it was her beau whose face registered some discomfort. Ultimately, his human glove called for assistance.

"*Kylie!*"

The party's hostess, resplendent in a long, burgundy velvet skirt, black leather boots, a shiny plastic corset that stopped just below her boobs, which were held captive in a tight, long-sleeved fishnet shirt, strode over, and after seeing the problem firsthand, commandeered the situation and showed the ham-fisted boyfriend a better technique. The victim hollered, the cuckolded boyfriend looked on intently with arms folded, as Kylie went deep, well beyond the tan line from her wristwatch.

"You know, we can leave whenever you want," I said.

"No, really, I'm fine," said Charlotte, who'd been yawning all through dinner. "I think I got a second wind."

It was 10:30 p.m. in LA, 6:30 a.m. her time—GMT. We could have both used a line, but the party was billed as strictly drug- and alcohol-free. About ten feet in front of us, a blindfolded woman—naked save for a dog collar—was strung to a piece of scaffolding while a man with a braided ponytail and bowler hat methodically slapped her ass with his hand. He was putting a lot of thought into every slap, hopping around her body, turning his head this way and that, holding his chin thinking through his next move.

"I hope you're not too freaked out by all this?" I said, finally acknowledging the fact that we were in the midst of a bacchanal. A small handful of friends from home knew what I did for a living, one or two of them had even read about my exploits, but this was the first time one of them had been witness to the sort of bedlam I was paid to be involved in. Before that very evening, Grant Stoddard the sex writer would have been purely theoretical, perhaps farcical in Charlotte's mind. Since we'd arrived at the party, it had become simultaneously apparent to the both of us that I'd somehow become a bit of an old hand at this sort of thing: I'd absentmindedly stepped over a couple in coitus to get to the buffet; I nonchalantly sidestepped the reach of a cat-o'-nine-tails en route to the bathroom, and brushed past a man brandishing a monkey wrench and large container of lube without a pang of curiosity for how those items were related. Charlotte wasn't shocked at the situation so much as she was astounded to witness how comfortably I existed within it.

"I'm okay," she said, "I just . . . can't believe that this is what you . . . do."

In truth, this was not typically what I did. I was typically obligated to be the one being flogged on the rack, on the end of a leash, the one elbow-deep in a stranger's vagina. Charlotte knew that.

"If you need to . . . y'know . . ." Charlotte gestured toward the growing conga line of furiously masturbating men and strap-on-wielding women taking turns penetrating a prostrate and buxom partygoer. "I can wait in the car, if *you'd* prefer."

It was abundantly clear that it was *Charlotte* who would prefer to not see her childhood friend in any of the hard-core sexual acts erupting all around her, though it was awfully thoughtful of her to make it seem as if it would be my decision. That's English for you, polite to a fault. Mustn't grumble. I'd almost lost that sensibility entirely. I'd become very American in the way that I voiced my needs and sought to fulfill them posthaste.

Michael would be expecting me to participate, but even with Charlotte in the general vicinity, it was never going to happen. Though Charlotte never made me feel horrid about myself, I slipped into my old persona as soon as I saw her at the airport. I could fool strangers into thinking I wasn't formerly a social leper, but in the presence of any of my old pals I was suddenly Grunt Stoddard again: virginal, desperate, bucktoothed, acne-ridden, problem-haired, and prone to wearing his heart on his sleeve, invariably with tragicomic effect.

We stayed for a little longer until Charlotte's second wind died down to a gentle breeze and her eyes glazed over. She's so English. Even though she had almost fallen asleep twice while standing up, she insisted that we stay until I did what I had to do for the article.

"Honestly, honey," she said with eyelids drooping. "I was just resting my eyes for a bit."

I abused her good nature for just a minute or two longer, then thanked Kylie Ireland for having us over.

"Not at all, thanks for coming!" she said as a man with a goatee fucked her hard from behind.

"Take care!" he added.

With my homegirl now positively zombiefied, I practically carried her into the car and sped off toward the Valley.

We spent the night at Ross and Jord's before heading up to the ranch.

"Like I said, there's really not much to do up there," I said as we drove I-5 to a mountainous stretch of road known as the grapevine. "We're just going to chill."

"That's fine," she said. "Work's been so crazy, I could really use a bit of that."

Charlotte was part of the small minority of people from our town who went on to university. She moved to North London shortly afterward and worked for a hip PR company off of Tottenham Court Road. She consequently lost the last remaining vestiges of her Essex accent, though it wasn't very strong to start off with. Her parents were from Zimbabwe and she had been taught to speak quite properly. When we were sixteen, I knew that if any of my peers had the will and the where-withal to leave Corringham it would be her.

"Can you believe we're here?" I said as the fire finally started kicking out some heat and I poured us each a glass of supermarket cabernet sauvignon. We relaxed after the four-hour drive.

"It's really lovely, Grant," she said. "You're so bloody lucky."

"Wait until the morning," I said; we'd arrived in darkness. "It's beautiful outside. You're going to freak out. There's an open outdoor shower that overlooks the valley. It's an amazing way to start the day."

As the fire died down to embers, I gave Charlotte the option of sleeping in my bed or in the room on the other side of the house. Even though she'd spent the previous decade tactfully assuring me that we would never sleep together, I sort of hoped that the wine, the romantic, rustic setting, the jet-lag, my California tan, and the unabashed carnality of the previous evening would conspire to cloud her judgment, weaken her resolve. But, as I suspected, she chose to sleep in the bedroom way over on the other side of the house.

I woke up at 3:31 a.m. to Charlotte shouting. Through two closed doors and the large expanse of the living room I couldn't make out any specific words, though she clearly sounded angry, upset. I half listened as the shouting stopped and started over for several minutes. Then silence. I'd promised myself that I'd get up and wake her if it started again. I was pretty sure that it was during sleep*walking*, not sleep*talking*, that you shouldn't wake someone, but I wasn't one hundred percent positive. I was a sleepwalker as a ten-year-old and once urinated in the kitchen garbage during a dinner party my parents were throwing. My parents made sure not to wake me then as their friends all watched me in stunned silence.

There was no more sleeptalking from Charlotte, however, and I fell back to sleep. It was just before five when I awoke again to a soft knock on my bedroom door.

"Grant," she whispered. "Can I come in?"

"Sure," I said, praying that she'd finally caved. "What's up?"

"Can I sleep in here with you?" Her brow was furrowed. "It's gotten a bit chilly in there."

"Sure," I said. She slid into the king-sized bed in her pajamas and stayed to one side.

I woke her the next morning for coffee on the porch, just as sunlight began to pour into the valley. The sky was blue, the air crisp, the snow-peaked mountains looked close enough to touch. I folded my arms and gauged Charlotte's reaction. I felt proud to show my paisan where I'd landed in the world. I couldn't have been more proud if I had created the vista myself and dug out the valley with my own bare hands.

"It's really gorgeous," she said, taking it all in. She seemed somehow troubled.

"Are you all right?" I asked.

"I'm fine," she said. "I just didn't sleep all that well last night."

I hoped she wasn't referring to how I'd overzealously tried to spoon her.

"Yeah, I heard you talking in your sleep. Do you always do that?"

"Sometimes," she said.

We spent the rest of her four-day stay at the ranch futzing around the ranch and the house, going for drives, making dinner, getting drunk by the fire, popping into Fresno to watch a movie. It was somewhat uneventful but fun.

"I have to tell you something," said Charlotte as we passed by the relative civilization of Bakersfield on the way back to LA. "The first night . . . I wasn't sleeptalking."

"Well, who were you talking to?" I asked.

"I was shaken awake. I mean shaken really hard. I thought it was you, winding me up."

"I would never do that," I said.

I would *totally* do that sort of thing as a prank, though probably not to Charlotte.

"Well, what you heard was me telling you to fuck off and to stop messing about. But it wasn't you, was it?"

"No."

"Then the room got really cold, and I saw something go around the edge of the bed really fast."

"Are you winding *me* up?" I said.

"I'm not." She looked like she was on the verge of crying. "It felt like I wasn't alone in the room. I kept hearing little noises. That's why it took so long to get up the courage to run across to your room."

"I don't believe in ghosts, silly," I said, but her conviction was beginning to unnerve me.

"Neither do I. I didn't want to tell you, seeing as you are going to be spending a few months there, but I had to say something, I felt like I was going mad. But . . . I felt it, the whole time that we were there. Didn't you notice? I hardly left your sight."

It hadn't occurred to me until she said it, but Charlotte had been physically close to me the entire length of her visit. When she took a shower she asked me to talk to her through the bathroom door. But from a sunny California highway, her experience was easy to dismiss as a figment of her imagination, and after a few more miles I'd practically forgotten about it.

After another day or two in LA, I dropped Charlotte back at LAX. It was a few days before Christmas and I'd decided that although I dismissed the holidays as humbug, I certainly didn't want to spend them alone. Ross and Jordana were out and about doing family things, however, and I found myself kicking around the house without them. My Christmas in LA was infinitely depressing: plastic snowmen and reindeer next to palms, sixty-two degrees, drizzly and overcast. Christmas is sort of a bigger deal in England and especially within my family. They were all stunned when I didn't come home for the first time but had begrudgingly gotten used to it over the years. The phone was passed around to almost all of their fourteen guests, who all asked if I was having a lovely "Crimbo."

I told them all that I was having a great time.

Ross found some time to have a semblance of a Christmas dinner with me at the International House of Pancakes on Sunset before continuing on with his errands. I'd resigned myself to the idea of spending the rest of the day moping around when I got a call from Jane Chung. I'd met Jane at a karaoke party in New York a few months earlier. We went on a date, a few drinks on the Lower East Side. We had a very nice time and kissed. Jane was eighteen and had no idea that I had spent the past three years as a sort of literary gigolo, which made our evening sort of sweet. It made me realize that I hadn't had a date that wasn't somehow spun off from my column in a long while. Jane was in Pasadena, back from NYU and visiting with her parents for the holidays. She needed to escape from a family that was too close to her, I needed a distraction from one that suddenly seemed too far away. I drove inland, picked her up, and we went to see a movie. It was something terrible and before too long we were down each other's pants in the back row. After the movie Jane snuck me up to her bedroom adorned with posters, cheerleading paraphernalia, and other trappings of an archetypal Californian mall rat. Whispering, so as not to arouse the suspicions of her strict Korean parents, Jane told me that she was—somewhat regrettably—a virgin. It seemed that the karmic surplus I'd accrued over a sexless youth had come to bare in a solitary moment, though it was abundantly clear that the venue was not here, the time was not now. I contemplated taking her to Ross and Jordana's, plotting ways in which we could keep from waking them or Dashiell up. I finally understood how difficult it must have been for my peers to have sex while still living with their parents. Ten years after the fact I had a sudden respect for the pluck, resourcefulness, and tenacity that must be a huge part of the teen sex experience.

"You should come to the ranch!" I said, not realizing the brilliance of the idea until the words actually tumbled out of my mouth.

"Really?" she said.

Really. An idyllic setting, total privacy, an element of danger, a sexually experienced older, European man; in a moment of unchecked narcissism, I actually began to covet the theoretically perfect experience I was going to give to this young colt. Not only would this be an excellent way to stave off the loneliness and put off doing any writing, but it would also be a chance to make up for the last botched opportunity I had to successfully stamp somebody's V-card. Plus, Jane was incredibly cute, smart, and fun, and it seemed a good time was virtually assured.

Jane began working out a series of lies to tell her parents in order to spend a long weekend away from home, and I picked her up under the guise of being her best friend's adopted brother and drove her the three and a half hours north to the ranch. A moonlit sky, an open fire, a bottle of red wine, somebody I could truly care about. Over the past three years most of my sexual dalliances had been slapdash, tawdry, loveless, careless, or bizarre. But being alone with Jane in the middle of nowhere and doing it right helped to pry off the adopted persona I'd taken on with my job.

We spent our time at the ranch canoodling, making extravagant meals, getting drunk, sleeping in, sunbathing on the ranch, sledding in Yosemite, but mostly talking about our passion for New York and our shared longing to return. In the morning we'd collect fresh eggs from across the ranch and pick rosemary from Jordana's herb garden.

I drove Jane back to Pasadena and put some last-minute voice-over material on the show at VH1 in Santa Monica. My MTV staff pass had expired, so Ross had to come and collect me from the front entrance. I'd realized by this point that Los Angeles is a fine town to be in if you happen to be busy or feel in some way useful. Not being allowed access to the building helped to reinforce that sentiment. After we'd shot the show, everyone involved with *Granted* was on to the next project, and aside from the occasional V.O. I was left kicking around until the execs in New York had decided what they were going to do with the show, where I was going to live, what I was going to do, who I was going to be, and so on.

The last voice-over session was booked to redo the British-sounding exclamations that would appear with a translation at the bottom of the screen throughout the show. Everyone seemed to be convinced that these would be a charming addition.

"Blimey!" I said into the mic.

"Again," said Ross. "More bemused than shocked."

"Blimey!" I said again for the twentieth time. To my ear it was the same as the previous nineteen.

"That's it!" said Ross. "Does everybody love that one?"

Everyone in the sound room nodded their agreement.

"Great! Okay, next one, Grant," he said.

I looked down at the cue sheet.

"I'm knackered!" I said.

"Again," said Ross. "Remember, we're going for tired here, but ultimately satiated."

The drive to and from the ranch was becoming ingrained in my mind. The 101 to the 10 to the 405 to the 5 to the 90. I was on autopilot when my phone rang. It was Michael Martin from Nerve. For some weeks he'd been voicing concern over the drop-off in decent subject matter for the column. Two issues had converged to potentially spell the end of the column: my having already done all there is to do sexually and choosing to live in isolation in the California wilderness. I'd been to orgies, sex parties, porn sets, BDSM retreats; I'd used cock rings, prostate massagers, and tantra; attempted "injaculation," tried to induce female ejaculation, had sex on a pupu platter of drugs, had a happy ending massage, received relationship coaching, watched twenty-four hours of porn, trawled Craigslist for a casual hookup, taken pictures of couples having sex, worn a chastity harness, taken pictures of girls posing nude, made out with a guy, offered myself up at a gay bar, given lap dances at a male revue, been a cock model, a foot model, had a threesome, had sex with a lifelike mannequin, had sex on the subway, been treated like an infant, and sploshed. There were of course some other things to do, but by and large we were scraping the bottom of the barrel in terms of fresh ideas. Michael had seen the end of the column some months prior, but being my only income, I'd clung to it for dear life.

"What have you got for me?" asked Michael.

"Well, I mean, it's difficult up here," I said.

Because of the money situation, I had to take my rental car back to Oakhurst, meaning that aside from trips to the grocery store in the pickup truck, I would be effectively marooned at the ranch.

"What?" he said. "You're breaking up." Beyond the Fresno city limits, cell reception was patchy at best.

"I said it's hard because I'm on my own up here."

"Okay. . . ."

I was spending money hand over fist and couldn't afford the column to end, but I was clearly reaching. The account of the porn star Christmas party was in Michael's words "a bit of a snooze," a complaint he'd been voicing more frequently over the past few months.

"How about phone sex?" I said.

"No, boring, next."

"Um . . . Fresno has a Craigslist. I could try to do a—"

"If you couldn't do it in New York you won't do it there. You're on a ranch, right?"

"Yeah."

"Will you fuck an animal?"

There was little I'd said no to as my column had gotten progressively more daring, but trying to have sex with livestock was totally and utterly out of the question.

"Are you fucking nuts?"

"At least it'd be *interesting*," said Michael.

"What with the foot-and-mouth. . . ."

"Well, okay then, what's the plan?" he said. Michael had had a huge amount of patience with me in the past but it seemed to be suddenly waning.

"Give me a few days to think about it."

"Huh?"

"Give me a—"

I finally lost service as I branched off onto Road 200.

Without my car, cell reception, Jane, and no prospect of another visitor, the ranch seemed suddenly and overwhelmingly daunting. I arrived back there just in time to collect kindling before the sun went down. For the first few weeks of my stay there, I'd left it too late and often found myself poking around the brush with a flashlight, content that the rustles in the bushes were just deer, but since the Kesselmans' tales of bloodthirsty mountain lions, I'd become much more cautious.

I convinced myself that now that the distractions were gone and weeks of near solitude stretched out before me, I'd really try and knuckle down and get some serious writing done, but I was unable to get myself out of bed the next morning. Over the next few days I found myself in the midst of a deepening existential crisis. I'd always assumed that I was far too shallow a person to dip a toe into any real introspection, but it was clear that I'd been saved from my own company by the white noise of my life all this time. My livelihood was hanging by a thread, there was no money coming in, Ross had begun to pessimistically manage my expectations regarding the show, and my column, which had provided such a framework for who I was, was ending, and for the first time ever I felt completely and utterly alone.

As I lay paralyzed on the carpet in front of the dying fire, I didn't want to admit that I was suffering with some manner of mental episode, though that's clearly what was happening: an anxiety attack. Whatever crippling self-doubt I was experiencing seemed to be amplified by the quiet and the solitude. Charlotte's insistence that she'd experienced a malevolent spirit made me aware of a sinister presence, be it mental or supernatural. Ross had told me that someone had in fact died in the house. My increasingly fragile mental state contributed to my completely freaking out when a bat flew out of the chimney one evening and buzzed my head several times. I screamed and ran into the bedroom before plucking up the courage to throw a bath towel over the tiny mammal and release it outside. My self-image as a latter-day Davy Crockett was now just an embarrassing memory.

Jane wrote me letters and sent me DVDs to watch, which helped me immensely. I wrote her long letters and e-mails. She had become the focal point for my homesickness and it became unclear to both of us whether I was primarily missing her or missing home.

On the rare occurrences that the land line would ring, I would attempt to keep the person on the phone for as long as possible, though

I had nothing to say. They were on New York time and, as supportive as they tried to be, they had shit to do.

After a few more days passed and my mania worsened, I was talking to myself, prone to hysterical crying fits followed by long periods of despondency. Ross was now talking about the future of the TV show in decidedly bleaker terms; Rob had left VH1 for a position at Fuse; Lauren was on maternity leave; Ross was in LA; there was no one left to vouch for *Granted*. I couldn't conceive of what I'd be doing with my life, going forward. I'd attempted to pitch articles to other magazines but largely came up empty-handed. For the first time in years I flirted with the idea of going to Defcon 4 and calling my parents, requesting that they spirit me home. But in those years, where they lived and where I was raised had ceased to be my home. I was a New York City boy.

On Sunday, I finally took the Kesselmans up on their open invitation to join them for morning meditation in their zendo. I have an aversion to anything even vaguely spiritual or New Agey, but I was so completely starved for human interaction that I'd been looking forward to seeing them for days. I was hoping that a few girls my own age might even show up. But there, atop their barn, a rather motley, baby-boomer congregation sat in silence amid the chanting and the ringing of bells. The agenda was a half hour of meditation, fifteen minutes of walking meditation, a second half hour of mediation, then a talk about the meditation with jasmine tea, baby carrots, and those glazed, Japanese seaweed snacks. I walked back feeling slightly disappointed that the meditation gathering hadn't yielded the sort of human interaction I was hankering for. The upside, however, was that Hank gave me a pile of Steve McQueen movies to distract me from myself.

Michael finally called to see what I'd come up with in terms of new column ideas, but I had nothing to offer.

"How about that girl, the fair maiden?" he said.

I'd told Michael all about Jane and my seemingly altruistic plan to make her first time special.

"What about her?" I asked.

"Well, did you make a woman out of her?"

"She's not a virgin anymore, if that's what you mean."

"Well, that's a *great* column, right there."

This would be the first time an experience from my own life had been misappropriated into column inches, after the fact. The idea of blending my personal life—not to mention the personal lives of the unsuspecting girls I was dating—into my job was simultaneously meta and incredibly distasteful. What made the column interesting—as far as I could tell—was my dependable reluctance to engage in any given activity; the sense of shame, self-doubt, and embarrassment I carried with me into the BDSM dungeon, the gay bar, the dating coach's office, the orgy. If it wasn't for the column I'm sure I wouldn't have had a fraction of the sexual experiences I'd crammed into the past two and a half years.

"The poor girl! Hasn't she been through enough?" I said.

I was already thinking through the conversation I'd have with Jane, coaxing her to agree to me spilling something almost sacrosanct into the public sphere for my financial gain. Even the hypothetical conversation made me feel quite disgusting.

"Just ask her," said Michael. "She knows what you do for a living, right? It's not beyond the realm of possibility that anyone you hook up with may or may not appear in your writing, right? You're a sex writer and them's the breaks."

As my work and personal life had become ever more interdependent over the recent months, the girls who had come in and out of my life had made a point of saying that it was or wasn't kosher to write about the sex we had, were immediately about to have, or—most disconcertingly—were in the process of having. Excepting my alleged hoodwinking at Leather Camp, however, I'd never written an unsuspecting civilian into an installment of the column.

"It sort of negates the whole me-making-it-all-nice bit though, doesn't it? I mean it was atypically special, if I do say so myself."

"Then surely she'd be thrilled if you recorded it for posterity, no?"

After years of getting me to agree to throw myself into some alarming, even dangerous situations, Michael knew precisely how to manipulate me.

"You'll change her name, the setting, anything identifiable."

As much as I didn't want to sell Jane out, my financial outlook was grim. The utility bill was becoming astronomical, not to mention four straight months of car rental. Being in California had proved to be just about as pricey as my living costs in Manhattan, costlier once I factored in my deteriorating mental health and its cancerous effect on my productivity.

Jane called that evening from the relative civilization of her NYU dorm by the South Street Seaport. She told me that huge ice floes were drifting down the East River, making me homesick for the cold.

"Jane," I began my pitch with some trepidation. "Would it be okay if I wrote about what we did up at the ranch for my column?"

Silence.

"Wait," she said. "You did *me* for science?"

"No, no, no!" I said. "I did you for . . . I mean, I didn't *do* you for anything."

Silence.

"Look, the truth is, I've run out of money and it looks like the column is going to end if I can't think of anything to write about. I'll change names, situations and stuff, but if you don't want me to write about this, I totally understand."

"Well, what are you going to say?" she asked. "I mean, *good* things?"

"Jane! Of *course* good things. I had an amazing time up here with you. It was the best."

It was true.

"Hmmmm. I guess it might be okay then. Let me sleep on it."

"Thanks, baby."

Ross called to say that VH1's ninety-day option on the show had expired and that they had extended it for yet another ninety days. This meant we would most likely not know whether we had a TV show until early summer, and therefore were to remain in limbo. There was certainly no way I could stay in isolation at the ranch for months on end, so I began making plans to go back to New York as soon as some outstanding checks came in to cover the airfare. I gave the girl living in my place five weeks' notice and started counting down the days in the same excited way that I counted the days between my November birthday and Christmas as a child.

With some hesitance and several conditions with regard to her anonymity, Jane generously gave her blessing to my recounting the loss of her virginity in a humor column. I also managed to get a smallish but extremely welcome freelance assignment from Nerve cofounder Genevieve Field, who was now an editor at *Glamour*. That combined with an end in sight for my self-imposed exile in California did wonders for my mental state and the debilitating personal crises were somewhat abated. I filed my virginity piece, worked on the *Glamour* article, and continued puttering around the house.

My friend Jamye Waxman asked if she could come and stay at the ranch with me to write and of course I jumped at the opportunity to have someone to talk to, not to mention escape to the comparative metropoli of Oakhurst or Fresno with. Jamye wasn't arriving for another three weeks, so in order to preserve my hard-won sanity, I cut hours, days, and weeks up into chunks of time allotted to certain endeavors. I decided that it was the lack of structure that was loosening my grip on reality, so I put in place a fairly rigid activities roster.

I would rise at 9:00, take coffee on the porch until 10:00, prepare and consume breakfast until 11:00, check e-mail and surf the Internet until 12:30, run until 1:15, shower until 1:45, prepare and consume lunch until 2:30, take phone calls until 3:30, work until 7:00 with one fifteen-minute break, which I spent collecting kindling and firewood. Make and eat dinner until 9:00. Watch a DVD until 11:00, yoga and/or calisthenics until 11:45, which allowed me a fifteen-minute period of leisure time before bed at midnight. Days were demarcated by the people I would like to talk with. I e-mailed them all and asked if they had a time slot they'd prefer, A friends getting twenty-minute slots, B friends ten. Jane got as long as she wanted. On Sunday mornings I spoke with my parents.

Michael called to tell me to be on the lookout for a package he had had sent to the ranch.

"It's a make-your-own-dildo kit," he said quite matter-of-factly.

"You want me to make a model of my own you-know-what?" I said.

"For starters," he said. "Then have someone strap it on and fuck you with it. It's brilliant. Go fuck yourself: the 'I Did It for Science' finale! Can you find someone to help you out with that?"

As luck would have it, Jamye was the perfect person to assist me. She was a sex educator, completely uninhibited, and perhaps most important, a dear friend.

"Yeah, my friend Jamye arrives in a few days."

"Okay, well, you kids get it on and gimme a call to let me know how it goes. Remember, this one has to be a doozy."

Given the circumstances leading up to this moment, fucking myself was spectacularly apropos, poetic even.

As I'd suspected, Jamye didn't even flinch when I asked her to bugger me. I even got the sense that she was rather looking forward to it.

Three days later, the day of Jamye's arrival, I awoke to find that one of the cowboys had left the Make Your Own Dildo Kit on the front porch. The box had been damaged in transit and its contents—a plastic tub with the mold, plaster, and other apparatus with a picture of an erect penis on the outside—were clearly visible. I cringed at what whoever delivered it must have thought when they drove into North Fork to pick up the mail from the post office. These were tough yet wholesome manly men, men I had always aspired to become like. It's no wonder they gave me funny looks as I pranced around the ranch on my daily jogs.

Fairly early on in my freelance writing career I learned that the sooner one files an article, the sooner one gets paid. To that end, Jamye and I got to work on the dildo project almost as soon as she'd dropped her bags and I'd given her a cursory tour of the interior. Neither of us batted an eyelash, carrying on our dinner discussion as I masturbated to a full erection and she mixed the plaster with water that had to be at a precise temperature.

"Wait until morning," I said, my fist pumping away. "We'll go for a drive, you won't believe how beautiful this place is."

"I can't wait," said Jamye, carefully stirring the porridgelike mixture. "I'm really looking forward to writing and chilling out for a week or two."

"Well, there's plenty of R and R to be had out here. We could go horse riding one day," I offered.

"Really? That'd be so cool. Okay. Thermometer says it's almost the right temperature. Are you ready?"

"Yeah, I think so. . . ."

"Well, it looks pretty hard to me," she said. She batted my hand away and pushed the tip toward the floor with her index finger, felt the resistance for a second and released, my penis snapping back skyward like a ruler on the end of a desk. I half anticipated that *ber-doi-oi-oi-oi-nggg* sound.

"Let's do it," I said.

Jamye handed me the mold and I plunged my unit into the tepid ivory-colored slime.

"Oooohhh. It's a bit chilly!"

I had to maintain my erection for two minutes. Jamye kept an eye on the microwave timer as I conjured up lewd images in my mind. The last ten seconds or so, I definitely sensed that the lukewarm mixture was taking its toll.

"Okay, that's two minutes!" Jamye said and helped my pull off the mold. With some effort on her part and a slurping, sucking sound, the mold finally came off, and after a few more minutes we filled the void with a rubber solution and put it on a shelf to harden overnight. While I took a shower Jamye washed the mixing bowl we'd used for the plaster so that I could mix the eggs, cream, chives, black pepper, pancetta, and parmesan for the linguine carbonara recipe that I'd perfected during my tenure at the ranch.

The next evening, immediately postcoitus, I looked over my shoulder at my penis as it proudly jutted forth, spent yet unflagging from between Jamye's legs.

"Are you okay?" she asked.

"Yeah," I lied as I tried to reconcile the vulnerable and empty feeling my penis's clone had left me with. "I think I just need to lie here for a minute or two."

"I'll get you some water," she said and walked to the kitchen, dismantling the harness that held the prosthesis to her body.

Michael said that he'd continue to call on me to write freelance bits and pieces for Nerve, but the real end of my career there was ushered in with Jamye's final pelvic thrust. My ass, like my whole future, was up in the air. It was at this moment that I began to experience the sensation of freefall I'd gotten every time I'd taken a leap out of my ever-expanding comfort zone, the fear and exhilaration of the unknown. Any pang of shame I might have felt from the circumstances was overridden by the question I asked myself over and over. I'd always told myself that in this day and age, my being a former sex worker would not be a strike against me in an interview situation, but now that I would presumably be putting this to the test, I was suddenly less secure in the assertion. When I began writing the column I was too concerned with having a roof over my head and a little pocket money to think about my time as a gonzo sex columnist being a great dirty stain on my résumé. Where would I go from here? How long could I coast before having to make some possibly difficult decisions.

Over the next two weeks Jamye and I hung out and worked on our respective projects while I counted down the days until I would eventually leave the rustic idyll of the Circled W ranch and get back to New York. I'd missed it immensely and found myself constantly daydreaming about my return: the plane's wheels touching the tarmac, the frigid February air filling my lungs, treating myself to a cab back to Manhattan. I felt that the new me, sans column, already resided there, and I was eager to get back to Manhattan and see what he would be all about.

ACKNOWLEDGMENTS

Many thanks to Ross and Jordana Martin, Lisa Carver, Michael Martin, and Nerve, my agent, Claudia Cross, at Sterling Lord Literistic, Kelly Harms, my editor, Jeremy Cesarec, Jeff O'Connell, Drew Reed, and Antony Topping for your largely undeserved patience and support.

Love and thanks to the entire Stuehler Family, my boys, David Fateman, Chris Apostolou, and Bran Battjer, for keeping me fed, clothed, housed, and inspired during numerous rough patches. You are the personification of good old American hospitality. Thanks to Jennifer Choi for your thoughtful guidance and tutelage.

A very special thanks to my family for their love, support, and promising never to mention that they've read any farther than this page.

Insights,
Interviews
& More . . .

About the author

About the book

Read on

A Conversation with Grant Stoddard

How did you first learn about sex?

It was when I was eight or nine. This kid found a dirty porno mag under his dad's bed and brought it into school and disgusted everybody with it because it was, frankly, grotesque. These sorts of hirsute, rotund continental women and super sleazy guys. So this kid shows this to a group of third graders! We all saw it and freaked out and he informed us that that's what everybody's parents do, and I was forever traumatized. It was eventually confiscated by the headmaster. I don't think I got any real parental talk. Maybe two or three years after that, by which time I saved them the trouble and told them I'd seen it all, and then some. In our school we had a lesson called P.S.E., which stood for personal and social education. It was taught by our gym teacher, this little Welsh dynamo named Mr. Power. He was my favorite teacher even though I routinely disappointed him in football, rugby, tennis, track . . . everything. He eventually threw me out of the P.S.E. class when I couldn't keep it together when required to put a

Me, about three years old, suffering from advanced malnutrition

condom on a banana. I remember my report card saying that I didn't possess the maturity to deal with the subject of sex and adult relationships. Prophetic.

In high school did you know this would be your destiny?

Um . . . no. I strongly suspected I would die a virgin. I really did think that. Up until it actually happened the prospect of actually having sex was becoming more remote by the day. It didn't help that I looked like Garth from *Wayne's World*. I wish that someone would have staged an intervention back then; made me over into a less vile prospect as a sexual partner.

When did you lose your virginity?

I was around eighteen. She worked at a stable and smelled of horse shit half the time. It was a group of firsts. First kiss, first everything. It all came at once.

Was that when your destiny became clear?

Not at all. I was actually kind of underwhelmed by the experience, as I'm sure she was.

So you went to college and lived with this ancient woman—Did this arrangement preclude sexual adventures?

It would be easy to use Mrs. Montague as a scapegoat. I think I did a thorough job of staving off any prospects on my own. I just had no game. I really felt awkward in my own skin, and people pick up on that immediately. ▶

Meet Grant Stoddard

© Jake Bronstein

At twenty-one, perennial virgin GRANT STODDARD came to the United States in pursuit of true love. Within eighteen months he was a couch-surfing ne'er-do-well, scavenging scraps of food and living in danger of being deported back to England. His saving grace appeared in the form of his winning an online trivia competition, resulting in his appointment as New York's most intrepid sex columnist, despite having little experience in either sex or writing. He lives in New York City. ༄

A Conversation with Grant Stoddard
(*continued*)

How did the metamorphosis come about?

Your line of questioning assumes that I somehow changed at some point. I really don't think that's the case. When I go home, I automatically snap back into that mode. It's being here that gave me a chance to leave a lot of that behind.

So you were corrupted by an American girl, and then America was your destiny?

Yeah. I always kind of had, from family vacations to the Midwest when I was a kid, the amount of oohing and aahing over me. People actually took an interest, which was very novel. I felt like I was included.

What was it about you that got you out of Essex and to America?

This is going to sound dumb, but years ago in England there was this TV commercial for British Airways, or maybe it was Virgin Atlantic, I'm not sure. Anyway, there's this guy and he's walking down the street and someone's lifting a grand piano into an eighth-floor apartment and the rope breaks and the piano comes hurtling toward him, and just prior

Sharing yet another secret with my mother

4

to impact, the action freezes. Then the viewer sees all these fast cut vignettes of him in exotic locales, running along a beach with these beautiful women, hang-gliding over Rio, going nuts at Mardi Gras in New Orleans, on a camel in Morocco, etc., doing these crazy death-defying things, and the tag line was something like; "When your life flashes before your eyes, make sure you have something to watch." As corny as that is, it stuck with me. I guess I just wanted that; I wanted to stockpile adventures. When my friends and I

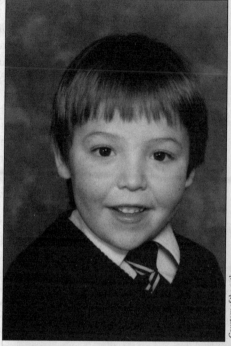

Me in the colors of Herd Lane Primary School

were around eighteen or nineteen we went through this period of doing things based primarily on how good a story it would be when we recounted it at the pub.

You wrote in the book about your encounter with Lisa Carver that led to a position with Nerve and, later, the column "I Did It for Science." You described it as very much accidental. But it takes a special kind of person to do that.

By that point I'd learned that the very occasions when I just throw caution to ▶

5

A Conversation with Grant Stoddard
(continued)

the wind and hope for the best—these are the moments when it all seems to work out fantastically well. Where I'm from, people aren't conditioned to take giant leaps of faith or stray very far from a predetermined life path. Various members of my family have, however, and I suppose they were supportive in breaking out of that mold. So with regards to the column it was just another opportunity that plopped into my lap that I felt compelled to take. All the other interns at Nerve would have given anything to get their writing published and I just thought it was funny that that the only intern who had no aspirations to write is the one who ended up with the opportunity to do so. I would never have had the guts to do any of those things under my own steam. Some of the "experiments" that the editors were suggesting were actually things that I had an interest in doing. Having it be my job made my feel less creepy and disgusting about it because I was required to do it. It was a great alibi to have. It also kind of allowed me to play catch-up for all the years that I was a wallflower.

Are you an exhibitionist? Some might say you're the very definition of an exhibitionist.

My hair as birth control

No. I dunno. I always imagined an exhibitionist would revel in it. During everything I've ever done I was nervous to the point of nausea. I was always hoping that somehow I wouldn't have to go through with it, right up until the last moment. I always thought an exhibitionist would feel some sort of joy. I was terrified about doing everything. A friend of mine said it's not an adventure until you're wishing that you were back at home tucked safely in your bed, and there's probably some truth to that.

My life in heavy metal

Would it be fair to say that without Lisa Carver's praise of your oral sex skills, you would not be where you are today?

I think she was just being nice. I dunno. Whatever skills I had then I think I've lost since. But I dunno, she recommended me for a job based on little else, so I suppose I did *something* right.

Did IDIFS make you more or less saleable on the dating market? ▶

A Conversation with Grant Stoddard
(continued)

It was certainly a great icebreaker. It's one of the most insane jobs, practically untoppable at a dinner party: "I'm paid to have bizarre sex with strangers and write about it." In addition to being a great icebreaker, I suppose it gave me more confidence. There was a period in which girls who were fans of the column were making it extremely easy for me to have sex with them. I certainly couldn't have foreseen that happening.

Have you gotten feedback from anyone you grew up with who wrote you off?

Aside from my own immediate family I'm not sure my friends from home actually have any idea. It's difficult. I got a Myspace message from a friend I hadn't seen in eight years who said, what have you been up to? And I kind of skirted the question because I think it would be difficult for them to get their minds around the idea of me and my bizarre lifestyle. At a certain point, the story becomes unrelatable to a large portion of my friends.

What experiment do you regret?

The orgy. I took the wrong girl, had the wrong mind-set, and I wish I had enjoyed it more, because it's something I may never do again.

Are you scarred for life by your experiences? Is there any hope for you to have a monogamous sex life?

I think that I was more scarred by the period when I was a sexual persona non grata.

66 There was a period in which girls who were fans of the column were making it extremely easy for me to have sex with them. I certainly couldn't have foreseen that happening. 99

A period of time I like refer to as the 1990s. I think that was the most damaging. If any damage happened to my psyche, it happened then. The opportunity to be reborn as a sort of literary gigolo actually resulted in my having a healthier mindset.

Are you not more impressed with yourself than you used to be?

Um . . . I suppose. I think that I'm most impressed with how I've been able to adapt. When I take inventory of all the amazing opportunities that have come my way since arriving in America, I can't help feeling electrified by the unordinary life I've found and I feel quite invincible for a minute. ∿

On Writing
Working Stiff

IT'S FITTING THAT *WORKING STIFF* came about in the same manner as all of the other wonderful opportunities I've had since arriving in America from England in the late nineties. Like leaving my staid little hometown, moving to New York City, getting a record deal, becoming a sexpert, and having Viacom fund my eponymous TV pilot, taking stock of my experiences in a memoir was something that somebody simply thought I should have a crack at. Whether it's my accent, the cut of my gibe, or just good old American hospitality at work, time and time again people ask me to do things I'm in no way qualified to do. It came as quite a shock to me that I was the type of person to run with any opportunity that came my way.

Working Stiff is primarily about the three years I spent writing my experiential sex column, "I Did It for Science," for Nerve.com. I eventually wrote thirty installments of the column, though I'd only written about six when the idea of writing a book was first mentioned by a man whom I'd just witnessed urinating on a masturbating stranger, ostensibly for episode number seven. He put me in touch with a literary agent in London, whom I met with on my next trip home in the summer of 2002. Before meeting me, the agent envisioned an anthology of my columns, but over lunch I expanded on my journey from the perennial wallflower to accidental sexplorer and he suggested that this transformation should be the main theme of the book, not just the columns themselves. As

> **I eventually wrote thirty installments of the column, though I'd only written about six when the idea of writing a book was first mentioned.**

the column—and the transformation—was ongoing and with my humiliation growing exponentially with each installment, I decided that writing an account of the experience at that point would have been blowing my figurative wad too soon.

As my column grew in popularity, I found myself writing sex and relationship features in several other publications and making TV appearances as some kind of expert on sex, to the startled amusement of anyone I'd gotten into bed. My raised profile had my employers at Nerve thinking of spin-offs into other media: audio, TV, and books. It was at this point that I left Nerve.com full-time and seconded to Los Angeles to make a TV pilot that had less to do with sex and more to do with my propensity for being immersed in bizarre situations. The TV show *Granted* was created and produced by Ross Martin. Ross introduced me to Claudia Cross of Sterling Lord Literistic in New York, who seemed enthused about representing the project I had recently started referring to as *Working Stiff*.

This created tension with Nerve.com and derailed their plans to spin off "I Did It for Science" and something called the "Grant Stoddard character" into other Nerve-branded media. However, as I was a popular columnist on Nerve, I continued to write "I Did It for Science" on a freelance basis.

Once the pilot was shot and my days as a columnist for Nerve were clearly drawing to a close, I was given an opportunity to disappear into Ross's vacation home in California's Central Valley to commence work on the book that several people wanted to read. Three months in the seclusion of a 4,000-acre ranch seemed like an opportunity to write *Working Stiff* while awaiting the fate of the ▶

On Writing *Working Stiff* (continued)

TV show. But it soon transpired that I was losing my mind in isolation, and I arrived back in New York without my bread-and-butter column, anything towards my memoir, or the TV show being picked up for production. Once back in Manhattan, I made a semblance of a living writing for *New York* magazine, *Muscle and Fitness, Glamour, Black Book, Men's Health, Playgirl, Vice, Vitals,* and the British edition of *GQ,* leaving me little time to concentrate on *Working Stiff,* though it had been almost three years since the idea was first floated. Interested parties redoubled their efforts to have me squeeze out a proposal, though with my being flat broke, I felt that I needed to concentrate on paying the rent. To that end, I got a temp job as a filing clerk at a French bank and some weeks later bizarrely became the managing editor of *Playgirl* magazine. It was in between hours of shuffling through nude pictures of oiled beefcakes and editing hausfrau erotica that I finally put a proposal together, and Claudia Cross deftly sold the project to HarperCollins. I quit my job at *Playgirl,* having clocked up five and a half weeks there, and began writing.

I completed *Working Stiff* some four years after the project was conceived, though the timing was

Brian Battjer

Me on my last day at Nerve, cleaning out my desk

opportune. I had never had a clear idea of the book's shape until the column had truly ended and I had been given a buffer of time in which I could make sense of what had happened to me, the mania slowing down just enough to see the story with some clarity. ∾

> 66 Flat broke, I felt that I needed to concentrate on paying the rent. To that end, I got a temp job as a filing clerk at a French bank and some weeks later bizarrely became the managing editor of *Playgirl* magazine. 99

"I Did It for Science"

THE BULK OF *WORKING STIFF* is about the three years I spent writing my column "I Did It for Science." I think I explained the concept in the body of the book, but here's an idea of what it actually looked like.

Experiment:

To subject myself to the rigors of a full-body massage and attempt to get a manual release.

Hypothesis—state your hypothesis in the form of a prediction that can be verified by the results of the experiment:

No really, it's not my bag! But the thought of a hot stranger getting her hands on the goods is a little naughty. Is this what they mean by hands-on reporting?

Materials—please list all the materials required for this experiment (including, if applicable, how they were obtained):

Massage parlor (one).

Method—in this portion of your report, you must describe, step-by-step, what you did in your lab. It should be specific enough that someone who has not seen the lab can follow the directions and re-create the same lab.

Trying to find a massage establishment that offers a "happy ending" is no easy task, especially if you're not intimately familiar with a city's seedy underbelly. Luckily, Isabella just happened to know a "friend of a friend" who was aware of such a place. As directed, I went to a faceless building in midtown Manhattan, feeling more than a little sheepish. Although the thought of being interfered with by a beautiful, skilled masseuse was exciting fodder for my teenage dreams, by the day of reckoning I was a bundle of nerves.

I walked into the building's lobby and was greeted by a rotund man in a crumpled blue shirt that sported a blob of every condiment in the Heinz rainbow. I asked where the massage place was. He gestured to the basement, his verbal skills compromised by the two or three knishes he seemed to be masticating simultaneously. I headed down a flight of stairs that ended with an unmarked gray door. This led to another flight, and another and another. Curiouser and curiouser, I thought as I opened the final door into the softly lit lobby of a spa. The room contained a counter and a plush leather sofa that snugly accommodated four attractive Korean women between the ages of twenty and forty. "Hello," chirped the most senior both in age and standing, and she hopped up to get behind the counter. "Hi, I'd like the full massage," I stuttered, placing a clumsy and unnecessary-in-hindsight emphasis on the word "full." The younger women smiled at each other and me with a kind of curiosity that I would encounter on several more occasions this afternoon.

I was asked if I had been to the spa before. It was then that I became conscious, nay, extremely paranoid that anything I said could blow my cover. I said I hadn't. "Seventy-five dollar, cash," said the woman, who handed me a fresh towel, a crisp robe, and a locker key affixed to a comically large chunk of lumber. "You follow me," she ordered and led me into the men's locker room. I use the words "locker room" loosely, as I'd never seen its like before. The "lockers" were made of an ornately carved, heavy dark wood; the floor was granite. A large marble sink and counter was covered with expensive soaps, aftershaves, deodorants, razors, and shaving gels. I don't know what this says about the circles I run in, but this was the fanciest joint I'd ever seen! In the middle of the attractively lit room was a low bench with twenty pairs of sandals underneath it. "You shower, lock locker real good and keep key all time," the woman commanded. I nodded a little too much. She left the room, and I got changed. Looking around the changing room for signs of any other clients, I spied a pair of large black dress shoes tucked into the row of sandals. I hardly recognized my reflection as I stared back at the kimono-wearing dork in the mirror. I was just a ponytail and a copper bracelet away from becoming Steven Seagal.

Wearing a pair of grossly oversized sandals, I shuffled through an opaque glass door into a large granite-and-marble shower room. Five huge shower heads—the ones the circus uses for hosing down elephants—adorned the walls, and a steam room and sauna were nearby. With the Japano-futuristic look of the place, the gaggle of uniformly dressed Asian beauties around and the perception that I was several miles below the Earth's crust, I started to believe that I was living out one of my numerous James Bond-inspired dreams: Trapped in the belly of an evil corporation's lair, treated with the utmost courtesy while my movements are monitored by a team of beautiful-yet-deadly double agents.

I made my shower last. The water pressure at my apartment provides little more than an occasional moody trickle, so I took advantage of the ▶

high-pressure jet and used every soap, shampoo, conditioner, exfoliating body scrub, washcloth, and loofah at my disposal. Feeling fresh as a daisy, I left the changing room and was assigned a masseuse. She was one of the older women, possibly in her late thirties, short and slight with a bob haircut and dressed in a clinical white uniform. She led me down a hallway to a small, demurely lit room, then told me to disrobe and lie stomach-down on the table, where there was an opening for my face. I skimmed my hand against the starched white tablecloth to see if there was a corresponding hole for my unit. Until this point, I hadn't really thought about how the pleasure would be administered. Simultaneously, all my daydreams about being on her majesty's secret service evaporated as I realized how quickly I crumble under questioning.

"My name Jung, what your name?" asked my inquisitor as she began to rub my neck. "Er . . . Jeff," I replied. Jeff? Where the fuck did that come from? "Oh," she said, sounding surprised and skeptical. Had she been through my locker and seen my ID? I started to sweat. "You live here, work here?" she asked as she covered my body in a thin, crisp linen sheet. "Yeah," I said, "in . . . Soho." "Oh," she replied. "What you do?" Butcher, baker, candlestick maker—any of those would have sufficed, but instead I blurted out, "I work for a magazine." Fuck! Fuck! Fuck! What a total fuckwit. I might as well have told her that I was with the NYPD vice squad. I quickly followed up by qualifying that I worked for a publication about fishing. "Oh ma gah!" said Jung, sounding disturbingly interested. Christ! Who was Soho Jeff from *Rods and Reels*? What's with the third degree already? I decided that as long as Jung didn't start questioning me about the ins and outs of koi carp, I would shut my stupid mouth and get this experiment back on track.

Jung went to work, digging her fingers into the painful nooks of my neck and shoulders. I heard a muffled guy's voice in the room next to mine. First, it sounded like the teacher in the Peanuts cartoons, but after a few sentences, I could pick out certain words. "Wah wah wah Wall Street," "Wah wah banking wah," and, most memorably, "wah wah you're a very beautiful girl wah wah." Ew. Other than that, all I could hear was the purr of the air conditioning and the popping sounds emanating from each of my joints that were subjected to Jung's digitry. During a few neck adjustments, I thought I could hear an offensive line prancing over ten yards of bubble wrap.

Jung rubbed my body through the sheet, first with her hands and then with her feet. She walked on my back, steadying herself by holding onto a ceiling-mounted pole. I couldn't enjoy her mastery; my mind was too preoccupied with the impending transition from massage to handjob. At one point, she stopped touching me for about fifteen seconds, and I couldn't tell where she was in the room. Out of nowhere, she grabbed my thigh, and I flinched. "You nervous!" she chuckled and gave me two firm pats to the buttocks. She wasn't wrong. I could hear my heart pounding in my ears. Jung's touch felt great, but I wasn't turned on in the slightest. She removed the sheet and traced her fingers up and down my legs, bum, inner thighs, and any parts of my undercarriage that she could get her crafty fingers on. I could hear the door to the little room open and close. Being face down and looking the opposite way, I couldn't see what was going on. Was Jung exhibiting some unnoticed birthmark to her coworkers? "You sunburn!" said Jung, and she started picking at the peeling skin atop my shoulders. "Oh ma gah!" she whispered.

That's not sexy. For a second I thought she was going to have a pick at my bacne too. She turned my head to inflict some more pain to my neck area, and we saw each other face-to-face for the first time in forty-five minutes. Jung was very attractive and kind looking; she wore plum-colored lipstick. "Oh ma gah!" she exclaimed. "You just boy! How old you?" Jeff, like me, is twenty-five.

Observations/Results—quantify the effects of the experiment:

"You want everything?" she asked in a slightly hushed voice. Thank Christ for that. I was almost ready to employ the same downward-pointing motion the slob at the door had used an hour earlier. "Yes!" I said. "Really?" she sounded surprised. "Young boy like you? Oh ma gah!" She told me to turn over and I did. As Jung turned her back to get the necessary lotion, I looked down, horrified at my uninterested rig. My nerves had gotten the better of me, and it seemed that I wouldn't be giving Jung much to work with. She sat her bum down on the table, her feet either side of my torso. She applied the cream to my twig-and-berries and gently started to run her fingers around them with a motion that was, in truth, a little too effective. I propped myself up on my elbows to get a better look. I stared at her face and tried to make eye contact, but Jung was looking at what she was doing: a rubbing, coaxing, snake-charming type maneuver, in absolute silence. In a matter of seconds, I had gone from willing my old chap to look alive to thinking about baseball. But Jung ▶

"I Did It for Science" *(continued)*

had a mind to get it all over with, and within an embarrassingly short period of time, she took me from a standing start to an orgasm. So deft was the operation that I wasn't even at full mast when I dropped sauce. It all felt pretty weak, the ejaculation rather unexplosive. Jung pointed my knob up and off to one side until I was all done. She cleaned up with a paper towel as I closed my eyes and tried to come to terms with her brand of blitzliebe.

I opened my eyes and saw her leave the room. I felt like calling out, "This is the bit where I like to hug," but it probably wouldn't have done any good. Jung was all business. I got back into my robe and padded out into the main area. Smiling, Jung handed me a fresh towel and directed me into the shower room. Passing one silver fox in the changing room and another in the shower room, I headed straight into the sauna to think about what had just happened and gleek onto the hot coals. I looked through the sauna's window at the tan, manicured moneymen whiling away another Tuesday lunchtime. A coiffed gent joined me in the sauna for a minute, going "phew" every few seconds and spreading his legs as if he were exhibiting some rare breed of plum in a nest of salt-and-pepper-colored pubes. After the heat and steam, I took a cool shower and got dressed. Jung was waiting behind the counter. I gave her my fold of bills, which she unabashedly counted twice before giving me a wink, a thank you, a business card and a "we see you again soon, I know!" Her smiling coworkers waved good-bye as I began my climb to the Earth's surface.

Conclusion—summarize your findings, don't forget to attempt to identify possible variables that could result in different findings for others trying to re-create your test results:

I really felt like a fish out of water at the spa, considering that I was a decade or two younger than most of the clientele and didn't carry enough pocket lettuce to buy Belgium. My excitement and arousal during the experience was somewhat compromised by a creeping feeling of sleaziness despite, or perhaps because of, the spa's ritzy ambience. The whole geisha-girl feel of the place—and the way the high-finance geezers lapped it up—made me feel like more of a john than I would have liked. I was left with questions about how Jung and the other women view the happy ending. Sure, it's probably pretty nonsexual and mechanical for them, like helping someone scratch an itch. But for most of their clients, it's undoubtedly more than that. I wondered how far the girls go in accommodating their clients' needs. In my case, Jung treated me to a couple of suggestive, "Oh ma ga's!" and a series of winks, but she stopped short of casting her eyes anywhere near mine when doing the deed. I wonder how the women's husbands and boyfriends deal with their profession. Are they as pragmatic and unimpressed as the women seem to be? I wonder if the full massage is viewed differently in Korea. In India, for example, it used to be common for barbers to fellate their customers after a shave and a haircut. Ultimately, I had to deal with the fact that I crossed a line. It's a terrible cliché, but I found that sex without any emotional attachment, or even mutual satisfaction, was a slightly chilling experience. ❧

> 66 I wonder if the full massage is viewed differently in Korea. In India, for example, it used to be common for barbers to fellate their customers after a shave and a haircut. 99

A Disturbance at Leather Camp

AFTER MY "Letters from Leather Camp" articles appeared on Nerve.com, I received thousands of e-mails from members of the BDSM community, a majority of them expressing their extreme displeasure at how I'd gained entry to Leather Camp, an event forbidden to reporters.

As its inclusion in *Working Stiff* provides a new outlet and a new audience for my take on the experience, I wanted to include an e-mail that expresses the viewpoint of the National Coalition for Sexual Freedom (NCSF).

The following template letter appeared on the NCSF website in the hours after Nerve.com posted my story; BDSM community members were encouraged to send it to Michael, Rufus, and myself.

NCSF Sample Letter to Nerve.com

Re: Letters from Leather Camp

I was very upset to see you sent a reporter, Grant Stoddard, to a private adult event and are now publishing articles about this event. It's like sending an undercover reporter to a private party at someone's house and then reporting on it. Leather Camp is a place for adults to go and explore their fantasies in a safe, sane and consensual setting. Your reporter violated the trust of every individual he spoke to, lying in order to obtain their private confidences and activities then publishing them for everyone to see. In the future, please give private events within

> **"I received thousands of e-mails from members of the BDSM community, a majority of them expressing their extreme displeasure at how I'd gained entry to Leather Camp, an event forbidden to reporters."**

the SM-Leather-Fetish community the respect they deserve.

Sincerely,
[*Your Name*]

[*Your phone number (for verification purposes only)*] ∽

A project of NCSF and the NCSF Foundation National Coalition for Sexual Freedom (NCSF) is a national organization committed to altering the political, legal, and social environment in the United States in order to guarantee equal rights for consenting adults who practice forms of alternative sexual expression. NCSF is primarily focused on the rights of consenting adults in the SM-Leather-Fetish, swing, and polyamorous communities, who often face discrimination because of their sexual expression.

Talk Like the Author!
Useful Phrases for One's Stay in Essex

[1]**bottle** *verb*: to smash a bottle into a person's face, very often a beer bottle after a drinking spree.

[2]**bottle** *noun*: courage, confidence, e.g., "John's scared, he's lost his bottle."

boy racer *noun*: a young man who has a penchant for fast cars and reckless driving.

chav *noun* [Orig. Southwest. Popular from early (2000s)]: a person, usually of poorly educated, working class origin, who dresses casually in designer sportswear and vulgar jewelry. [Chavs are generally viewed as an ignorant underclass with a propensity for criminal or loutish behavior.] (*Usually derog.*)

cunting *adjective*: an intensifier, e.g., "If this cunting weather doesn't improve within the next twenty-four hours, we'll have to cancel the whole trip."

geezer *noun*: a gregarious man about town.

ginger knob/minge *noun*: a person with ginger hair. Male being *ginger knob* (also ginger nob), and female, *ginger minge*. (*Derog.*)

mug *noun*: a hapless fool.

minge *noun* (1900s.): the female genitals.

Derived from dialect, which ultimately may have its roots in the Romany, minj.

minger *noun, pronounced with a hard G*: a physically undesirable, smelly, or ugly person, e.g., "It wasn't 'til we woke up the next morning, that I realized quite what a minger she was."

muppet *noun*: an idiot, an objectionable person.

nonce *noun*: 1. a sexual deviant, having been convicted of a sex crime against children. 2. an objectionable or contemptible person, by extension of the definition in noun 1.

pikey *noun* [South-east England/Kent use. (*Dialect*)]: 1. a gypsy. 2. a vagabond, vagrant. (*Derog.*)

[1]**ponce** *verb*: to beg or freeload, e.g., "He's been poncing off shoppers up the high street, saying he's homeless."

[2]**ponce** *noun*: 1. a contemptible person. 2. an effeminate male. (*Derog.*) 3. an ostentatious male. (*Derog.*)

slapper *noun*: a promiscuous woman.

wide boy *noun*: someone who flashes material wealth without any obvious means of acquiring it.

Don't miss the next book by your favorite author. Sign up now for AuthorTracker by visiting www.AuthorTracker.com.